QuickCourse®

in Microsoft

Windows
2000 — Training Edition

Fast-track training® for busy people

Online Training Solutions, Inc.

PUBLISHED BY
Online Training Solutions, Inc.
2217 152nd Ave NE
Redmond, WA 98052
Phone: (425) 885-1441, (800) 854-3344
Fax: (425) 881-1642
E-mail: CustomerService@otsi.com
Web site: www.otsi.com

Copyright © 2002 by Online Training Solutions, Inc.

All rights reserved. No part of the contents of this book may be reproduced or transmitted in any form or by any means without the written permission of the publisher.

Publisher's Cataloging-in-Publication
(Provided by Quality Books Inc.)

Quick Course in Microsoft Windows 2000 : fast-track training for busy people / Online Training Solutions, Inc. -- 1st ed.
    p. cm. -- (Quick Course)
    Includes index.
    ISBN: 1-58278-009-9

    1. Microsoft Windows (Computer File) 2. Operating systems (Computers) I. Online Training Solutions (Firm) II. Title: Windows 2000

    QA76.76.063Q533 2002   005.4'469
                              QBI02-200077

Printed and bound in the United States of America

2 3 4 5 6 7 8 9 W I N 3 2 1 0

Quick Course® and Fast-Track Training® are registered trademarks of Online Training Solutions, Inc. Microsoft, Microsoft Press, and Windows are either registered trademarks or trademarks of Microsoft Corporation in the United States and/or other countries. Other product and company names mentioned herein may be the trademarks of their respective owners.

All names used in this book are fictitious. Any resemblance to an actual company or product name is coincidental and unintentional.

Content overview

PART ONE: LEARNING THE BASICS

1 Introducing Windows 2000   2

We set the stage with a discussion of some important operating system concepts. Then we start Windows 2000 and explore its desktop, icons, and windows. Finally, we explore the Windows 2000 Help system, and then show you how to safely shut down your computer.

2 Using Programs   28

While using WordPad to create a document, we discuss how to start programs and choose commands using menus and toolbar buttons. Then we start more programs to demonstrate multitasking. Finally, we show how to print files.

3 Managing Folders and Files   60

We track down and open existing documents using My Computer, My Network Places, and the Search feature. Then we show you how to get organized by creating folders and moving, copying, renaming, and deleting documents.

4 E-Mail Basics   92

After a discussion of internal and Internet e-mail concepts, we show you how to use Outlook Express to send, reply to, and forward messages. You also learn how to use the Address Book, attach files, and organize messages.

PART TWO: BUILDING PROFICIENCY

5 Increasing Your Efficiency   124

We create shortcut icons on the desktop for programs and folders, and then we add shortcuts to the Start menu, the Programs submenu, and the Startup submenu. Next we display more toolbars at the bottom of the screen and show you techniques for speeding up everyday tasks. Finally, we explore linking and embedding files.

6 Customizing the Way You Work   154

We discuss how to add hardware and install programs, how to set up the screen the way you want it, and how to customize the taskbar. Then we cover other common adjustments to tailor your computer to your own way of working.

7 Solving Common Problems   190

We discuss the steps you can take to reduce potential problems while working in Windows 2000. Included are discussions of backing up and restoring files; cleaning up, defragmenting and scanning hard disks for errors; and troubleshooting startup problems.

Index   214

Content details

PART ONE: LEARNING THE BASICS

1 Introducing Windows 2000 — 2
Why Do You Need an Operating System? 4
Navigating Through Windows 5
Starting Windows 6
Using the Desktop 7
    Setting Up the Desktop 8
        Changing the Style 8
        Turning on the Quick Launch toolbar 11
    Working with Icons 12
    Working with the Start Button 15
Learning Window Basics 16
    Sizing and Moving Windows 17
    Arranging Windows 20
    Displaying the Desktop 21
    Closing Windows 21
Getting Help 21
Turning Off Your Computer 26

2 Using Programs — 28
Starting Programs 30
Command Basics 33
    Choosing Commands from Menus 33
        Using Menus on the Menu Bar 33
        Using Dialog Boxes 35
        Using Shortcut Menus 43
    Choosing Commands with Toolbar Buttons 45
Multitasking 47
    Switching Among Running Programs 48
    Sharing Information Among Programs 51
Using Printers 56
    Printing from a Program 56
    Adding a Printer 58
Quitting Programs 59

3 Managing Folders and Files — 60

- Understanding Storage 62
- Opening Recently Used Files 64
- Searching for Files 65
  - Using My Computer 66
  - Using the Explorer bar 69
  - Using My Network Places 74
    - Sharing Folders 74
    - Connecting to Shared Folders 76
    - Stopping Sharing 77
  - Searching for Documents 78
- Organizing Folders and Files 80
  - Deciding on a System 80
  - Creating New Folders 82
  - Selecting Folders and Files 82
  - Moving and Copying Folders and Files 83
  - Renaming Folders and Files 86
  - Deleting and Undeleting Folders and Files 87
- Customizing the My Computer Window 90

4 E-Mail Basics — 92

- Learning E-Mail Concepts 94
  - Knowing the Difference between Internal E-Mail and Internet E-Mail 95
  - Understanding E-Mail Addresses 96
- Setting Up Internet E-Mail 98
  - Starting Outlook Express for the First Time 101
- Customizing the Outlook Express Window 104
- Sending Messages 106
  - Using Contacts 109
  - Attaching Items to Messages 112
    - Attaching Stationery 112
    - Attaching Files 113
  - Sending Messages Stored in the Outbox 114
- Receiving and Handling Messages 115
  - Replying to Messages 117
  - Forwarding Messages 118
  - Organizing Messages 118
  - Deleting Messages 120
- Communicating with Instant Messaging 121

PART TWO: BUILDING PROFICIENCY

5 Increasing Your Efficiency — 124
- Getting Started Quickly 126
  - Using Shortcuts 126
    - Creating Quick Launch Toolbar Buttons 126
    - Creating Desktop Icons 129
    - Deleting Shortcut Icons and Buttons 132
  - Using Start Menu Shortcuts 132
    - Adding Shortcuts to the Programs Menu 133
    - Adding Shortcuts to the Startup Menu 136
    - Removing Startup Menu Shortcuts 136
  - Using Favorites 137
    - Deleting Favorites 138
  - Creating Custom Toolbars 138
    - Displaying Custom Toolbars 139
    - Customizing the Taskbar 140
- Working Faster 141
  - Creating Instant Documents 142
  - Associating Documents with Programs 144
  - Reusing Information 146

6 Customizing the Way You Work — 154
- Adding or Removing Hardware 156
- Adding or Removing Programs 159
  - Adding or Removing Application Programs 160
  - Adding or Removing Windows Components 161
- Tailoring the Display 163
  - Changing the Number of Colors and
    the Resolution 163
  - Changing the Background 164
  - Displaying a Screen Saver 168
  - Changing the Color Scheme 170
  - Accessing the Web from Anywhere 171
- Customizing the Taskbar and Start Menu 174
  - Moving the Taskbar 174
  - Changing Taskbar and Start Menu Properties 175

Making Other Adjustments 177
　　　　Changing the Date or Time 178
　　　　Adjusting the Mouse Buttons 180
　　　　Adjusting the Mouse Pointer 181
　　　　Adjusting the Keyboard 183
　　　　Accommodating Different Abilities 184
　　　　　　Using Magnifier 186
　　　　　　Using the On-Screen Keyboard 187
　　　　Adjusting Sounds and Audio Devices 188

7 Solving Common Problems   190

　　Backing Up Your Files 192
　　　　Creating a Full Backup 193
　　　　Creating an Incremental Backup 197
　　　　Restoring Documents 201
　　Optimizing Your Hard Disk 202
　　　　Scanning Your Hard Disk for Errors 202
　　　　Using Disk Cleanup 204
　　　　Using Disk Defragmenter 205
　　　　Scheduling Maintenance Tasks 206
　　Troubleshooting Startup Problems 209
　　　　Creating an Emergency Repair Disk 209
　　　　Using Special Start Modes 210
　　　　Keeping Windows Up to Date 211

Index   214

PART ONE
LEARNING THE BASICS

In Part One, we show you the techniques you need to be able to find your way around Windows 2000. After completing these chapters, you will know enough to put Windows 2000 to work on a daily basis. In Chapter 1, you explore the desktop, icons, windows, and Help. In Chapter 2, you create a document in WordPad, experiment with multitasking, and then print out your work. Chapter 3 teaches you how to organize your files using several Windows programs. In Chapter 4, we introduce you to Outlook Express, and you try your hand at sending e-mail messages.

INTRODUCING WINDOWS 2000

We set the stage with a discussion of some important operating system concepts. Then we start Windows 2000 and explore its desktop, icons, and windows. Finally, we explore the Windows 2000 Help system, and then show you how to safely shut down your computer.

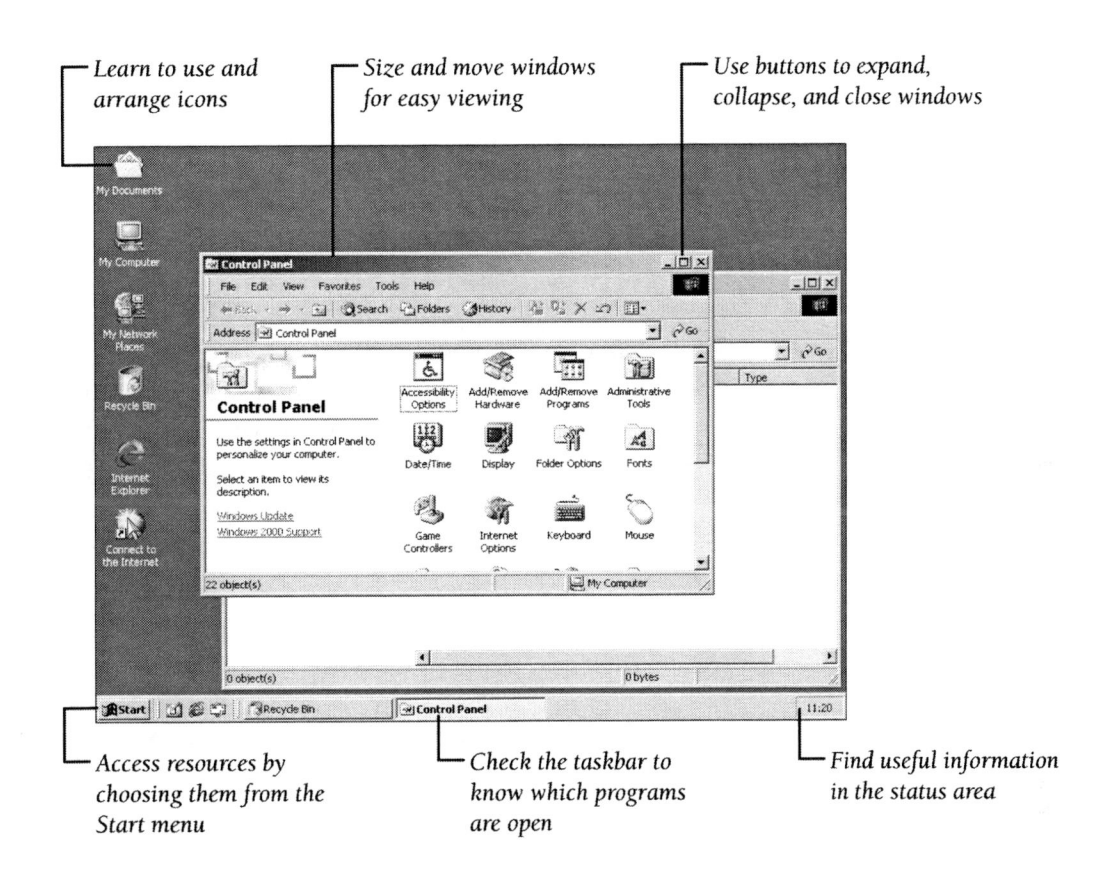

- Learn to use and arrange icons
- Size and move windows for easy viewing
- Use buttons to expand, collapse, and close windows
- Access resources by choosing them from the Start menu
- Check the taskbar to know which programs are open
- Find useful information in the status area

Since the initial development of Microsoft Windows in the early 1980s, computers have become faster, more powerful, and less expensive. Meanwhile, the range of computing technologies has become broader, with greater emphasis on the Internet. To keep pace with these developments, Microsoft has updated Windows, its flagship operating system, not only to improve existing features but also to realize the potential of full integration with the Internet.

WHY DO YOU NEED AN OPERATING SYSTEM?

So what exactly is an *operating system*, and why do you need one? Your computer's operating system is an intricate set of *software* programs that coordinate all your *hardware*. Your hardware consists of a central processing unit (CPU), memory chips, hard drives, floppy drives, CD-ROM drives, a monitor, a keyboard, a mouse, and any other devices that are part of your computer system. In addition, the operating system works as a liaison between your hardware and the other software programs that run on it.

When you work on your computer, you work with two kinds of software: *application programs* and *system programs*. An easy way to distinguish between these programs is to remember that applications are normally run by you, while system programs (also called *utilities*) are run by your computer.

- **Application programs.** You use these programs to perform specific types of tasks. For example, you can construct financial models with spreadsheet programs such as Microsoft Excel, and you can write reports with word-processing programs such as Microsoft Word.

- **System programs.** These programs control the computer and run application programs.

An operating system is a collection of system programs that are designed to work together. By managing files and hardware devices and overseeing basic functions, an operating system provides a foundation for the application programs that work with, or *run on,* it. So if an application program works with your operating system, you can be certain it will also work with your CPU, monitor, sound card, and so on.

CHAPTER 1   INTRODUCING WINDOWS 2000

Well, that's enough preamble. You are probably anxious to get started and see what the Windows 2000 operating system is all about. Because we assume that Windows 2000 is already installed on your computer, we don't cover the details of installation in this course. Instead, we focus on what you need to know about Windows 2000 to do useful work. We do give some background information for new computer users; those of you who are new to Windows 2000 but not new to computers can simply skim over those sections. Let's get going.

NAVIGATING THROUGH WINDOWS

The mouse is a fundamental piece of equipment for working with Windows and the applications that run on Windows. (You can also give instructions using the keyboard.) Your mouse is electronically connected to your computer, and the movements of your mouse are represented on the screen by a *pointer*. As you move the mouse, the pointer moves correspondingly on the screen, allowing you to point to the item you want to work with. The pointer often looks like an arrow, but it can take other forms, such as an I-beam when it is over text, a hand when it is over an item that can be selected, or an hourglass when you need to wait for Windows or another program to process information. You can also customize the pointer in accordance with a graphic theme or personal preference. When the pointer is where you want it, you can click one of the mouse buttons to tell the computer that you want to do something with the item under the pointer. These are the different ways of clicking:

SEE ALSO...
Customizing pointers, page 181

- **Clicking.** Clicking means pressing and releasing the primary mouse button once. In this course, we assume that you are using a standard mouse in which the left mouse button is the primary button and the right mouse button is the secondary button. So when we say *Click the Recycle Bin icon*, we mean *Move the pointer over the Recycle Bin icon, and click the primary button once.*

SEE ALSO...
Reversing the mouse buttons, page 180

- **Right-clicking.** You right-click by pressing and releasing the secondary mouse button once. When we say *Right-click the desktop*, we mean *Move the pointer to a blank area of the desktop, and click the secondary mouse button once.*

- **Double-clicking.** To double-click, you quickly click the primary mouse button twice.

STARTING WINDOWS

Windows 2000 can be used on a single, stand-alone computer, but it is designed to be used on computers running on a *network*, which is a group of computers that are set up to "talk" to each other. Each network is identified by a *domain name*. To be part of a network, you must have a *user account* that is identified by a unique *user name* (meaning that no other user on the network can have that name) and a *password*. Usually, the network's administrator controls your user name, and you control your password. Whether or not your computer is part of a network, your computer might be set up with only one user account or with multiple user accounts, depending on whether more than one person uses it.

User accounts are an important part of the Windows security system because they determine what each user is allowed to do on the network—which files the user can see and work with, what computer settings the user can change, and which of the network's components (called *resources*) the user can access.

Assuming that you know your user name, password, and network domain name (if you need them), follow these steps to start Windows:

1. Turn on your computer.

    If your computer has been set up as a stand-alone machine without a user name and password, Windows starts and after a minute or so, displays its opening screen. However, if your computer has been set up as part of a network or with more than one user account, you see a screen that says "Welcome to Windows."

2. Hold down the **Ctrl** and **Alt** keys, and press the **Delete** key to display a log on screen.

    From now on, we'll designate key combinations by separating the key names with plus signs, as in Ctrl+Alt+Delete.

3. Enter your user name and password in the boxes provided, and in the **Log on to** box, fill in the domain name of your

---

REMOVING OR CHANGING YOUR PASSWORD

If your computer is connected to a network, you must log on using your network user name and password. If your computer is not part of a network and only one user account is set up on it, you don't have to enter a password each time you log on to Windows. You can easily remove the password by simultaneously holding down the Ctrl, Alt, and Delete keys, and then clicking Change Password. Type your password in the Old Password box, leave the New Password and Confirm New Password boxes empty, and click OK. Use the same procedure to change the password.

Chapter 1 Introducing Windows 2000

network. (If your computer is part of a network and the **Log on to** box is not visible, click the **Options** button to make it appear.)

4. When you have filled in the required information, press the **Enter** key.

5. If you now see a Getting Started window, close it by clicking **Exit**.

    The Windows opening screen appears.

Using the Desktop

The Windows opening screen is called the *desktop*. This name is designed to make using the tools available with Windows 2000 seem no more intimidating than using the tools found on a typical desk. (If you are already familiar with Windows 95, Windows 98, or Windows Me, you'll instantly recognize many of the items on the desktop.)

The Windows 2000 desktop looks something like this:

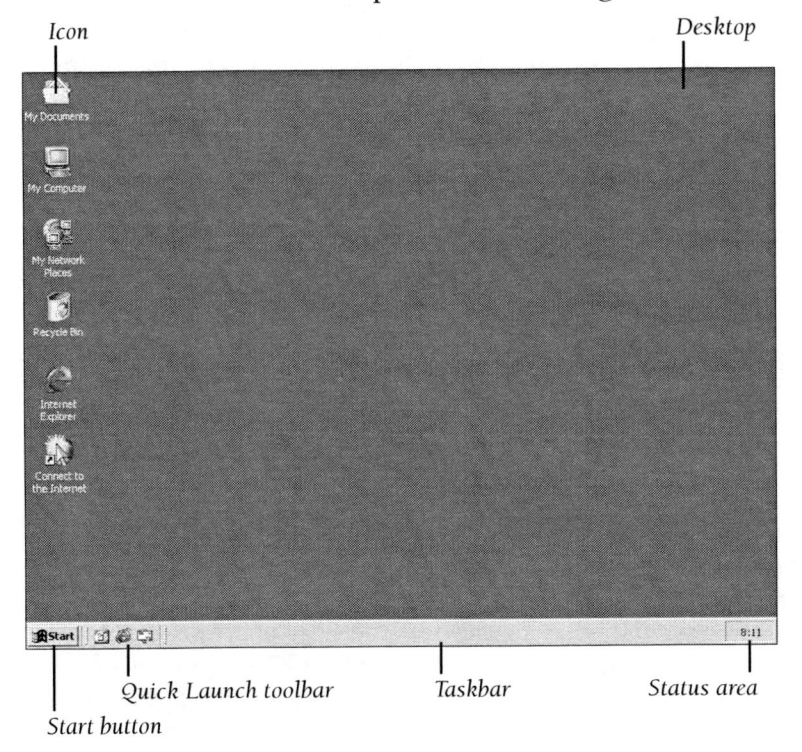

Icon — *Desktop*

Start button — *Quick Launch toolbar* — *Taskbar* — *Status area*

Program window instead of desktop?

If you log on to Windows and a program starts automatically, that program has been added to the computer's Startup folder. You can click the Close button at the right end of the program window's title bar to close the program and display the desktop. If you don't want a particular program to start automatically when Windows starts, click the Start button, click Programs, and click Startup to display a list of programs that start automatically. Right-click the program you want to remove from the list, and click Delete.

On the desktop are *icons* that represent commonly used Windows tools. Running horizontally across the bottom of the screen is the *taskbar*, which has a *Start button* on the left and a *status area* on the right. The status area probably displays the time, and it might contain other items depending on your computer's setup. The taskbar probably also displays the *Quick Launch toolbar*, which provides easy access to programs and the Internet. As you'll see as you work through this course, the taskbar changes to reflect the current task, so don't worry if your taskbar doesn't always look the same as ours.

Setting Up the Desktop

Your desktop might look different from ours for a variety of reasons. For example, someone might have changed the default screen colors, or you might be working at a different screen resolution. (The resolution determines the size of elements on the screen and is measured in *pixels*, which are the dots on the screen that make up an image. The illustrations in this course show the screen at 800 pixels wide by 600 pixels high.)

More About...
Screen colors, page 163

More About...
Screen resolution, page 163

Some desktop differences will have no effect on your ability to work your way through the exercises in this course. Others might make the steps a bit harder to follow. So the first thing we need to do is make sure we are all looking at the same desktop.

Changing the Style

If you have upgraded from an earlier version of Windows, your desktop might be set to a different style than ours, and the style can affect how the desktop works. Older versions of Windows

Moving the taskbar
By default, the taskbar is displayed across the bottom of your screen. If you prefer, you can move it and attach (or *dock*) it at the top, left, or right side of your screen. The taskbar then changes from horizontal to vertical orientation, as appropriate. To move the taskbar, point to an empty area of the taskbar, hold down the left mouse button, and drag it where you want it.

No taskbar?
If you don't see the taskbar on your screen, it might be hidden. When the taskbar is nowhere in sight, you can display it temporarily by pointing to the edge of the screen where the taskbar is currently docked. Move the pointer away from the edge of the screen to make the taskbar disappear again. To make the taskbar appear with the Start menu already open, press Ctrl+Esc. Press Esc to close the Start menu but keep the taskbar visible. If you want to permanently display the taskbar, right-click the taskbar, and click Properties. On the General tab of the Taskbar and Start Menu Properties dialog box, click the check mark in the Auto Hide check box to remove the check mark (an action known as *deselecting* an option), and then click OK.

Chapter 1 Introducing Windows 2000

were not designed to take advantage of and mirror the style of the Internet, and Windows 2000 might have carried forward older settings when it was installed. If you want to follow along with our examples without any glitches, you need to set your screen to the same style as ours. Were going to lead you quickly through a series of steps for doing that, without much explanation. Don't worry if you don't fully understand what's going on at this point. We'll explain things in more detail later. Here goes:

1. Click the **Start** button at the left end of the taskbar to display the Start menu, which contains a list of programs, folders, and other options.

2. Click **Settings**.

   The Settings submenu appears.

3. Click **Control Panel**.

   Windows displays the Control Panel window shown here:

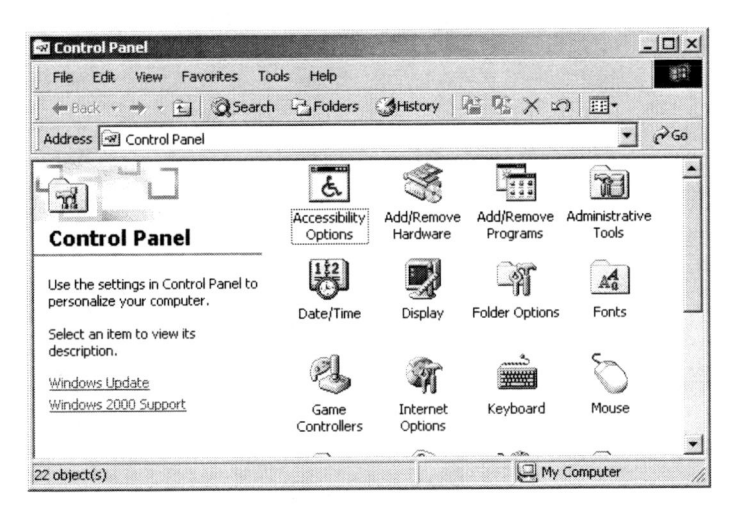

   Don't worry if your Control Panel window is a different shape or size than ours.

4. Click **Tools** on the menu bar at the top of the Control Panel window.

   The Tools menu drops down, displaying a list of choices.

More About...
Control Panel, page 10

5. Click **Folder Options**.

   Windows displays the dialog box shown in this graphic:

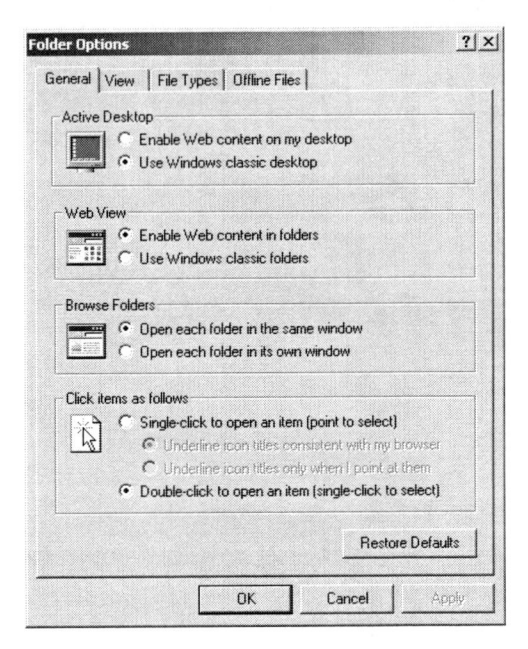

   You use dialog boxes to supply additional information about how Windows should carry out your instructions.

WHAT DOES CONTROL PANEL CONTROL?

You can use the tools in the Control Panel window to tailor your computer to fit your needs:

- **Accessibility Options.** Manipulate views, keyboard and mouse functions, and sounds to accommodate disabilities.
- **Add/Remove Hardware.** Install, remove, and troubleshoot hardware connected to your computer.
- **Add/Remove Programs.** Install or remove applications, and install or remove Windows components.
- **Date/Time.** Set the date, time, and input options for your geographic location and time zone.
- **Display.** Customize your desktop's appearance, colors, screen area, and related visual effects, including screen savers and background graphics.
- **Folder Options.** Change the way that files and folders look and respond to commands.
- **Game Controllers.** Add, remove, and configure game controller hardware such as joysticks and gamepads.
- **Internet Options.** Configure your Internet connection and display settings.
- **Keyboard.** Customize your keyboard settings.
- **Mouse.** Customize your mouse settings.
- **Phone and Modem Options.** Provide information about and configure location-specific telephone dialing rules.

Chapter 1 Introducing Windows 2000

6. Check the setting in the Active Desktop area, and if it isn't already selected, click the button to the left of the **Use Windows classic desktop** option.

   This option displays folders and files in the style that you might be familiar with if you've worked with Windows 95 or Windows 98.

7. Click **OK** at the bottom of the dialog box.

   The dialog box closes, and if you changed the Active Desktop setting, you will notice some changes in the appearance of your screen.

8. Click the **Close** button in the top right corner of the Control Panel window to close the window.

Turning on the Quick Launch toolbar

The Quick Launch toolbar sits at the bottom of the screen on the left side of the taskbar. You can use it to open frequently used programs or files with just on click. If you don't see the Quick Launch toolbar on your screen, here are the steps to turn it on:

1. Right-click an empty area of the taskbar.

What does Control Panel control? *(continued)*

- **Power Options.** Configure energy-saving settings, enable hibernation, and monitor your Uninterruptible Power Supply, if you have one.
- **Regional Options.** Customize the way languages, numbers, times, and dates are displayed.
- **Scanners and Cameras.** Install and configure scanners and cameras.
- **Sounds and Multimedia.** Assign sounds to events and configure audio devices.
- **System.** View and change system information and environment settings.
- **Users and Passwords.** Add or remove user accounts and passwords, and change user account permissions.

Links to the following folders are also available:

- **Administrative Tools.** Access tools that administrators use to configure computer settings.
- **Fonts.** See all the fonts that are installed on your computer.
- **Network and Dial-Up Connections.** Configure your network or dial-up connection and display settings.
- **Printers.** Add, remove, and configure your local or network printers.
- **Scheduled Tasks.** Create and manage a list of tasks that are scheduled to occur on a regular basis.

2. Click **Toolbars**.

3. If there is no check mark beside **Quick Launch** in the list, click it. Otherwise, click away from the lists to close them.

   The toolbar appears, displaying buttons for a few of the programs that come with Windows 2000.

WORKING WITH ICONS

Windows 2000 is very easy to work with, in part because of its use of *icons*—little pictures that represent programs and the files you create with them. Clicking an icon is a shortcut way of starting a program or opening a file. In the default installation of Windows 2000, you see several icons on your desktop, some of which represent the storage locations available to your computer and some of which represent programs.

If you purchased your computer with Windows 2000 already installed, the computer manufacturer (also called the *OEM*, for original equipment manufacturer) might have added other icons to your computer's desktop, or if you upgraded from a previous version of Windows, icons might have been carried over. As you install applications on your computer, their setup programs might also add icons to the desktop, to such an extent that your efficiency can suffer because of the clutter. You need to know how to add, remove, and manipulate icons so that the Windows desktop contains the tools you need to get your work done efficiently and so that it stays neat and tidy. Try this:

1. Point to the **My Computer** icon.

2. Hold down the primary mouse button, move the pointer to the top right corner of the desktop, and release the button.

   This hold-move-release action is called *dragging*. As you move the pointer, a shadow image of the My Computer icon moves with it, and when you release the mouse button, the icon jumps to its new location.

3. Point to the **Recycle Bin** icon.

   Notice that Windows displays a pop-up box describing the item's function.

4. Drag the **Recycle Bin** icon below the **My Computer** icon.

   Your screen now looks something like this graphic:

CHAPTER 1   INTRODUCING WINDOWS 2000   13

[Screenshot of Windows 2000 desktop showing icons: My Documents, My Computer, Recycle Bin, My Network Places, Internet Explorer, Connect to the Internet, with Start button and taskbar showing 8:20.]

5. Move other icons slightly out of line on the desktop.

As you can see, your icons don't have to be aligned precisely. But if you want, you can tell Windows 2000 to keep your desktop neat by nudging the icons into straight lines. Try this:

1. Right-click an empty area of the desktop.
2. Click **Line Up Icons**.

   Windows straightens up the icons on the desktop.

If you don't like the way the icons are arranged, you can tell Windows to rearrange them for you, like this:

1. Right-click the desktop, and click **Arrange Icons**.
2. Click **by Name**.

   Windows arranges all the icons on the left side of the desktop.

If you want Windows to act like a drill sergeant and automatically keep your icons straight, this is what you do:

1. Right-click the desktop, click **Arrange Icons**, and then click **Auto Arrange**.

   Nothing seems to happen. However, behind the scenes Windows is now on duty.

ICON SPACING

You can control how close together the icons are. Right-click the desktop, click Properties, and then in the Display Properties dialog box, click the Appearance tab. Click the down arrow to the right of the Item box, and then click Icon Spacing (Horizontal) or Icon Spacing (Vertical) in the drop-down list. In the Size box, click the up or down arrows to specify the number of pixels between the icons, and click OK.

2. Drag the **My Network Places** icon to the middle of the desktop.

   When you release the mouse button, the remaining icons move up to fill the spot left vacant by My Network Places, and My Network Places snaps back to the left side of the desktop, but at the bottom of the column.

3. Right-click the desktop, click **Arrange Icons**, and then click **by Name**.

   The original pecking order is restored.

4. Right-click the desktop, click **Arrange Icons**, and click **Auto Arrange** to turn it off.

   Windows is now off duty, and you can move the icons wherever you want them.

Being able to shuffle icons on the screen is all well and good, but why are they there? Icons are not just cute little pictures; as we said, they represent programs and other computer elements, such as hardware, storage areas, or documents. Double-clicking an icon carries out a specific action, such as starting a program or displaying the contents of a storage area. Here's an example:

- Double-click the **Recycle Bin** icon.

   The window shown in this graphic opens:

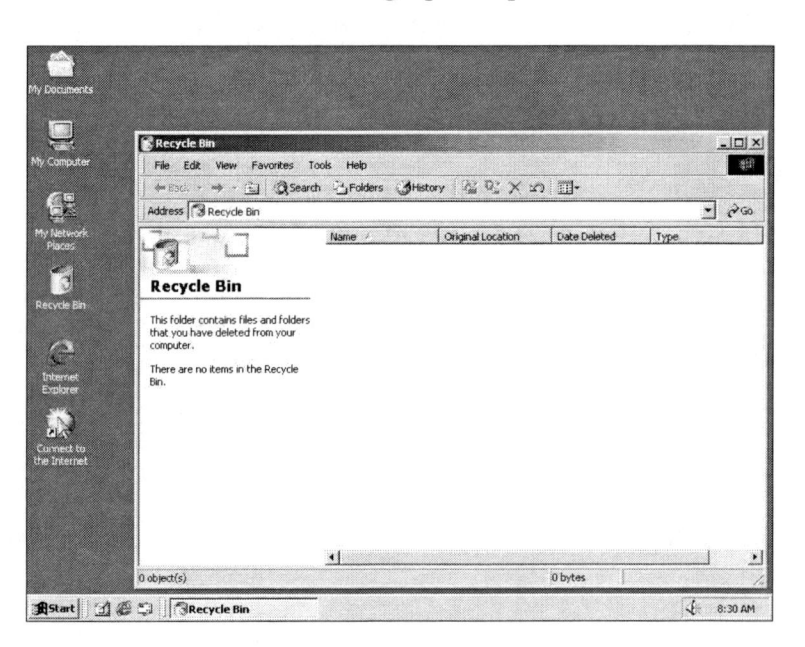

Chapter 1 Introducing Windows 2000

The Recycle Bin is an area on your hard disk to which files are moved when you "delete" them. (Files aren't permanently deleted until you empty the Recycle Bin.) The Recycle Bin shown on our screen is currently empty, but yours might contain deleted items.

Notice that a button representing the Recycle Bin window has appeared on the taskbar at the bottom of the screen. We'll talk more about this button in a moment.

Leave the Recycle Bin window open for now, and watch what happens to it as you work through the next section.

More About...
Recycle Bin, page 88

Working with the Start Button

An important feature of the desktop is the Start button. As its name implies, you can start many tasks by clicking this button. You already used this button when you set the style of your desktop, but let's take another look at how the Start button works:

1. Click the **Start** button at the left end of the taskbar.

    Windows displays the Start menu shown in this graphic:

    This convenient list provides a fast way to carry out common computer tasks, such as starting programs, finding and opening files, changing system settings, and getting information.

2. Click **Settings**, and then click **Control Panel**.

Start menu variations
Your Start menu might look different from the one we show, depending on what programs are installed on your computer and whether your Start menu has been customized. For example, if your Start menu doesn't have Windows 2000 Professional written down the left side and its icons look smaller than our icons, don't worry—it just means that your Start menu is set to show small icons and ours is set to show large ones. To change the look of your Start menu, right-click the taskbar and click Properties. In the Taskbar and Start Menu Properties dialog box, select or deselect the "Show small icons in Start menu" check box, and click OK.

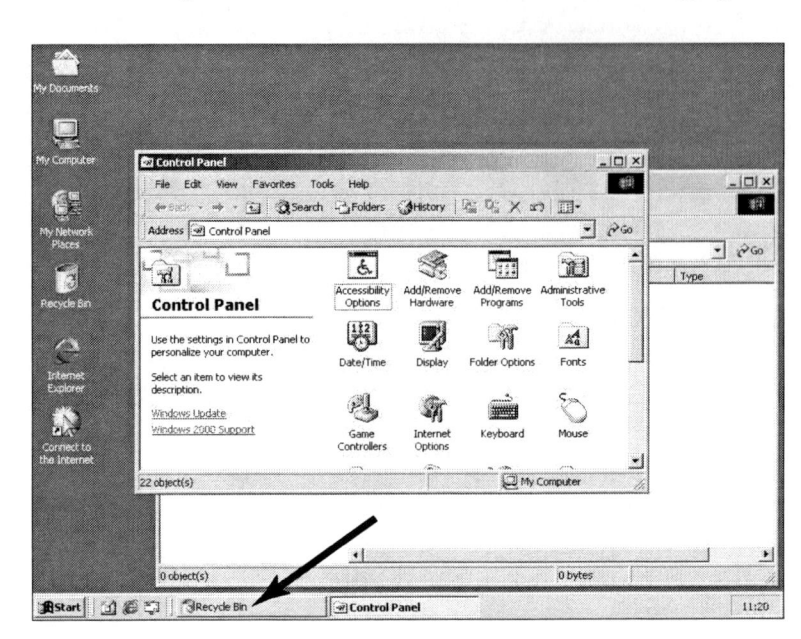

Your desktop now looks like the one shown in this graphic:

Notice that you don't have to close an open window before you can open another one. Although the Control Panel window obscures the Recycle Bin window, the Recycle Bin is still open, as indicated by the presence of its button on the taskbar.

Leave the Control Panel and Recycle Bin windows open as we move on to the next section.

LEARNING WINDOW BASICS

As the operating system's name implies, when you're working with a program that runs on Windows, you are always working in a *window*. A window is a frame of information that can be displayed, resized, or hidden away. A window can contain text, graphics, dialog boxes, scroll bars, buttons, and various other features that make it possible to move within and among windows. This arrangement enables you to have several items of information and several programs available at the same time, because each is displayed in its own window. To make efficient use of windows, though, you need to know how to manipulate them. So while we have two windows open, we'll take a few minutes to learn some basic windowing skills before we go any further.

> **INTERNET INFLUENCE**
>
> On the left side of the Control Panel window, Windows Update and Windows 2000 Support are underlined to indicate that they are links. When you move the mouse pointer over these links, the pointer changes to a hand with a pointing finger (or another symbol that indicates an active link, depending on your mouse settings). These visual cues mirror those you can expect to find on the Internet and suggest the influence that the Internet has had on Windows. This influence is also reflected in the toolbars. For example, the Favorites menu and Address bar found in many Web browsers are now part of Windows 2000.

CHAPTER 1   INTRODUCING WINDOWS 2000   **17**

SIZING AND MOVING WINDOWS

You'll often want to work in a window that occupies the entire screen so that you can see as much of your work as possible. Sometimes, however, you'll want the window to take up less of the screen so that you can see other items on your desktop. You can use two of the buttons clustered in the top right corner of most windows to quickly contract and expand the windows. You can also size the windows manually. To try various ways of resizing a window, follow these steps:

1. Point to the **Maximize** button in the top right corner of the Control Panel window.

   When you hold the pointer over the button, Windows displays a pop-up box, called a *ScreenTip*, that shows the name of the button. This feature is a big help in getting to know your way around Windows 2000 and the applications that run on it.

2. Click the **Maximize** button.

   The window expands to fill the screen, with the Maximize button replaced by the Restore Down button, like this:

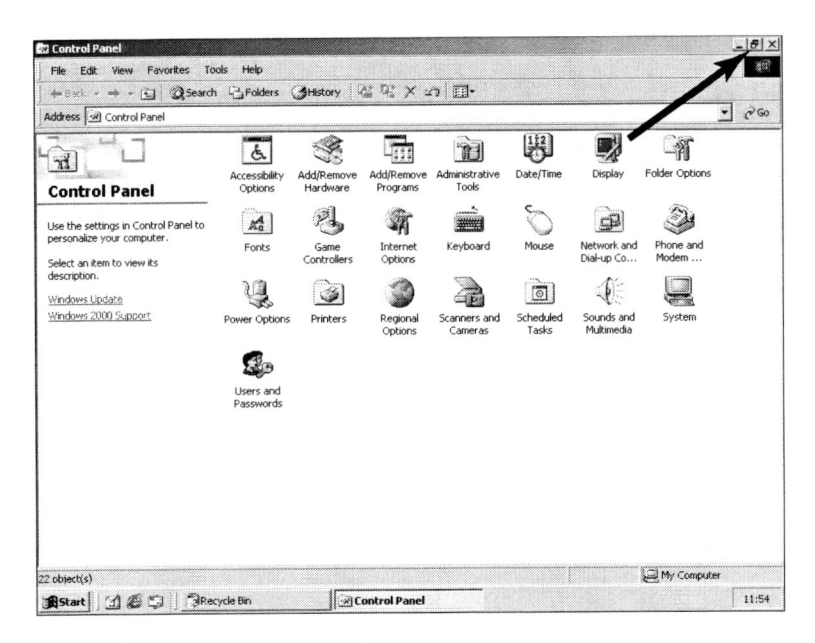

3. Click the **Restore Down** button.

   The window shrinks to its former size, and the Maximize button reappears.

When a window is maximized, you can restore it to its previous size by double-clicking its title bar. Double-clicking the title bar of a window that does not fill the screen maximizes the window.

4. Click the **Recycle Bin** button on the taskbar to bring its window to the forefront, as shown in this graphic:

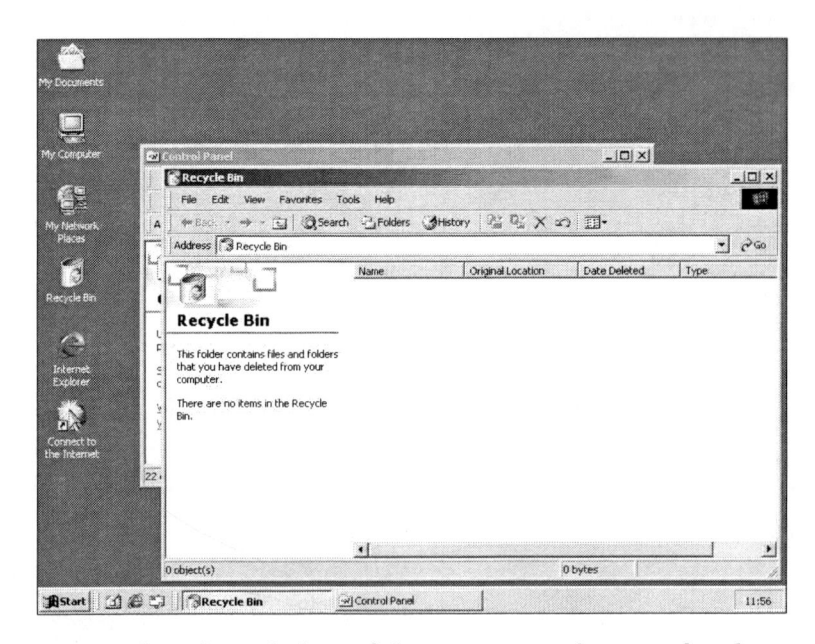

Notice that the title bar of the active window is a brighter color than that of the inactive window. Also notice that the active window's button on the taskbar is lighter in color and appears to be "pressed."

5. Click the Recycle Bin window's **Maximize** button to expand the window to fill the screen.

6. Click the **Control Panel** button on the taskbar to make its window active.

Except for the windows of some simple programs, all windows that don't occupy the entire screen have *frames*, which can stretch and shrink. As you move the mouse pointer over different parts of a resizable frame, the pointer becomes a two-headed arrow, indicating the directions in which you can move

A FULL TASKBAR

If you open several windows, the taskbar can get pretty full of buttons. Windows then abbreviates the button names to accommodate them all. If you can't tell which button belongs to which window, point to the button for a brief moment, and the full window name will pop up as a ScreenTip.

CHAPTER 1 INTRODUCING WINDOWS 2000

the frame to change its size. You can move the sides of the frame to the left and right, move the top and bottom of the frame up and down, and move the corners up and down diagonally. This technique works only with windows that are not maximized. Let's experiment with this now:

1. Point to the right side of the Control Panel window's frame.

   The pointer changes to a double-headed arrow.

2. Hold down the primary mouse button, move the pointer to the left to make the window narrower, and release the mouse button.

3. Point to the bottom of the frame, and drag it upward until the window is about 3 inches tall.

4. Point to the diagonal lines in the bottom right corner of the window, and drag in a diagonal direction to change the window's height and width simultaneously.

5. Point to the window's title bar, and drag in any direction.

   The window moves to its new location.

6. Now click the **Maximize** button to expand the window so that it fills the screen.

   Notice that a maximized window doesn't have a frame, so you can't manually resize it.

You can shrink a window to its minimum size and tuck it out of sight under its button on the taskbar. Although the window isn't visible, the minimized window is still accessible, as the following steps show:

1. Click the **Minimize** button at the right end of the Control Panel window's title bar.

   The window appears to shrink under its taskbar button, which now appears inactive. The only other open window, the Recycle Bin, becomes active.

2. Redisplay the **Control Panel** window by clicking its button on the taskbar.

MOVING WINDOWS WITH THE KEYBOARD

A window that's not maximized can accidentally be moved so far off the screen that you can't grab its title bar and move it back. If that happens, press Alt+Spacebar, click Move, press the Arrow keys to move the window back onto the screen, and then press Enter.

Arranging Windows

What if you want an unobstructed view of all the open windows? You could size each window in turn, but here's an easier method:

1. Right-click a blank area of the taskbar, and click **Cascade Windows**.

2. Right-click the taskbar, and click **Tile Windows Horizontally**.

3. Now right-click the taskbar again, and click **Tile Windows Vertically**.

   The result is shown in this graphic:

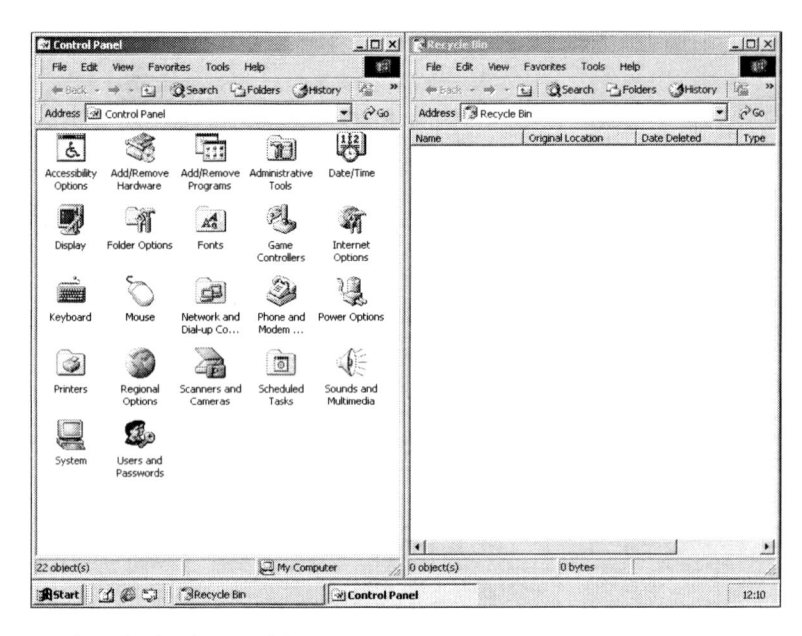

4. Right-click the taskbar again.

   As you can see, after you arrange your windows in a particular way, a command to undo that arrangement is added to the list.

5. Click **Undo Tile**.

   The previous arrangement is restored.

6. Right-click the taskbar, and this time click **Minimize All Windows** to minimize both windows.

> **MINIMIZED WINDOWS ARE NOT ARRANGED**
> If any open programs are minimized or if they have open dialog boxes, their windows are not included in screen rearrangements carried out using the Cascade Windows, Tile Windows Horizontally, or Tile Windows Vertically commands.

Displaying the Desktop

You have just seen how to display the desktop by minimizing all open windows. But there is a faster way. As we said earlier in the chapter, the Quick Launch toolbar holds buttons that quickly start programs and open files. By default, this toolbar includes one very useful button that quickly hides all the open windows and displays the desktop. Suppose you need to access an icon on your desktop. To see the desktop, you could right-click the taskbar and click Minimize All Windows, which requires two steps. But here's how to access the icon with just one click:

- Click the **Show Desktop** button at the end of the Quick Launch toolbar.

   The open windows shrink under their buttons on the taskbar, revealing the desktop.

Closing Windows

When you no longer need to work with a particular window, there is no point in keeping it open. You've already seen how to use the Close button to close a window. These steps provide another way:

1. Right-click the **Recycle Bin** button on the taskbar.
2. Click **Close** to close the window.
3. Click the **Control Panel** button on the taskbar, and leave its window open for now.

Getting Help

Using Windows 2000 is fairly straightforward. Most of the time, you will have a good idea about what to do and how to do it. However, for those times when you stumble, you'll want to consult the Windows 2000 Help system. Think of this feature as an encyclopedia-sized directory in which you can look up just about any topic. You can access Windows 2000 Help topics like this:

1. Click the **Start** button.

2. Click **Help** on the Start menu to display the window shown in this graphic:

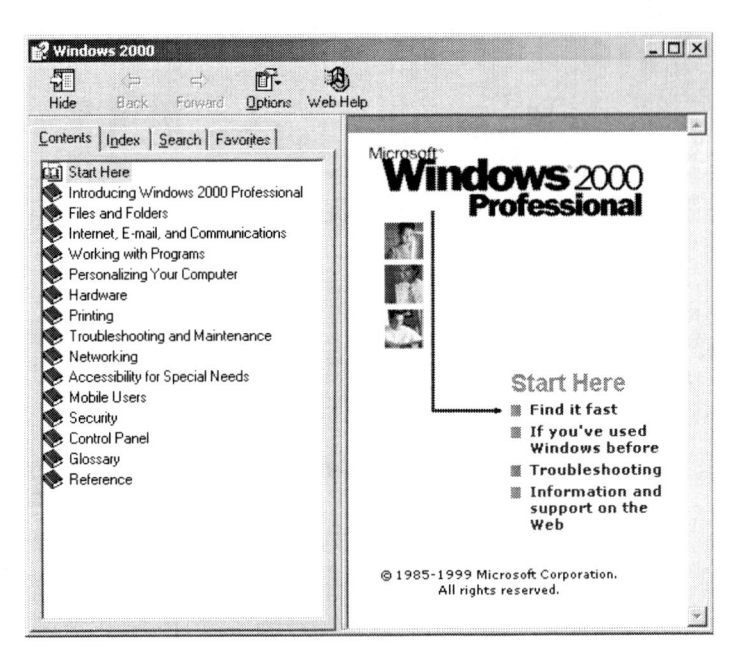

In Windows 2000, the old Help system has been given a new look. The left pane of the Help window contains a list of links to general topics that serve the same function as the table of contents in a book. Other tools that make Help easier to use are also accessible from this window. You use the toolbar buttons at the top of the window to navigate, and you click the tabs across the left pane to choose between different ways of finding information, including:

- **Contents.** You can search the expandable list of topics and link to the information on that topic in the table of contents.

- **Index.** You can browse an index of Help topics the same way you would browse the index of a book.

- **Search.** You can search for a specific topic by keyword. You can combine keywords with the words *and* and *or*.

- **Favorites.** You can create a personalized list of those topics to which you most commonly refer. You add a topic to your favorites list by displaying the topic, clicking the Favorites tab, and then clicking Add.

HELP WITH PROGRAMS
Most programs that run on Windows have Help features that function in much the same way as Windows 2000 Help. In many programs, you can press the F1 key to instantly access the program's Help window.

CHAPTER 1 INTRODUCING WINDOWS 2000

Here's an example of how to search for topics:

1. Click the **Search** tab.

2. Type *wordpad* in the **Type in the keyword to find** box, and click the **List Topics** button.

   The window now looks like the one shown in this graphic:

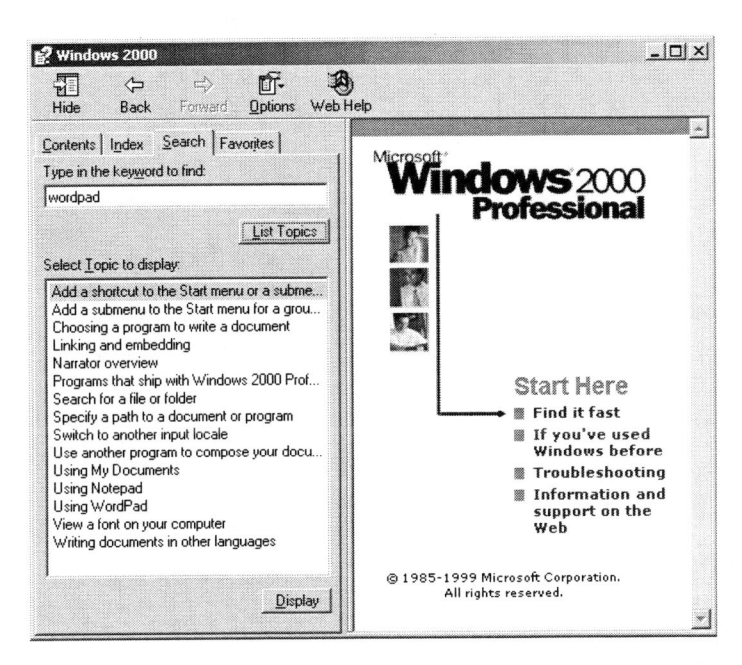

   All the topics that contain the word *wordpad* are listed in the "Select Topic to display" list.

3. Click the **Using WordPad** topic, and then click the **Display** button.

   In the right pane, Windows displays a topic page that provides information about editing short documents in WordPad.

4. Click the shortcut link to start WordPad in a separate window.

   You will often be able to open windows or dialog boxes directly from a Help topic.

CHANGING THE HELP WINDOW DISPLAY

Click the Hide button on the Help window toolbar to shrink the Windows 2000 Help file window so that only the topic page is visible. This is especially useful if you want to view a program window or dialog box and a Help topic's instructions at the same time. Click the Show button to redisplay the left pane.

PRINTING HELP FILE TOPICS

To print a Help topic, click the Options button and click Print. In the Print dialog box, make your printing selections, and click the Print button.

24 **QUICK COURSE IN MICROSOFT WINDOWS 2000**

5. You use WordPad later in this course; for now, close the window.

6. Back on the Using WordPad topic page, click the **Related Topics** link.

   In the pop-up box, Windows displays a list of topics related to the current topic.

7. Click any one of the topics to display its page.

8. To return to the opening Help screen, click the **Options** button on the toolbar, and then click **Home**.

Instead of searching for information, you can look it up in Help's index, like this:

1. Click the **Index** tab.

   You see the window shown in this graphic:

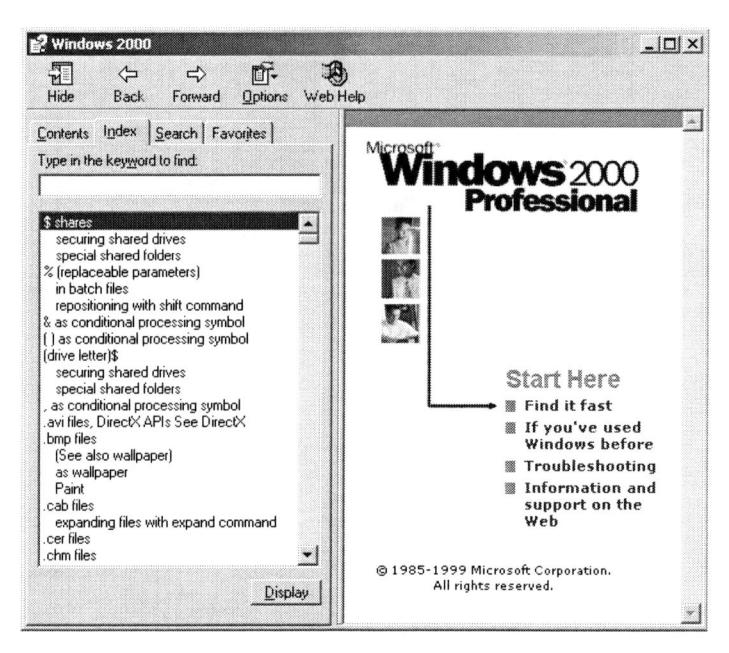

NOT FINDING WHAT YOU NEED?
To find the latest information about Windows 2000, useful tips, and practical advice for users, you can consult the Windows 2000 Help resources on the Web. You can contact the Microsoft Windows 2000 product support team; download updates, new features, and drivers; search for Windows 2000–compatible software and hardware; learn how to utilize Windows 2000 within an organization; view the Windows 2000 Resource Kit; and learn more about accessibility resources. To access these online resources, click the Web Help button. On the Online support and information page, click the topic you want to view. You need an active Internet connection to do this, because you are connecting to live Web sites.

2. Press the **Down Arrow** key to move down the keyword list. When you see the **24-hour time format** topic, double-click it.

   You can also click the topic and then click the Display button or press the Enter key to display the topic in the topic

CHAPTER 1 INTRODUCING WINDOWS 2000

panel. And if you want to move through the list without using the arrow keys, you can use the scroll bar to the right of the keyword list.

MORE ABOUT...
Scrolling, page 37

3. Next, click at the left end of the **Type in the keyword to find** box at the top of the left pane, press **Delete** until the current entry is erased, and type the words *turning off*.

   The list of keyword entries scrolls to the one that matches, or most closely matches, the words you typed, as shown in this graphic:

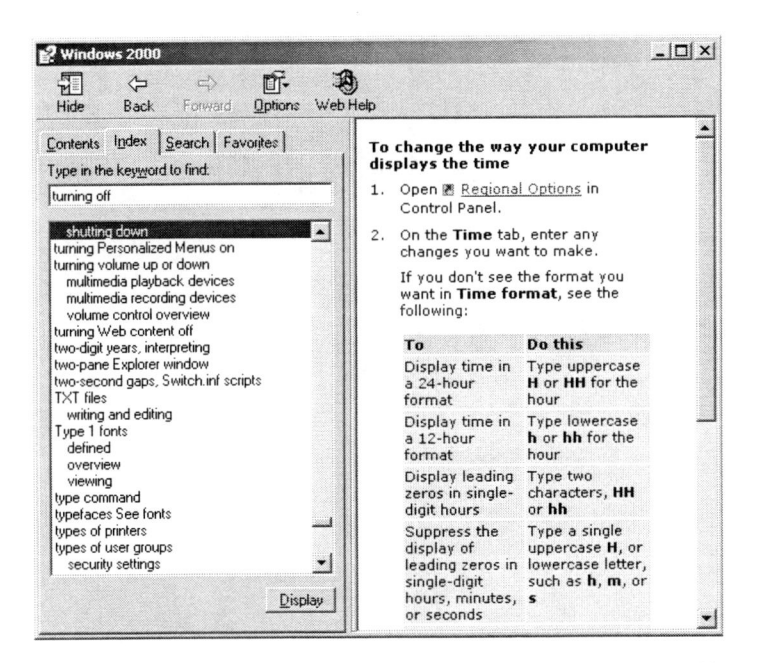

   In this case, there is no Help topic with *turning off* as its exact title, but there are several related topics.

4. Double-click **shutting down** to display its page.

5. To return to the previous topic page, click the **Back** button at the top of the window.

6. To redisplay the shutting down topic page, click the **Forward** button.

7. Explore the Windows 2000 Help system on your own for a bit.

8. When you have finished, click the **Close** button to close the Help file window.

Turning Off Your Computer

Well, this section is going to be easy, because you've already learned from the Windows 2000 Help file how to turn off your computer. A word of warning: Never turn off your computer by pressing its on/off button without first running through the shut-down procedure. Windows does a lot of housekeeping at the end of each session to ensure that your computer will function properly the next time you turn it on. If you simply turn it off, none of the housekeeping gets done, and there's no telling how future sessions might be affected. Here's how to shut down correctly:

1. Click the **Start** button, and on the Start menu, click **Shut Down**.

   Windows displays the Shut Down Windows dialog box shown in this graphic:

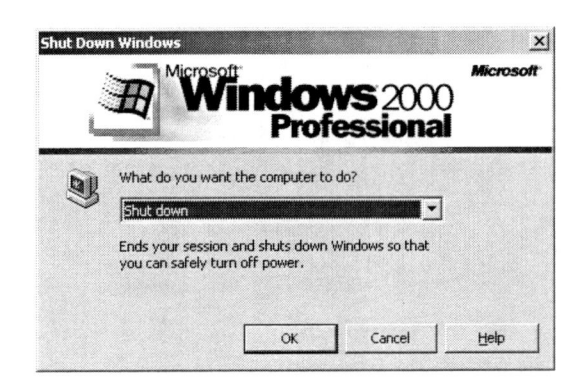

Other Shut-Down Options

If you are going to stop working on your computer for some period of time, you have other options in the Shut Down Windows dialog box:

- You can click the down arrow and click Log off, which closes down any running programs and returns the computer to the logon screen. (Save your work before logging off.)
- You can click Stand by. This option runs your computer on low power for a short period of time. (Before switching to Stand By mode, you should save your work.) To resume working, press any key. Windows wakes up with all the program windows in the state (open or minimized) in which you left them.

If you just want to turn your computer off and then on again right away, you have this option:

- You can click Restart, which is the one-step equivalent of shutting down and turning your computer back on again.

To quickly access the Shut Down Windows dialog box, you can press Alt+F4. You might be prompted to close any open windows. If you have several windows open, it's faster to click Shut Down on the Start menu.

Chapter 1 Introducing Windows 2000

2. Check that **Shut down** appears in the box below **What do you want the computer to do?**

3. If it doesn't, click the down arrow at the right end of the box, and click **Shut down** in the drop-down list.

4. Click **OK**.

   Windows records information about this session. Then your computer will either turn off automatically or display a message telling you that it is safe to turn off your computer.

5. If you see the message, turn off your computer manually.

That's it for your introductory tour of Windows 2000. In the next chapter, we'll focus on running programs.

USING PROGRAMS

While using WordPad to create a document, we discuss how to start programs and choose commands using menus and toolbar buttons. Then we start more programs to demonstrate multitasking. Finally, we show how to print files.

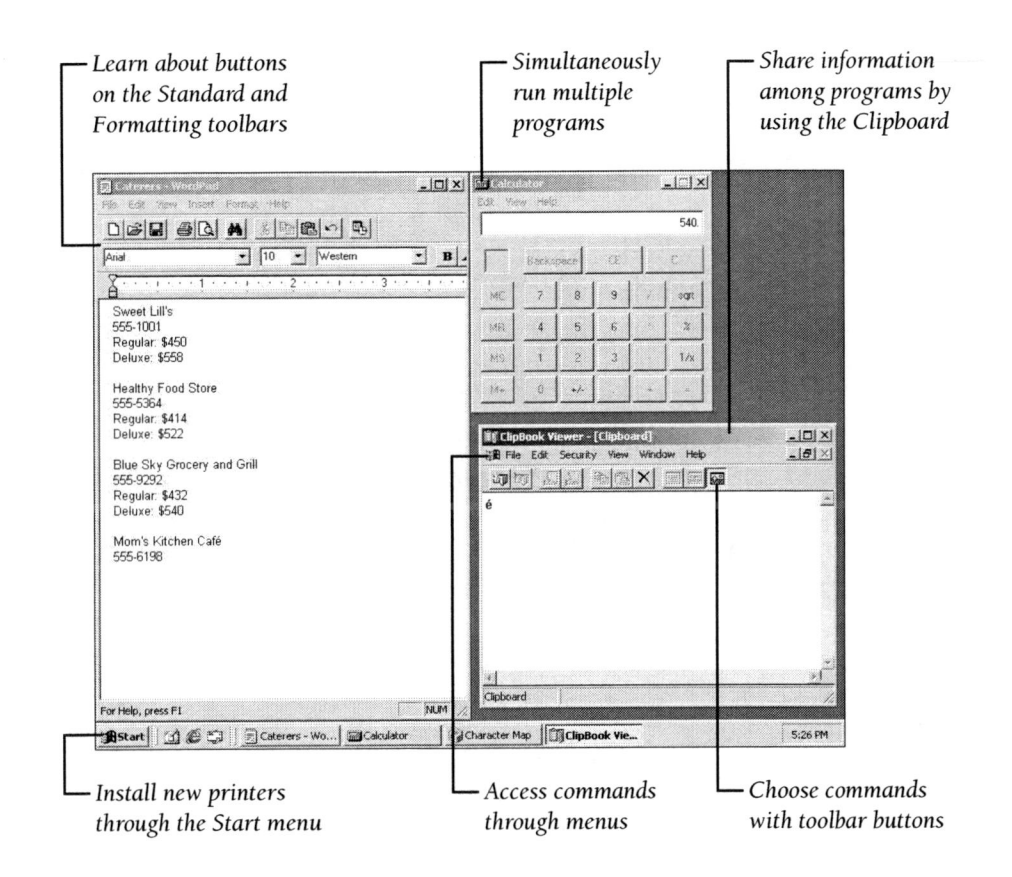

- *Learn about buttons on the Standard and Formatting toolbars*
- *Simultaneously run multiple programs*
- *Share information among programs by using the Clipboard*
- *Install new printers through the Start menu*
- *Access commands through menus*
- *Choose commands with toolbar buttons*

SEE ALSO...
Adding and removing programs, page 159

MORE ABOUT...
The Startup menu, page 7

STARTING MS-DOS PROGRAMS

If you want to use programs that run on MS-DOS, you can access a version of this operating system while working in Windows 2000. To start MS-DOS, click Start, Programs, Accessories, and then Command Prompt. MS-DOS opens in a window. You can press Alt+Enter to switch to full-screen mode and press Alt+Enter again to restore the window. You can then run programs and give commands in MS-DOS without leaving Windows. For example, to start the MS-DOS Editor program, type *edit* at the command prompt, and press Enter. To close the command prompt window, click the window's Close button. To start an MS-DOS program without going through Command Prompt, click Run on the Start menu, type the program's file name in the Open box, and then click OK.

Most people use computers as tools for accomplishing practical tasks. They want to send a letter, jot down notes for a meeting, draft a report, or analyze income and expenses for the month. So it's likely that the first thing you want to know about Windows 2000 is how to start programs and create, save, and print documents. In this chapter, you'll learn how to use the programs on your computer to carry out common tasks.

If you shut down your computer at the end of Chapter 1, the first thing you need to do is turn your computer back on. Notice that Windows 2000 remembers that Control Panel was open when you shut down your computer, and it displays the Control Panel window when it starts up. (Windows does this for some of its own programs, but it does not automatically reopen applications like word processors unless they are on the Startup menu.) Note that all applications are programs, but not all programs are complex enough to be called applications. In this course, we use the term *program* in a generic sense and the term *application* when we want to single out the type of software packages you might purchase for tasks such as word processing or accounting.

STARTING PROGRAMS

One of the simplest ways to get going is to start a program from the Start menu. (Starting a program is sometimes referred to as *running*, *executing*, *launching*, or *loading* a program. Generally, these terms can be used interchangeably.) Here are the steps:

1. Close any open windows.

2. Click the **Start** button at the left end of the taskbar to display the Start menu.

3. Click **Programs**.

   Windows displays a submenu of programs and program groups. Clicking a program name starts that program, and pointing to or clicking a program group name (indicated by a right-pointing arrow after the name) displays yet another submenu.

4. Click **Accessories** at the top of the submenu.

   Windows displays another submenu that lists the components that are assigned to the Accessories program group.

CHAPTER 2 USING PROGRAMS 31

Your screen now looks something like the one shown in this graphic:

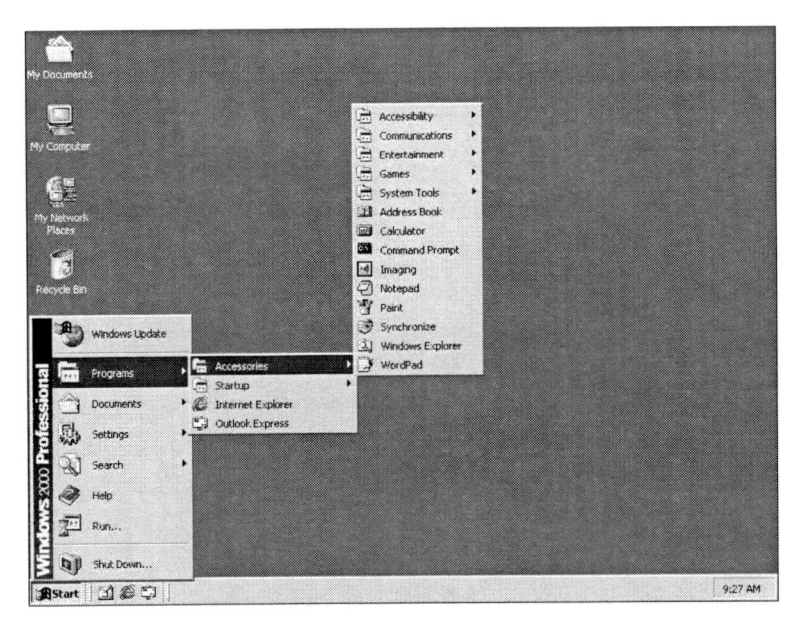

5. Click **WordPad** to start the simple word processor that comes with Windows 2000.

You see the window shown in this graphic:

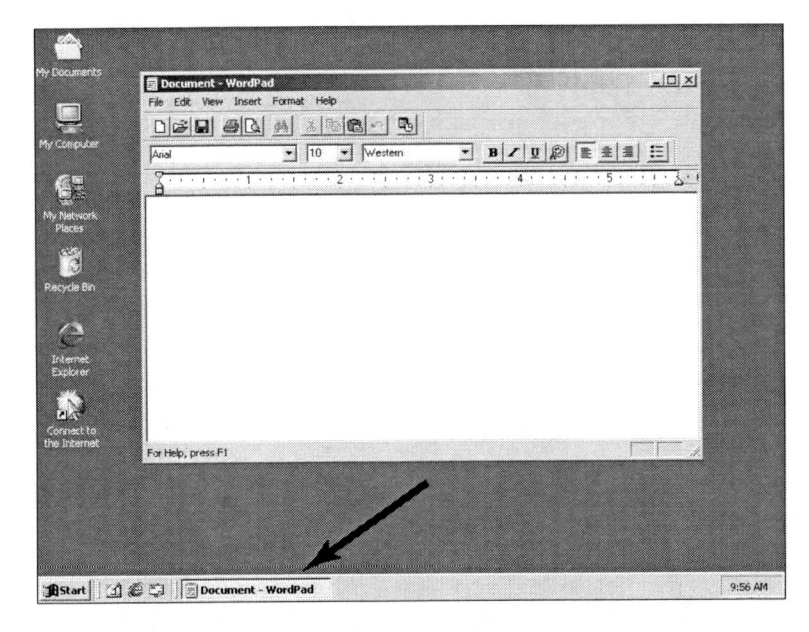

Notice that a button representing the WordPad window has been added to the taskbar. (Don't worry if your window is not the same size as ours.)

PROGRAMS SUBMENU VARIATIONS

The Programs submenu in our graphic is for a new computer on which no application programs have been installed. Each time you install an application, its installation program will probably add an item or a group to the Programs submenu. If Windows detects that you use the Programs submenu to start only a few programs, after a while it might hide all the programs you haven't started in this way. You can access these programs at any time by clicking the chevrons at the bottom of the Programs submenu to redisplay the hidden options.

MORE ABOUT...
Sizing windows, page 17

6. Maximize the WordPad window.

   The window now appears as shown in this graphic:

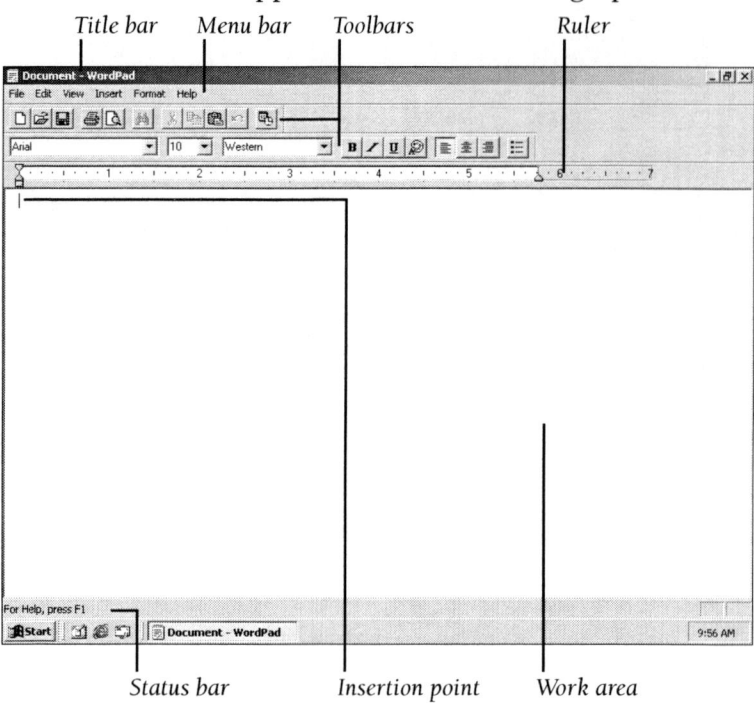

   Title bar   Menu bar   Toolbars   Ruler

   Status bar   Insertion point   Work area

The window now on your screen has many of the characteristics of a typical application window. It has a *title bar*, which in this case tells you that the window contains a WordPad document. Below the title bar is the *menu bar*, which contains the menus available for WordPad. Below the menu bar are two *toolbars*, which are collections of *buttons* that you can click to quickly carry out commands. (We'll talk about the various ways of giving commands in a moment.) Below the toolbars, you might see a *ruler*, a handy measuring tool that helps you design documents that are more complicated. At the bottom of the window is a *status bar*, where the application posts various items of useful information. Occupying the majority of the window is the *work area*, where you create your document. In this area, a blinking *insertion point* indicates where the next character you type will appear. (Don't confuse the insertion point with the pointer, which moves with your mouse and doesn't blink.)

Back to the title bar: At the left end is the *program icon*. Clicking this icon displays a control menu of commands for sizing and moving the window and quitting the program. (The same menu is also displayed when you right-click the title bar.) At the right end of the title bar are the Minimize, Maximize/Restore Down, and Close buttons you used in Chapter 1. These buttons are common to all Windows-based programs.

Command Basics

To get any useful work done, you have to be able to tell the computer what to do. In the world of Windows, that means giving *commands*. Some commands are simple, and others are very complex, requiring multiple instructions and supporting items of information. Windows (and any program you run on it) provides a number of methods for giving these instructions, including choosing commands from menus, clicking buttons on toolbars, and pressing various key combinations. We'll look at the primary methods in this section.

Choosing Commands from Menus

In Chapter 1, we gave a quick preview of how to choose commands from menus, without explaining exactly what you were doing. You've already seen the Start menu and know that it's just a list of tasks you might want to perform, such as starting a program. Most applications that run on Windows have two types of menus: those on the menu bar, which group commands by type of task, and those on shortcut menus, which group commands by the type of object you are working with. In this section, we'll examine both types of menus in more detail.

More about...
The Start menu, page 15

Using Menus on the Menu Bar

In most programs that run on Windows, you can carry out tasks by choosing commands from the menus on the menu bar. You click the name of the menu, and its list of commands drops down. In most programs, the menus containing commands that carry out similar tasks have the same name and occupy the same position on the menu bar. For example, the File menu contains commands such as New (for creating new items, such as documents); Open (for opening existing documents); Save (for saving the current document); and Exit (for leaving the program). No matter what program you are working in, the File menu always appears at the left end of the menu bar.

To choose a command from a menu, you simply click the command. To close a menu without choosing a command, you either click an empty spot away from the menu or press the Esc key. To practice, let's take a quick look at WordPad's menus and choose a command or two:

1. Click the word **File** on the menu bar.

   The File menu drops down, as shown in this graphic:

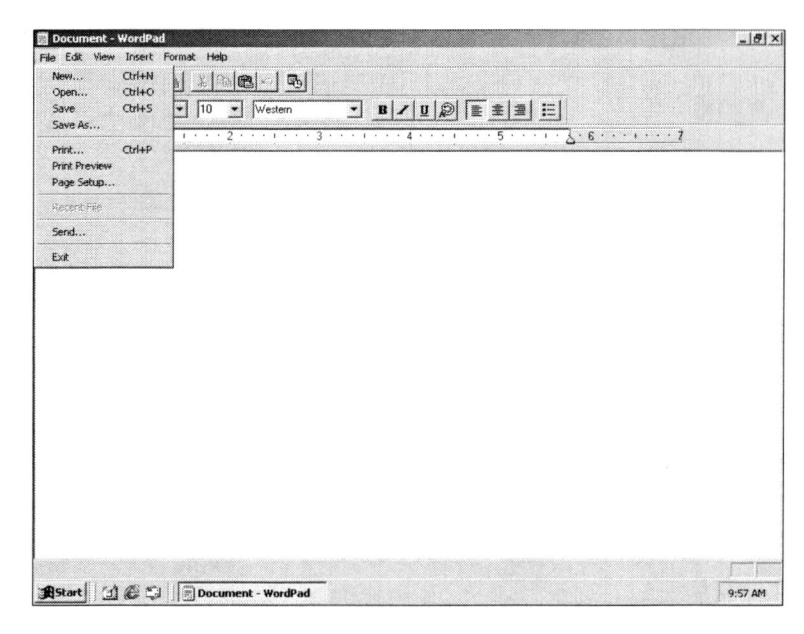

2. Point to the word **View** on the menu bar to display that menu.

   Notice that when one menu is open, you don't have to click to open another.

3. On the View menu, click **Ruler**.

   The menu closes, and the ruler is now turned off. (If the ruler was turned off, it is now turned on.)

4. On the menu bar, click **View** to display the View menu again.

5. Notice whether the Ruler command is preceded by a check mark. If it isn't, click **Ruler** to turn on the command and redisplay the ruler. If it is, press the **Esc** key to close the menu.

   The ruler is now turned on.

6. Click **View**, and make sure that check marks appear in front of the first four commands on the menu. (Click any that don't have check marks.) Then press **Esc** to close the menu.

   Commands that can be turned on and off in this way are called *toggle commands*. Turning on these toggle commands

HELP WITH COMMANDS

After displaying a menu, you can point to a command to display a description of its function in the program's status bar.

Chapter 2 Using Programs

ensures that your WordPad window displays all the elements shown earlier in the graphic.

All Windows-based programs present their menu commands in consistent ways and use the following visual cues to give you information about the commands:

- **Groups.** Commands that perform related tasks are grouped, and the group is separated from other commands by a line.
- **Unavailable commands.** Some commands appear in gray letters, indicating that they are not currently available. For example, many programs have Cut and Copy commands that appear in gray letters on their Edit menus until something that can be cut or copied has been selected in the active document.
- **Dialog boxes.** Some commands are followed by an ellipsis (...), indicating that you must supply information in a special kind of window called a *dialog box* before the command can be carried out.
- **Keyboard shortcuts.** Key combinations appear to the right of some commands, indicating that you can bypass the menu and carry out the command by pressing the corresponding keyboard shortcut.
- **Submenus.** Some command names are followed by a right-pointing arrow, indicating that the command has a submenu. (You saw how submenus work when you started WordPad.)
- **Toggles.** As you have just seen, some commands are preceded by a check mark, indicating that you can toggle the command on and off.

You'll become very familiar with these visual cues as you work your way through this course.

Using Dialog Boxes

As you saw in Chapter 1, you use dialog boxes to give Windows information or to select from several options so that a particular command can be carried out exactly the way you want it. To demonstrate, let's create a memo:

1. In WordPad, type *MEMO*, and press the **Enter** key twice.
2. Next type *To: All Staff*, press **Enter**, type *From: Julia*, and press **Enter**.
3. Now type *Date:* and a space.

CHOOSING COMMANDS WITH THE KEYBOARD
If you are more skilled at using the keyboard than the mouse, you can choose commands by pressing keys. First activate the menu bar by pressing Alt, and then open the menu you want by pressing the underlined letter in the menu name. Next choose a command by pressing the key for the underlined letter in the command name. If you change your mind, press Esc to close a menu without choosing a command, and press Esc again to deactivate the menu bar. After you have learned the letters for menus and commands, you can type the key sequence quickly to choose the command. For example, in many programs, pressing Alt, then F, and then X closes the program.

4. To insert the date in your memo, click **Insert** on the menu bar to display a list of the items that can be inserted in a WordPad document, and then click **Date and Time**.

WordPad checks your computer for the current date and time and then displays the date and time in various formats in the dialog box shown in this graphic:

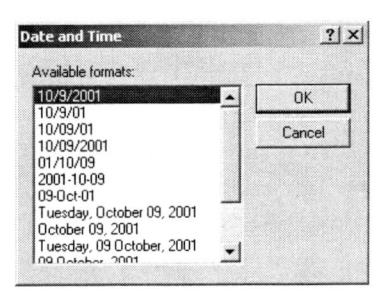

This dialog box is simple and presents only one set of options, but as you saw in Chapter 1, dialog boxes can be quite complex, like the one shown in this sample graphic:

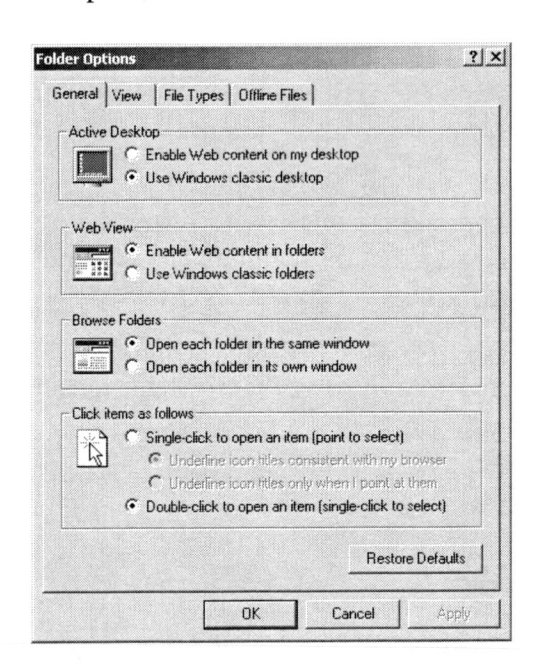

CORRECTING MISTAKES

If you make a mistake while typing the memo, the simplest way to correct it is to press the Backspace key until you have erased the error, and then retype the text correctly. If you need to move the insertion point, point to the place in the existing text where you want the insertion point to appear, and then click the primary mouse button. You can also use the Arrow keys to move the insertion point.

Because this dialog box has many options, they are arranged in logical groups on *tabs*. Here the General tab is displayed; clicking the View, File Types, or Offline Files tab displays that tab's options, just as you might display a different tabbed page in a binder.

Back in the Date and Time dialog box, you choose the look you want for dates by selecting a format from a list box.

Because the list of possible formats is too long to fit in its box, you use the scroll bar on the right side of the list box to scroll the list up and down to bring out-of-sight options into view.

5. Click the *scroll arrow* at the bottom of the scroll bar to see the other date format options, and then click the format that is the equivalent of October 09, 2001 to select it.

   Windows *highlights* your selection by changing it to white type on a dark background.

6. Click **OK**.

   WordPad inserts the current date in the selected format.

7. Next, press **Enter**, type *Subject: Directions to staff party*, and press **Enter** three times.

8. Type the following, and then press **Enter** twice:

   As promised, here are directions to Adventure Works. See you all there on Saturday!

9. Now type the following, pressing **Enter** where indicated:

   1. Take I-5 North to Alderfield. (Press **Enter**.)

   2. Take Exit 217, and turn right onto Route 24. (Press **Enter**.)

   3. Follow the road for 7 miles until you see the Alpine Ski Center on your left. (Press **Enter**.)

   4. Turn right onto Park Road, and the entrance to the park is immediately on the left by the totem pole. (Press **Enter**.)

SCROLLING

When a list box or window is not big enough to display all its contents, Windows provides vertical and/or horizontal scroll bars so that you can bring the rest of the contents into view. You use the vertical scroll bar to move the contents up and down and the horizontal scroll bar to move the contents from side to side. Clicking the arrow at either end of a scroll bar moves the contents a line or a column at a time. Clicking directly on the scroll bar on either side of the scroll box moves the contents a "windowful" at a time. You can also drag the scroll box. The position of the scroll box in relation to the scroll bar tells you where you are in the contents. When the scroll box is in the middle of its bar, the window is positioned about halfway through its contents. The size of the scroll box tells you about how much of the contents you can see at one time. For example, if the scroll box is half the length of the scroll bar, you can see half the contents. To alter the width of the scroll bar, right-click the desktop, and click Properties on the shortcut menu to display the Display Properties dialog box. Click the Appearance tab, click the down arrow to the right of the Item box, click Scrollbar in the drop-down list, and then change the setting in the Size box. Your change is reflected in the preview window. Click OK to close the Display Properties dialog box and change your settings.

When you finish typing, you see the results shown here:

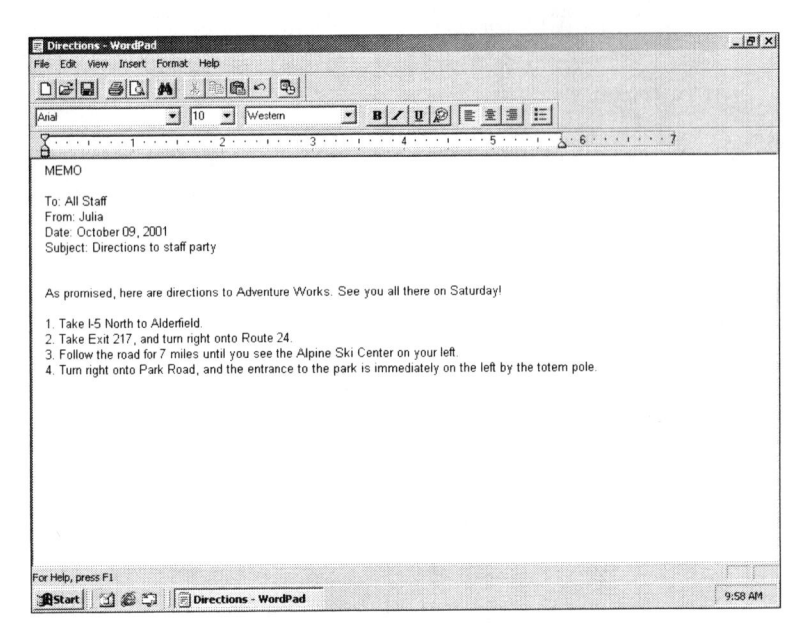

[Screenshot of WordPad window showing a memo document with the following content:

MEMO

To: All Staff
From: Julia
Date: October 09, 2001
Subject: Directions to staff party

As promised, here are directions to Adventure Works. See you all there on Saturday!

1. Take I-5 North to Alderfield.
2. Take Exit 217, and turn right onto Route 24.
3. Follow the road for 7 miles until you see the Alpine Ski Center on your left.
4. Turn right onto Park Road, and the entrance to the park is immediately on the left by the totem pole.]

In Windows, all dialog boxes request information in consistent ways and, like commands, provide visual cues to let you know the kind of information needed and how you should give it. Here's a list of the most common dialog box components:

- **Text boxes.** You enter information, such as a file name, by typing it in a text box. To replace an existing entry, select the entry and delete it, or overtype the old text with the new.

- **List boxes.** When you need to select from several options, the options are sometimes displayed in a list box. When you have more choices available than can fit in the list box, the list box has a scroll bar. For example, the list box in the Date and Time dialog box presents a vertical list of options with a vertical scroll bar. Regardless of the format of a list box, you select an option by clicking it. The option you clicked is then highlighted in the list.

- **Drop-down lists.** For space reasons, options are sometimes displayed in a drop-down list. A drop-down list appears initially as a text box containing an option. At the right end of the box is a down arrow that you can click to display a list of the other available options. To select an option, you simply click it. That option then appears in the box.

MORE ABOUT...
Selecting, pages 44 and 82

- **Combo boxes.** Sometimes a text box and a drop-down list box are combined to form a combo box. You can either type the information or select it from a drop-down list.

- **Check boxes.** Some options are presented with a check box (a small square) in front of them. Clicking an empty check box selects the associated option; a check mark appears in the box to indicate that the option is *active*, or *turned on*. Clicking the box again removes the check mark to indicate that the option is *deselected*, *cleared*, or *turned off*. Check boxes operate independently, so if a dialog box presents a group of check boxes, you can select none, one, some, or all of them, as required for the task at hand.

- **Option buttons.** Some options are presented with an option button (a small circle, also known as a *radio button*) in front of them. These buttons are used in groups of mutually exclusive options. When you click an option button, a dot appears in the button to indicate that the option is selected, or turned on. Because only one option in the group can be turned on at a time, the dot disappears from the button of the previously selected option.

- **Command buttons.** Most dialog boxes have at least two command buttons: one that carries out the command and one that cancels the command. Clicking either button also closes the dialog box. Some dialog boxes have additional buttons that you can use to refine the original command. As with commands on menus, if the label on a button is followed by an ellipsis (...), clicking the button opens another dialog box. A dark border around a command button indicates that you can press Enter at any time to implement that command.

USING THE KEYBOARD WITH DIALOG BOXES

In dialog boxes that require you to type information in text boxes, it is often quicker to move around the dialog box using just the keyboard than switching between the keyboard and mouse. You can move among the elements in a dialog box by pressing the Tab key. (An active text box contains either a blinking insertion point or a highlighted entry. Other elements are designated as being active by a dotted outline.) With a list box or a group of option buttons, pressing Tab takes you to the active option. You can then either press Arrow keys to move through the options one at a time, press Home or End to move to the first or last option, or press Page Up or Page Down to display the previous or next boxful of options. When the option you want is selected, press Tab to move to the next element. No matter which element is active, pressing Enter immediately implements the command button that has a dark border. Pressing Esc implements the Cancel button.

- **Spin boxes.** If a text box must contain one of a specific set of options (usually numbers), it sometimes has a pair of up and down arrows at its right end. You change the entry either by selecting the existing number and typing a new one or by clicking one of the arrows to increase or decrease the number.

- **Sliders.** Number settings can also be represented by the position of a slider on a horizontal or vertical bar. To change the setting, you drag the slider.

- **Toolbar buttons.** Some dialog boxes have toolbar buttons that you use to interrupt the current task and carry out a different one, or to modify the current task in some way.

To get some practice with a more complex dialog box, let's save the memo you have just created. In the following steps, you'll assign a file name to the document, specify where to store it, and create a folder to hold this and related documents. You'll also get an idea of how your computer's storage (the electronic equivalent of a filing cabinet) is structured. Here we go:

1. Click **File** on the menu bar, and then click **Save As**.

   WordPad displays the Save As dialog box shown in this graphic:

Because this document is brand new, WordPad suggests the name *Document* in the File name text box. Take our word for it: saving a document with a name that is too generic, such as *Document*, is a bad practice. Instead, you want to give the document a unique descriptive name and tuck it

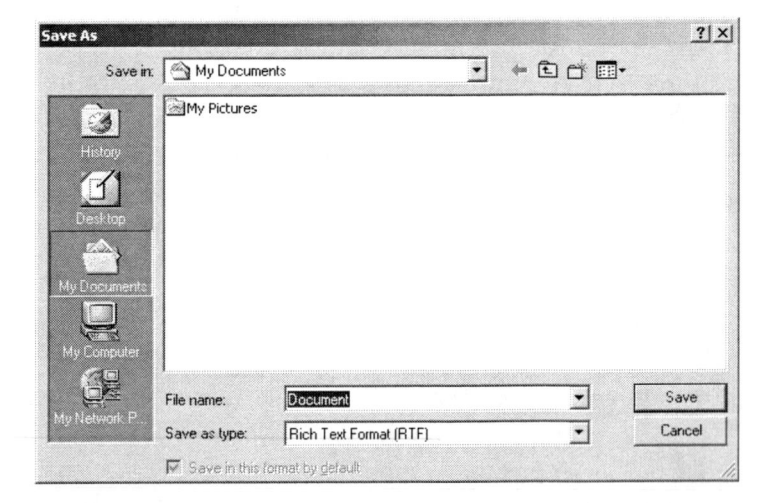

CHANGING YOUR MIND
If you change your mind about the settings you have made in an open dialog box, click Cancel or press Esc to close the dialog box. All the changes you made are discarded, and the previous settings remain in effect. You can then start over if necessary.

CHAPTER 2 USING PROGRAMS

in a predictable location with other related documents, so that it will be easy to find weeks or even months from now.

2. The word *Document* is selected in the **File name** box, so simply type *Directions* to replace it.

   You can type information in a text box only if a blinking insertion point or a highlighted entry indicates that the box is active.

   The Save in text box at the top of the dialog box indicates that WordPad will save the document in a folder called My Documents unless you specify otherwise. The list box shows any folders and files already stored in the My Documents folder, such as the My Pictures folder created automatically by Windows.

3. Click the down arrow to the right of the **Save in** box.

   A hierarchical list of potential storage locations appears, as shown in this graphic:

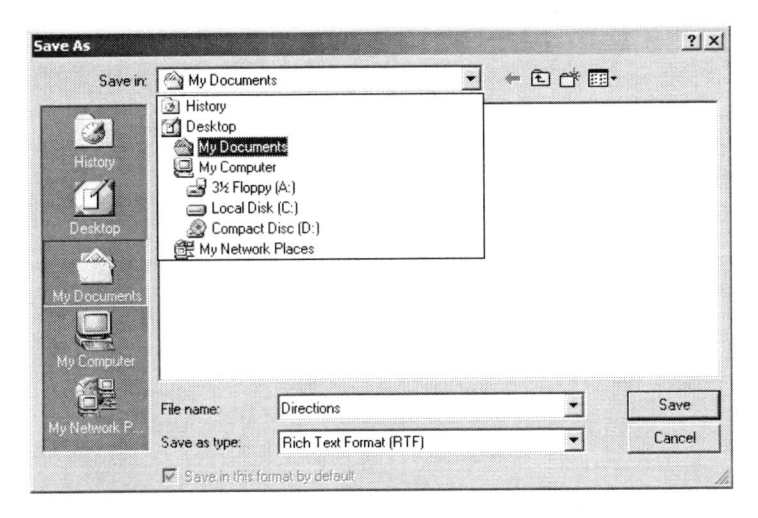

MORE ABOUT...
Naming files and folders, page 80

[Save As dialog box screenshot showing storage locations including History, Desktop, My Documents, My Computer, 3½ Floppy (A:), Local Disk (C:), Compact Disc (D:), My Network Places; File name: Directions; Save as type: Rich Text Format (RTF)]

The desktop has these storage locations: My Documents (the default storage folder for documents—*default* means the option your computer will use unless you specify a different setting); My Computer (your PC); and My Network Places (the PCs on any network to which you are connected). In turn, My Computer has several storage locations, which, depending on your particular hardware configuration, might consist of floppy disk drives, hard disk drives, CD-ROM drives, or DVD-ROM drives. If you are connected to other computers on a network, My Network Places might show several storage locations as well.

NAME CONVENTIONS
File names and folder names cannot have more than 215 characters, and they cannot contain these characters:

\ / : * ? " < > |

4. Click **Local Disk (C:)**, which designates the main hard disk drive in your computer.

   Local Disk (C:) replaces My Documents in the Save in box, and the list box displays a set of folders in which various files are already stored on drive C. (Your list will look different from the one in our graphics because yours reflects the folders and files on your drive C.)

   You could save the memo directly on drive C, but that's not a good idea. You wouldn't throw all your paper documents in one big pile if you expected to be able to easily find a specific document later on. Instead, you'd organize all the documents and store them in file folders. Likewise, you need to organize your computer documents for easy retrieval.

5. Click the **Create New Folder** button above the list box.

   Windows creates a new folder on drive C and highlights its title to indicate that it is selected, as shown in this graphic:

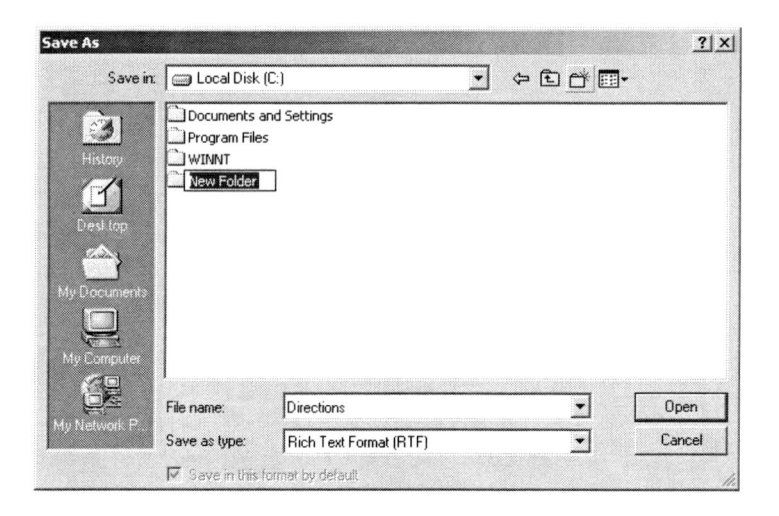

WHY DO YOU HAVE TO SAVE DOCUMENTS?

A document exists only in your computer's memory until you save it on a storage device such as a hard disk or floppy disk. Memory is temporary and can be erased deliberately by turning off your computer or accidentally by power surges and failures. Disk storage is more permanent and can be erased only by using specific commands or by fairly rare drive failures. If all you want to do is type a letter, print it, and send it, you might not need to store the letter on your hard disk. However, you'll want to save the file if you need an electronic record of what the letter said, if you want to use that letter as the basis for another letter, or if composing the letter is taking a while and you don't want to have to start over in the event of a computer glitch. The hard drives of the world are full of trivial documents that will never again see the light of day and that are not critical to "who said what to whom and when" audit trails. Your company might have a policy about which documents need to be saved and for how long. Otherwise, you can decide for yourself which documents to save.

Chapter 2 Using Programs

6. Type *Staff Party* to replace the selected title, and press **Enter**.

7. Now double-click the folder icon to the left of Staff Party to open the folder.

   Staff Party replaces Local Disk (C:) in the Save in box; the list box is empty because nothing is stored in the new folder yet.

8. Ensure that **Rich Text Format** (**RTF**) is selected in the **Save as type** drop-down list.

9. Click **Save** to save the memo in Rich Text Format with the name Directions in the Staff Party folder.

   The dialog box closes, and you return to WordPad, where Directions has replaced Document in the title bar and on the taskbar button.

Using Shortcut Menus

Windows applications make extensive use of shortcut menus, which group together the commands you're most likely to use with a particular *object*. An object can be an icon on the desktop, a toolbar in a program window, a word in a document, and a variety of other things. Let's explore shortcut menus further:

1. Click **Edit** on the menu bar, and then click **Select All** to select the entire memo.

2. Move the pointer over the selection, and right-click to display its shortcut menu.

   As you can see in the graphic on the next page, this shortcut menu includes commands for manipulating the selected text.

File types and file name extensions

Depending on the application you use to create a file, you will have several file types from which to choose, including Document Template, Text Document, Rich Text Format, and Web Page. Most applications give you the option of saving as an application-specific file type, such as Excel Workbook or PowerPoint Show. Graphic files can be saved as a wide variety of file types, each of which has specific benefits depending on how you intend to use the graphic. The file type also determines the file name extension—the set of letters appended to the file name. For example, when you save a file as a Word Document, the extension is *.doc*. The extension then determines what programs can be used to open, edit, or display the file.

Rich Text Format

You save a document as a Rich Text Format (RTF) file when you don't know which word processor will be used to open it. In an RTF file, the formatting is translated into codes that can be interpreted by most word processors. Even if you work on the RTF file in another word processor, such as Microsoft Word, you will still be able to open it in WordPad.

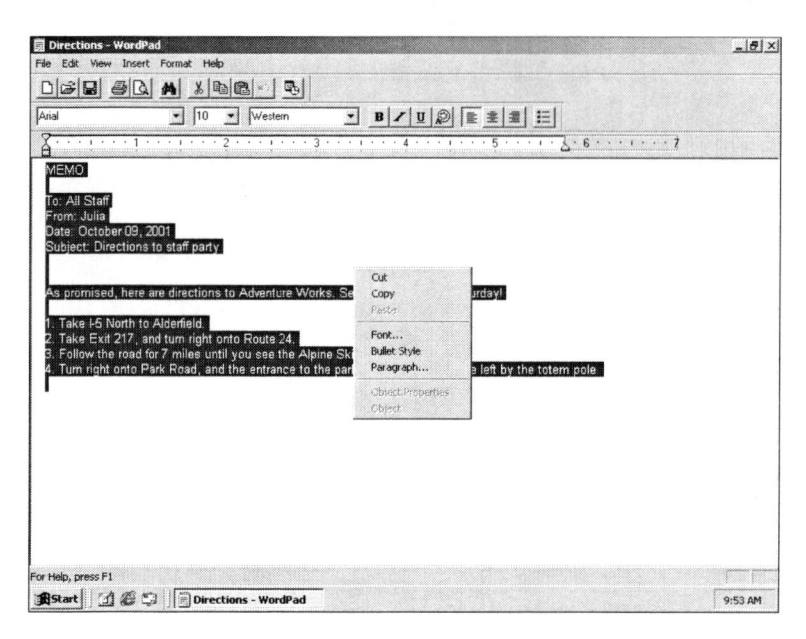

3. Click **Paragraph** to display the dialog box shown here:

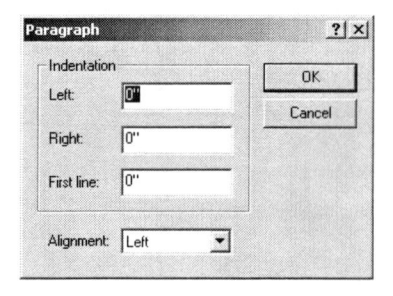

SELECTING TEXT

With Windows-based programs, you can use several techniques for selecting text. You can double-click a word to select it. You can triple-click a block of text to select it. You can point to the beginning of a block of text, hold down the left mouse button, and drag through the block, releasing the mouse button when the entire block is highlighted. You can *shift-click*—click to place an insertion point at the beginning of a block, hold down the Shift key, and click at the end of the block to select it all. And you can click an insertion point and hold down the Shift key while you use an Arrow key to highlight text.

PATHS

Some dialog boxes, such as the one that appears when you click Run on the Start menu, ask for the *path* of a program, file, or folder. Think of the path as an address. For files stored on your computer, this address starts with the drive letter and traces through folders and subfolders to the file's exact location, separating each storage level from the previous one with a backslash (\). For example, *C:\Staff Party\Directions.rtf* is the path of the Directions document stored in the Staff Party folder on drive C. If the path contains any spaces (such as the space between Staff and Party) you need to enclose the entire path in quotation marks so that Windows knows that it is one string of information. If you are working on a network, the path of a document stored on another networked computer starts with two backslashes and the computer name, followed by the drive letter, any folders and subfolders, and the document's file name (including the file name extension). When a dialog box requires that you enter a path, you can either type the path directly in the text box, or if you are unsure of the path (or are a slow typist), there is usually a Browse button you can click. In the Browse dialog box, you can navigate to the location of file and click Open to insert the path of the selected file in the text box, just as if you had typed it.

Chapter 2 Using Programs

4. Type *1* to replace the highlighted 0" in the **Left** text box, and click **OK**.

   Here's the result:

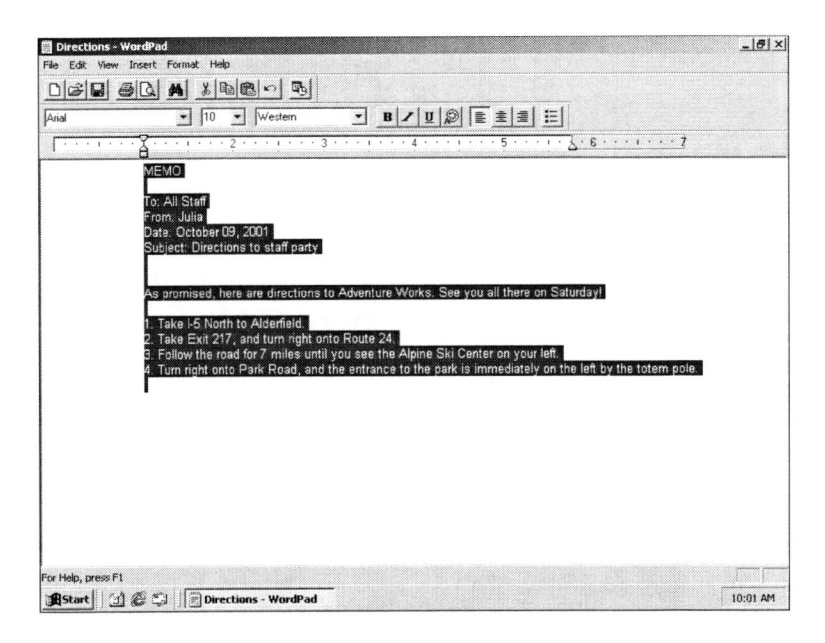

Choosing Commands with Toolbar Buttons

Most programs that run on Windows 2000 have toolbars, which display buttons and boxes that you can use to carry out common commands. Clicking a button carries out its command with the predefined, or default, settings. When you want something other than the default settings, you must access the command on its menu. Here's how to familiarize yourself with the buttons on the WordPad toolbar:

1. Point to each toolbar button in turn, pausing until the button's name appears in a box below the pointer. (These boxes are called *ScreenTips*.)

2. Look at the status bar at the bottom of the window, where WordPad displays a brief description of the button you are pointing to.

To demonstrate how to use toolbar buttons, we'll introduce you to an important button. The one-inch left indent you just set looks a bit goofy. You could repeat the previous set of steps to reverse the Paragraph command, but here's an easier way:

1. Click the **Undo** button on the top toolbar, which most applications call the *Standard toolbar*.

WordPad resets the left indent to 0.

Clicking the Undo button is the equivalent of choosing the Undo command from the Edit menu. (You can also press Ctrl+Z.) Many Windows applications include an Undo command, enabling you to reverse your last editing action. Some applications' Undo commands enable you to erase several of your recent actions. Knowing that you can always take a step backward makes experimenting less hazardous. It's worth checking out the Undo command of any application you use, so you'll know exactly what to do if you paint yourself into a corner.

2. Move the pointer to the left of *MEMO* at the top of the document, and when the pointer changes to a right-pointing arrow, click the left mouse button to select just that line.

3. Click the **Align Right** button on the bottom toolbar, which most applications call the *Formatting toolbar*.

The line jumps to the right side of the screen, and WordPad changes the look of the button on the Formatting toolbar so that it appears "pressed." (Looking at the buttons on the Formatting toolbar is a good way of telling at a glance what formatting is applied to selected text.)

4. Click the **Undo** button to move the line back to the left side of the screen.

Now the Align Left button appears pressed.

5. Click the **Bold** button on the Formatting toolbar to make the text bold.

6. Click a blank area of the document to see this result:

UNDO VARIATIONS

The capabilities of the Undo button—which actions it can undo and how many changes it remembers—vary between applications. When working with a new application, you might want to experiment with less critical documents so that you know how far you can backtrack. When the Undo button has a down arrow to its right, you can click the arrow to select from a list of recent actions that are available to be undone.

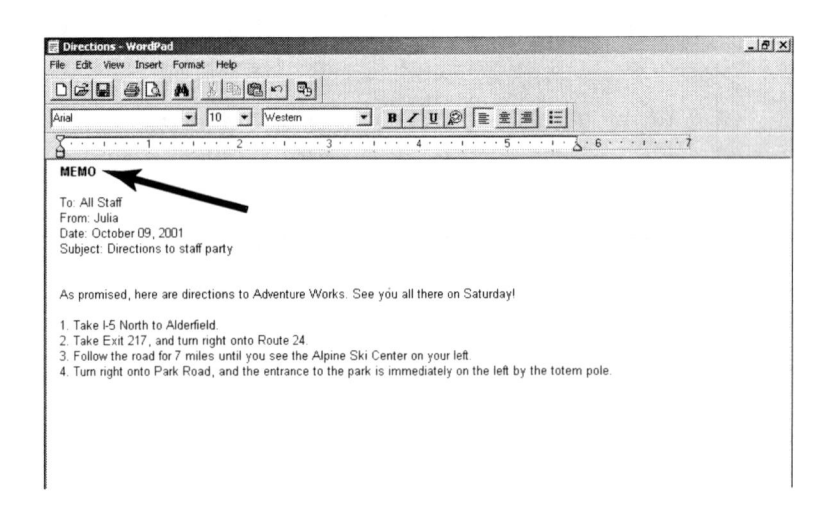

Chapter 2 Using Programs

7. Reselect *MEMO*, and try clicking other buttons on the Formatting toolbar and then clicking **Undo**.

8. When you are ready, click the **Save** button.

   WordPad saves the document with the current settings, including the file name.

For practice, you might want to create a new document and experiment with formatting commands.

More About...
Creating a new document, page 142

MULTITASKING

The term *multitasking* might sound intimidating, but the concept is simple: Multitasking is carrying out two or more tasks at the same time. For example, you might be writing a report while your computer is printing another document, or while your communications program is downloading information from an online service, or while your e-mail program is receiving an incoming message. In practice, most people don't often take advantage of multitasking. They usually open two or three programs and work with one while the others sit idly in memory, waiting until they are needed. The programs have been started and they are available, but they aren't actually doing any work.

Having several programs open at once saves you time by enabling you to keep all the information you need at your fingertips, whether it is stored in a report, in a spreadsheet, in a database, or in any other type of document. If you're in the middle of writing a letter and need to look up some numbers in a spreadsheet, you don't have to stop what you are doing, quit the word processor, load the spreadsheet, find the numbers, and then start your word processor again. You can simply switch between windows to get the information you need.

Although you can have more than one program running at the same time, only one program can run *in the foreground*, meaning that its window is active and receiving input from you. Any other open program runs *in the background*, meaning that it is behind the scenes, either carrying out another task or waiting for your next instruction. Let's use the keyboard to start another program and experiment:

1. Hold down the **Ctrl** key, and press **Esc** to open the Start menu.

2. Press the **Up Arrow** key until Programs is highlighted, and then press **Enter**.

The Programs submenu opens with Accessories selected.

3. Press **Enter** to open the Accessories submenu.

4. Press the **Down Arrow** key until Calculator is selected, and press **Enter**.

   Windows starts its mini number cruncher, which is shown in this graphic:

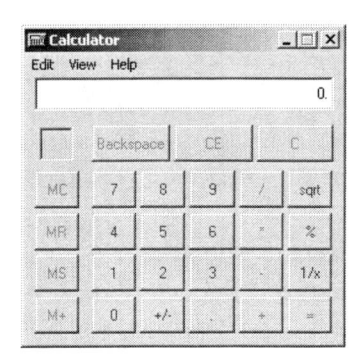

   [Calculator window image]

5. Click anywhere in the WordPad window to bring it to the foreground and make it active.

6. Click the **New** button.

7. When WordPad asks you to specify a format for the new document, double-click **Rich Text Document**.

   With WordPad, you can have only one document open at a time, so the Directions file closes, and the new document takes its place. If you had not just saved the changes you have made to the Directions document, WordPad would have displayed a message box asking if you wanted to save the current version.

SWITCHING AMONG RUNNING PROGRAMS

MESSAGE BOXES
Windows-based programs display message and warning boxes when a command you have chosen can't be carried out or there is a chance you might regret the choice (for example, when you delete files). You can click OK or Yes to acknowledge the message and continue the command. Click Cancel or No to close the message box and cancel the command.

As you just saw, it's easy to switch to a program when you can see part of its window. If you are working in a maximized window and can't see the windows of programs running in the background, you can use the taskbar buttons to switch among programs. As a demonstration, suppose you are responsible for providing appetizers for the staff party, and while browsing through the Yellow Pages, you use WordPad to take down information about potential caterers. Follow these steps:

1. In the new document, type *Sweet Lill's*, press **Enter**, type *555-1001*, and press **Enter** twice.

CHAPTER 2 USING PROGRAMS

2. Add a second caterer to the list:

   Healthy Food Store (Press **Enter**.)

   555-5364 (Press **Enter** twice.)

3. Add another caterer:

   Blue Sky Grocery and Grill (Press **Enter**.)

   555-9292 (Press **Enter**.)

   The WordPad window is shown in this graphic:

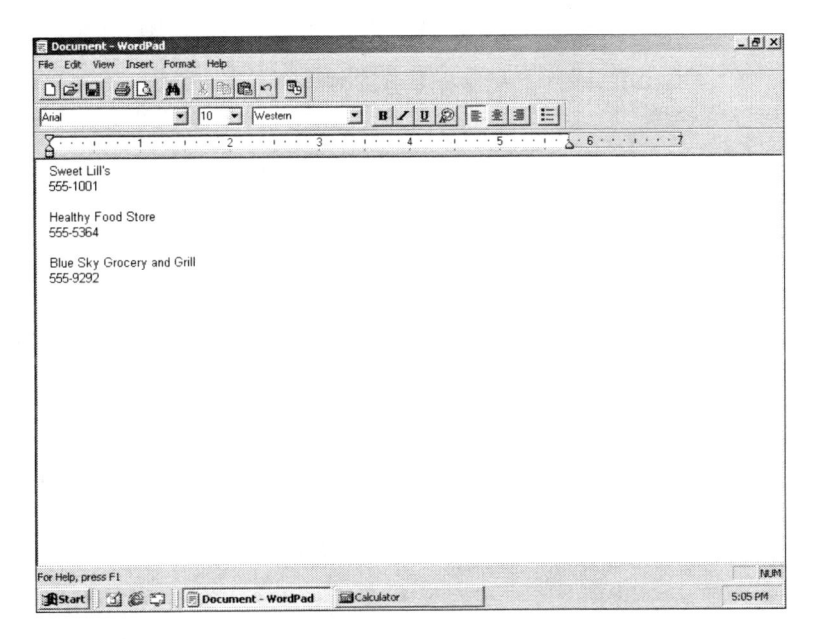

4. Click the **Save** button.

   You haven't yet named the document, so WordPad displays the Save As dialog box.

5. If Staff Party does not appear in the Save in box, click the down arrow to the right of the **Save in** box, click **Local Disk (C:)** in the drop-down list, and double-click **Staff Party** in the list box.

6. With Document selected in the File name text box, type *Caterers* as the file name.

   If Document is not selected, you can double-click it to select it.

7. With Rich Text Format (RTF) selected as the "Save as type" setting, click **Save**.

Suppose you are using your handy list to call the caterers and get estimates. The first caterer quotes you a per-person price of $6.25 for a regular assortment of appetizers and $7.75 for a deluxe assortment. You want to know the respective costs for 72 people. This is a job for Calculator:

1. Click the **Calculator** button on the taskbar to bring the Calculator window to the foreground.

2. Click the buttons for *72*, click the *x* button (the symbol for multiplication), click the buttons for *6.25*, and click *=*.

   You can also press the equivalent numeric-keypad keys if NumLock is turned on. The display bar shows the total, 450.

3. Click the **WordPad** button on the taskbar to display its window, which obscures the Calculator window.

4. Click at the beginning of the blank line after the first caterer's telephone number to position the insertion point there, type *Regular: $450*, and press **Enter**.

Here's another way to switch between open programs:

1. Hold down the **Alt** key, and without releasing it, press the **Tab** key.

   A window appears in the middle of the screen in which icons represent the open programs. A selection box indicates which program Windows will switch to when you release the Alt key (generally the last program that was active before the one you're currently using).

2. Still holding down the **Alt** key, press **Tab** again to move the selection box to the icon of the other program. Press **Tab** again to move the selection box back to the Calculator icon, and then release the **Alt** key.

3. In the Calculator window, click the **CE** (for clear entry) button, click the buttons for *72*, click the *x* button, click the buttons for *7.75*, and then click *=*.

   The display bar shows the total, 558.

4. Switch back to WordPad using the **Alt+Tab** combination.

5. With the insertion point at the beginning of the blank line after the regular cost, type *Deluxe: $558*, and press **Enter**.

Now suppose the second deli has quoted you a per-person price of $5.75 for a regular assortment of appetizers and $7.25 for a

---

ABOUT NUMLOCK

The numeric keypad at the right of your computer's keyboard serves a variety of purposes. For many people, particularly those who do a lot of work with numbers, the keypad provides an easier way to type numbers than using the standard number keys. To use the numeric keypad to enter numbers, NumLock must be turned on. (Simply press the NumLock key.) People who have difficulty using the mouse can use the numeric keypad to control the mouse pointer. For more information, search Windows 2000 Help for *Accessibility Options*.

Chapter 2 Using Programs

deluxe assortment. First we'll arrange the open programs so that you can see them both at the same time, and then we'll enter the information for the second deli:

1. Right-click a blank area of the taskbar, and click **Tile Windows Vertically** on the shortcut menu to arrange the open windows side-by-side.

2. Click the **Calculator** window's title bar to activate it, click **CE**, click the buttons for 72, click *x*, click the buttons for 5.75, and then click =.

   The display bar shows the total, 414.

3. Click the **Caterers** window, click an insertion point at the beginning of the blank line after the second caterer's telephone number, type *Regular: $414*, and press **Enter**.

4. Repeat steps 2 and 3 with the deluxe $7.25 amount to calculate the second caterer's deluxe cost, and then enter it in the document.

   Your screen looks like the one in this graphic:

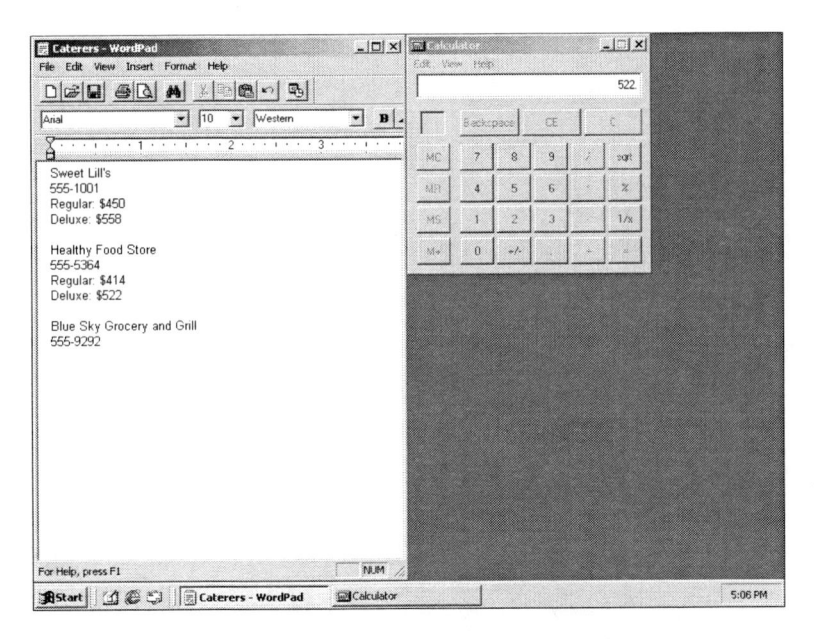

Sharing Information Among Programs

With Windows, it's easy to use the information from one program in another program. Need a logo for your letterhead? You

About Calculator

Calculator is capable of performing more complex functions than those we describe here, and it provides several buttons you can use to store calculations. To learn the exact function of a particular button, as well as its keyboard shortcut, right-click the button, and then click What's This? on the shortcut menu. To display a scientific calculator, click View, and then click Scientific.

can create one with a graphics program, copy it to a storage area in the computer's memory called the *Clipboard*, and then paste it into a word-processing document. Because you can run the graphics program and the word processing program simultaneously in Windows, moving from one program to the other is a simple matter of clicking the mouse button.

More About...
Transferring data among programs, page 146

You can experiment with transferring information by following these steps, which use WordPad and Calculator to complete the information for the third caterer:

1. Click the **Calculator** window, click CE, click the buttons for 72, click the *x* button, click the *6* button, and click =.

   The display bar shows the regular appetizer cost at $6 per person, 432.

2. Click Calculator's **Edit** menu, and click **Copy** to copy the value in the display bar to the Clipboard.

3. Click the **Caterers** window, click an insertion point at the beginning of the blank line after the third caterer's telephone number, and type *Regular:* followed by a space and $.

4. Click WordPad's **Edit** menu, and click **Paste** to paste the total from Calculator into the document. Then press **Enter**.

5. Repeat steps 1 through 4 to calculate the third caterer's deluxe appetizer cost at $7.50 per person and paste it into the document.

6. Save your work.

To give you more practice using multiple programs, we'll take a look at Character Map, a Windows-based program you can use to insert special characters in your documents. The following steps add an entry for a fourth caterer called Mom's Kitchen Café to the list:

About the Clipboard
The Clipboard is a temporary storage place in your computer's memory where data cut or copied from any open Windows-based program is stored. You can use it to transfer data within the same program or from one program to another. Because the Clipboard is a temporary storage place, shutting down your computer erases any information you have stored there.

1. With the Caterers window active and the insertion point at the beginning of the blank line below the third caterer, press **Enter**, and type *Mom's Kitchen Caf*.

2. Click the **Start** button, display the **Programs**, **Accessories**, and **System Tools** submenus, and then click **Character Map**.

   The window shown in this graphic appears:

CHAPTER 2 USING PROGRAMS   53

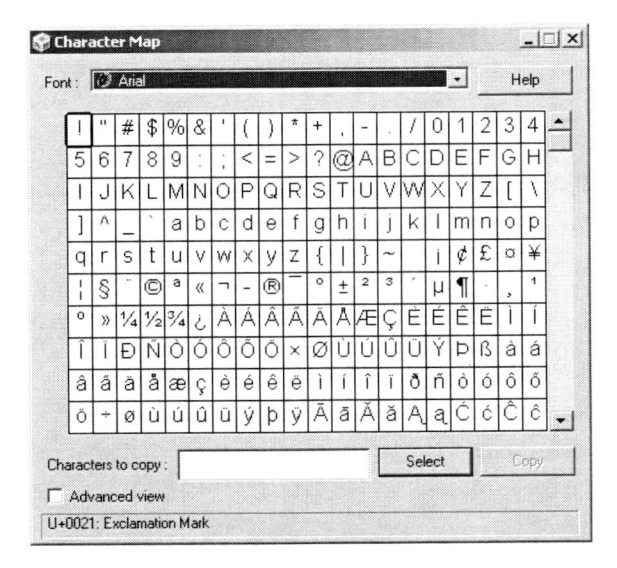

As you can see, the program displays all the characters available in the font specified in the Font box.

3. If the font currently shown in the box is not Arial, click the down arrow to the right of the **Font** box, and click **Arial** in the drop-down list.

4. If the **Characters to copy** box is not empty, double-click the existing entry, and press the **Delete** key.

5. Click *é* to enlarge the character so that you can verify that it is the character you want to insert, and then click the **Select** button.

The program enters *é* in the Characters to copy box, and the window now looks like the one shown in this graphic:

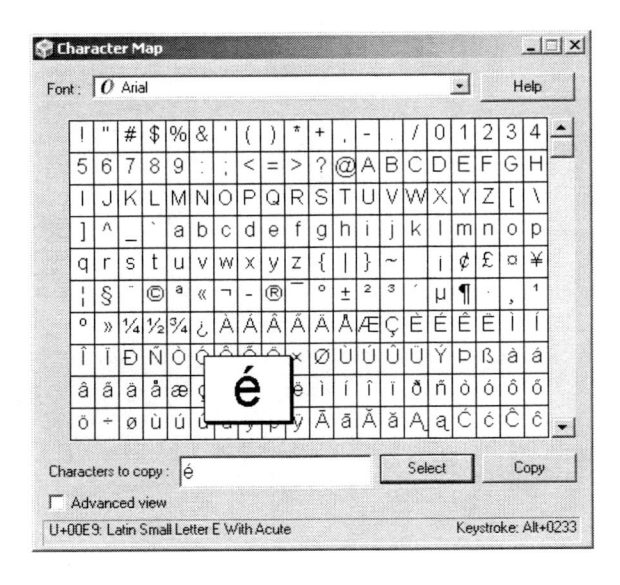

ENTERING CHARACTERS WITH THE KEYBOARD

The bottom right corner of the Character Map window displays the shortcut you can use to insert the selected character from the keyboard. For example, you could insert the *é* character without switching to Character Map by holding down the Alt key and pressing 0, 2, 3, and 3 (Alt+0233) on your keyboard's numeric keypad. (You can't use the number keys that are across the top of your keyboard.)

6. Click the **Copy** button to copy the character to the Clipboard, and then minimize the Character Map window.

7. With the Caterers document active and the insertion point at the end of the last line, click the **Paste** button on the toolbar.

   The character you copied in the Character Map window appears at the insertion point.

The font size of *é* is 13 points, but the rest of the text in the Caterers document is 10 points. To fix this problem, follow these steps:

1. Select *é* by dragging the mouse pointer over it so that it becomes highlighted.

   If you have trouble selecting a single character with the mouse, click to the right of the *é*, hold down the Shift key, and press the Left Arrow key.

2. On the Formatting toolbar, click the down arrow to the right of the **Font Size** box, and click **10** in the drop-down list.

Now let's complete the information for the fourth caterer:

1. Press the **End** key to move to the end of the current line, and then press **Enter**.

2. Type *555-6198* as the telephone number, and press **Enter**.

   The results are shown in this graphic:

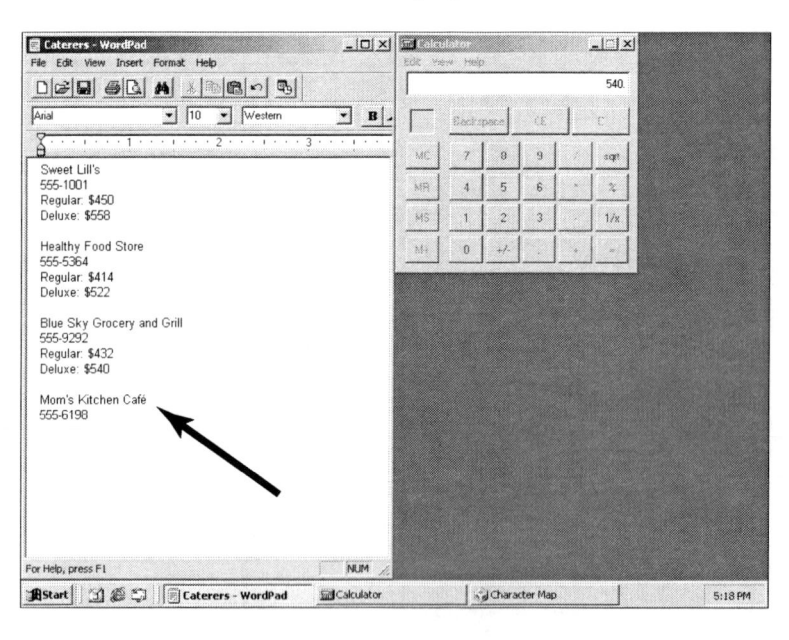

ABOUT FONTS

Windows 2000 comes with a standard set of fonts, and some programs install other fonts. In any program, you can see which fonts are available by clicking the down arrow to the right of the Font box. When you are not working in a program, you can display Control Panel and then double-click the Fonts icon to open the Fonts folder. To see a sample of a font, double-click the font's icon. To print the sample, click the Print button, select a printer, and then click Print. The sample includes a font description and examples in several sizes. Fonts are measured in terms of their height—the distance from the bottom of descender characters, such as *p*, to the top of ascender characters, such as *h*. The unit of measure is called a *point* (abbreviated *pt*), and 1 point equals 1/72 inch. So if the setting in a program's Font Size box is 12, the size of the characters is approximately 1/6 inch.

Chapter 2 Using Programs

The last item you copied, *é*, is still on the Clipboard and will stay there until it is replaced by the next item you cut or copy, or until you quit Windows.

Let's sidetrack here to see the copied item on the Clipboard:

1. Click the **Start** button, and then click **Run**.
2. Type *clipbrd* in the **Open** text box, and then click **OK**.

   Windows starts the ClipBook Viewer program, which initially looks like this:

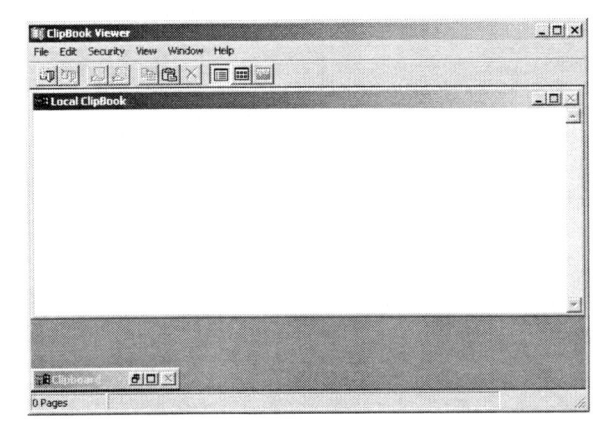

3. In the bottom left corner of the ClipBook Viewer window, click the Clipboard window's **Maximize** button and see the contents of the Clipboard displayed in the window.

4. Resize and move the ClipBook Viewer window so that your screen looks like the one shown in this graphic:

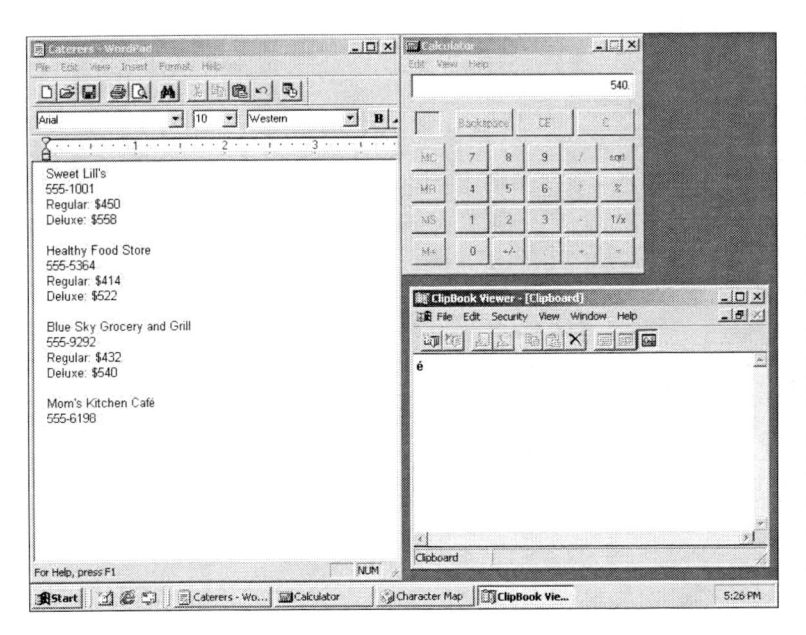

SAVING CLIPBOARD CONTENTS

Unlike the Clipboard, ClipBook Viewer can store several items. To save something you have cut or copied to the Clipboard for use at a later time, open ClipBook Viewer, which displays the copied text, click Save As on the File menu, enter a name and storage location for the item in the Save As dialog box, and then click Save. To access the item later, open ClipBook Viewer, and then click Open on the File menu. You can then copy the item and paste it into another program as usual.

5. Calculate the cost of regular appetizers at $6.50 per person, and copy and paste the result into the Caterers document.

   Notice that the copied item replaces the existing item in the ClipBook Viewer window.

6. Repeat step 5 to calculate the cost of deluxe appetizers at $8 per person, and paste the result into the Caterers document.

7. Save the document.

After you have created a document, you'll usually want to print it, so we'll discuss printing next.

Using Printers

Although computers were supposed to usher in the era of the paperless office, in our experience this has not been the case. Even with the proliferation of electronic mail and computer-to-computer faxes, most people still print at least some of their documents.

More About...
Changing the default printer, page 57

With Windows 2000, you can print in three ways: by using a program's Print command, by dragging a document to a printer icon, or by using the Send To command. Unless you specify otherwise, the document is printed on the default printer. If there is only one printer attached to your computer, that printer is usually the default. If you have a choice of more than one printer, the default is probably the one you use most frequently. In this section, we assume you have installed one printer that is physically connected to your computer (called a *local printer*), but the procedure for using a printer that is connected to your network (called a *network printer*) is basically the same.

Printing from a Program

You can print an open document from within a program by using the program's Print command. To see how this is done, follow these steps to print the Caterers document we've been working on in WordPad:

1. In the Caterers document, click **File**, and then click **Print**.

   The Print dialog box appears. This dialog box varies from program to program, but typically, it looks something like the one shown in this graphic:

CHAPTER 2 USING PROGRAMS

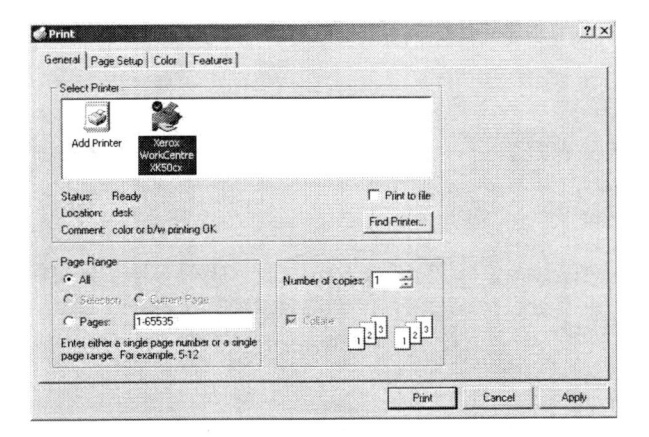

The Select Printer box shows the available printers and which printer is currently selected. The Status line tells you whether the printer is busy or ready to receive your document. The Location line indicates where the printer is physically located, as specified in the printer's Properties dialog box. Finally, the Comment line contains any notes you have made about this printer.

2. You want to print the entire document, so leave the **Page Range** option set to **All**.

   With multi-page documents, you can print a range of pages by selecting the Pages option and typing the page numbers in the text box—with individual pages separated by commas, and page ranges indicated by hyphens. You can select part of a document and print just that part by selecting the Selection option, or just print the page you are currently looking at by selecting the Current Page option.

3. Change the **Number Of Copies** setting to 2.

4. Click **Print** to print two copies of Caterers on your selected printer.

The Print dialog box offers printing options that vary depending on the application you're printing from. You can generally select printers from the Print dialog box, as well as check on the status and location of printers, and add comments regarding each printer on the network. By clicking the tabs (or in some programs the Preferences button), you can see even more details about the selected printer. (The Printing Preferences dialog box usually includes such settings as portrait or landscape orientation, paper size, and resolution.) Selecting the "Print to file" check box prints the current content to a file instead of to the specified printer. You can also specify the print range and

CHANGING YOUR PRINTER SETUP

To make changes to your printer setup, click the Start button, point to Settings, and then click Printers. Then right-click the icon for your printer to display its shortcut menu. If you want to rename the printer, click Rename, type the new name, and press Enter. To add a comment for the printer, click Properties, type the comment in the Comment box on the General tab, and then click OK. To make the printer the default, click Set as Default Printer. To delete the printer, click Delete, and click Yes to confirm the deletion. If Windows asks if you want to remove the files used for the printer, click Yes or No, depending on whether you will use that printer again in the future.

number of copies, and sometimes you can tell the printer to *collate* (to order numerically) multiple copies of documents.

ADDING A PRINTER

You can use the Add Printer Wizard to install a local or network printer on your computer. Wizards are programs that guide you step by step through a process, prompting you for all the information Windows needs to carry out a task that is too complex to accomplish in a single dialog box. Follow these steps to see how wizards work:

1. To start the wizard, click the **Start** button, point to **Settings**, and click **Printers** to open the Printers window. Then double-click the **Add Printer** icon to display the wizard's first page.

2. Click **Next** to display the second page of the wizard. Select the **Local printer** option, and then click **Next**.

3. Select the port to which your printer is connected, and then click **Next**.

4. Scroll through the **Manufacturer** list on the left side of the fourth page of the wizard, and select your printer's manufacturer. The **Printers** list on the right side of the dialog box changes to reflect the printer models produced by the manufacturer you chose. Select the correct model from the **Printers** list, and click **Next**. (If your printer is not listed, check the installation instructions that came with it. You will probably need to insert a disk and click the **Have Disk** button.)

5. Leave the printer name as is or type a new name in the **Printer name** text box, select **Yes** if you want to designate the new printer as the default printer, and click **Next**.

6. Indicate whether you want to share the printer, and then click **Next**.

7. To print a test page, click **Yes**, click **Next**, and then click **Finish**.

Windows might ask you to insert the Windows 2000 CD-ROM so that it can copy the driver for the new printer to your hard disk. You then return to the Printers window, where the new printer is now listed.

If you're on a network, here's how to access a network printer:

1. In the Printers window, double-click the **Add Printer** icon to start the Add Printer Wizard, and then click **Next**.

WHAT IS A DRIVER?

A driver is a program that tells Windows how to work with a specific piece of hardware. Windows 2000 ships with the drivers for hundreds of common types of monitors, printers, sound cards, and so on, and because Windows can usually detect exactly what's needed, you might never need to deal with drivers. However, if you buy an exotic piece of hardware, you might need to install its driver from a disk supplied by the hardware's manufacturer. Or if you buy a piece of hardware that didn't ship with Windows 2000–compatible drivers, you might need to download an updated driver from the manufacturer's Web site.

Chapter 2 Using Programs

2. Select **Network printer** on the wizard's second page.

3. On the wizard's third page, enter the location and name of the printer in the **Name** text box, or click the **Next** button and browse to the printer.

   (If a password is required to access the printer, you will have to supply it during this installation process.)

4. Specify whether the network printer should be the default.

5. Click **Finish** to close the Add Printer Wizard.

After the driver for the network printer is installed on your computer, you can print documents on the network printer as easily as you can on a local printer. If other documents are being printed, your document joins a *queue* (a temporary holding space for data) and must wait its turn. You can see the queue by double-clicking the printer icon that appears in the status area at the right end of the Windows taskbar.

Quitting Programs

When you finish working with a program, you will probably want to close it before moving on to some other task. As you have seen, closing a program—also called *quitting*, *leaving*, or *exiting* a program—is a simple matter of closing its window. Here's how to quit WordPad:

1. Click the **Close** button at the right end of the WordPad window's title bar.

   If you have done some work since you last saved the Caterers document, WordPad prompts you to save the current version.

2. If you see the message box, click **Yes**.

   The WordPad window closes, and its button disappears from the taskbar.

3. Close the other open program windows in the same way.

   You can also quit a program by pressing Alt+F4. For programs that display a File menu, you can quit by pressing Alt+F+X, or by clicking Exit on the File menu.

4. Close the minimized Character Map program by right-clicking its button on the taskbar and clicking **Close** on the shortcut menu.

QUITTING A PROGRAM THAT HAS CRASHED

If a program crashes, you can often close the misbehaving program and carry on working. To close the program, press Ctrl+Alt+Delete to display the Windows Security dialog box. Click Task Manager, select the program you want to close, and click End Task. You will lose any unsaved work in the program, but your work in other programs should be unaffected. If this key combination doesn't work, other programs might have become unstable, and your best bet is to shut down and restart Windows. A word to the wise: Save your work regularly to prevent mishaps from becoming significant setbacks.

MANAGING FOLDERS AND FILES

We track down and open existing documents using My Computer, My Network Places, and the Search feature. Then we show you how to get organized by creating folders and moving, copying, renaming, and deleting documents.

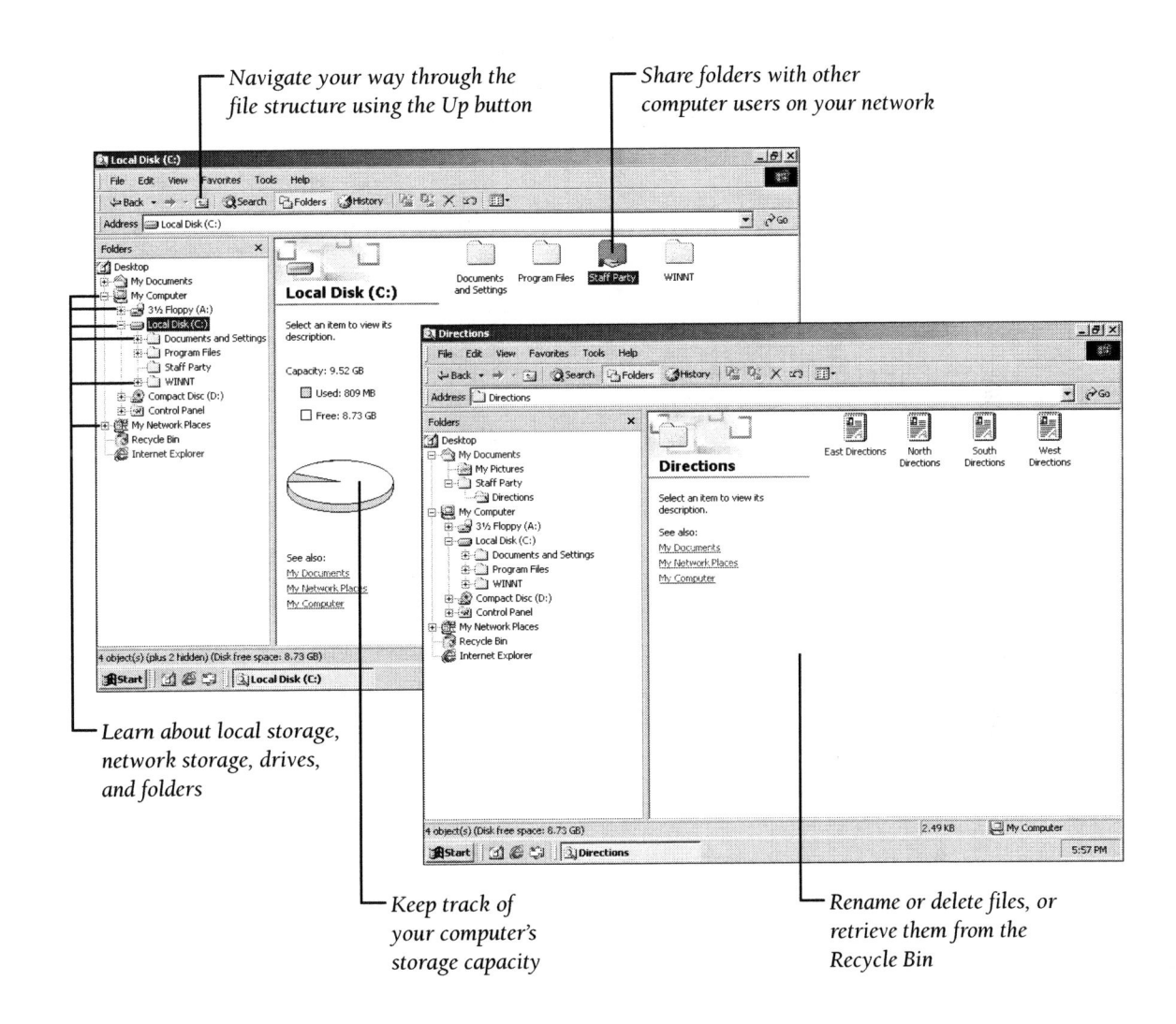

- Navigate your way through the file structure using the Up button
- Share folders with other computer users on your network
- Learn about local storage, network storage, drives, and folders
- Keep track of your computer's storage capacity
- Rename or delete files, or retrieve them from the Recycle Bin

For some people, organizing computer files is a difficult chore. They start a program, open a new document, save it with a name like *Letter,* and think that they'll be able to retrieve it without much trouble if they need it again. Because these people are busy, they often don't take the time to work out a file-naming system, and they might end up wasting a lot of time searching for a particular document. Is it *Letter,* or *Smith Letter,* or *July 12 Letter?* And is it stored in the Letters folder, the Smith folder, or the July folder?

With Windows 2000, you no longer have to trust your memory to organize and retrieve documents efficiently. You can use up to 215 characters, including spaces, in a file name. So you can use file names such as *Letter Written on 7-12-2001 to Smith Associates about the Hunter Project* to describe your documents. Additionally, Windows provides two organizational aids, My Computer and My Network Places, which you can use to shuffle documents into folders in any way that makes sense to you.

In this chapter, we first discuss some organizational concepts. Then we show you how to find and open documents. We also give basic instructions for accessing resources on other computers if you are working on a network. Finally, we look at organizational strategies and techniques that make locating your documents as easy as possible.

UNDERSTANDING STORAGE

When you saved documents in Chapter 2, you saw that your computer storage space is divided into logical groups. You can think of this division as taking place on five levels:

- **Level one.** The Windows desktop, by now familiar to you through our practice with the Show Desktop icon, provides access to all the storage resources available to you.

- **Level two.** On the desktop you'll find a My Computer icon representing your computer's storage, which we'll refer to as *local storage.* Also displayed is a My Network Places icon representing the storage of other computers that are available if you are connected to a network, which we'll refer to as *network storage.*

    Also at this level is the Recycle Bin, which, as you've seen, holds objects you've deleted.

Chapter 3 Managing Folders and Files

- **Level three.** Your local storage is divided into chunks of space called *drives,* which are designated by unique, single letters. Most computers have one floppy disk drive, designated as drive A, and one hard drive, designated as drive C. If you have other drives, such as a CD-ROM drive, they are also assigned letters: D, E, and so on. If your computer is on a network, the network's storage consists of chunks of space on other computers, which are designated by the computers' names. Those computers are further divided into drives designated by letters.

  Also at this level is Control Panel, which, as you've seen, stores tools for customizing the way you work with your computer.

- **Level four.** Divisions within drives are called *folders.* When Windows 2000 was installed on your computer, it created a folder called *Documents and Settings* in which it stores your *personal profile* (information about your user accounts). Included in this personal profile is a folder called *My Documents,* and by default Windows assumes that you will use this folder to store your documents. (It is the default save location in the Save As dialog box.) Some folders contain *subfolders.* For example, Windows created a subfolder called *My Pictures* within My Documents. (In this course, we use the term *folder* to mean any folder, designating folders within folders as subfolders only when the relationship is important.)

- **Level five.** The lowest level of storage consists of *files,* which are divided into two main categories: *program files* and *data files.* Program files contain the computer instructions that are written by programmers. Data files are the documents you create with a program, such as a letter written using a word processor or a picture drawn with a graphics program.

For example, you might write a report called *2nd Qtr Sales* and store it in a folder called *2000.* This folder is a subfolder of a folder called *Reports,* which is in turn a subfolder of the My Documents folder, which is stored in your personal profile folder on drive C of your computer. If your computer's name is *Sales1,* the path of the document is \\Sales1\C:\My Documents\Reports\2000\2nd Qtr Sales.

Keep these levels of storage in mind as we move on to explore ways of finding and organizing documents.

More About...
Control Panel, page 10

More About...
Paths, page 44

OPENING RECENTLY USED FILES

When you want to open a document you worked on recently, you don't have to know where you stored it. For example, in Chapter 2, you created a document called *Directions*. Suppose you now want to change some of the instructions in the document. Here's how to open it and make the changes:

1. Click the **Start** button to open the Start menu, and then point to **Documents**.

   Windows displays a submenu of the documents you have worked on recently, as shown in this graphic:

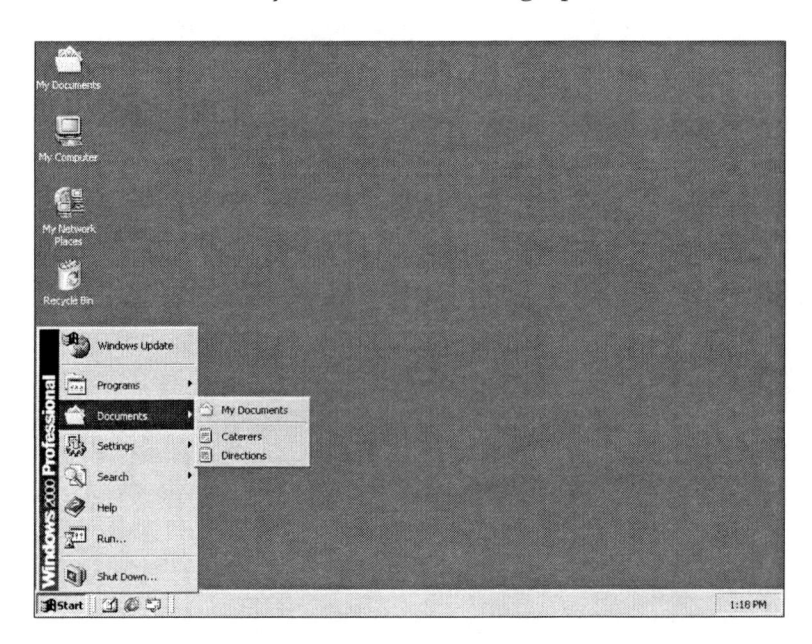

   Programs can record shortcuts to the locations of up to 15 documents on this submenu. (Not all programs use this feature.) When the submenu is full, shortcuts to older documents are deleted from the list as new ones are added.

2. On the Documents submenu, click **Directions**.

   Windows opens the document in its associated program so that you can begin editing. Notice that you don't have to first start a program and then open the document. Windows automatically knows which program is associated with the document and starts that program. (If Word is installed on your computer, Windows starts Word instead of WordPad because it assumes you want to use the more sophisticated

> **CLEARING THE DOCUMENTS SUBMENU**
>
> Sometimes you might want to start a Windows session with an empty Documents submenu to avoid the clutter of old documents you don't need. To clear the submenu, right-click a blank area of the taskbar, and click Properties on the shortcut menu to display the Taskbar and Start Menu Properties dialog box. Click the Advanced tab, click the Clear button in the Customize Start menu area, and then click OK to close the dialog box.

CHAPTER 3   MANAGING FOLDERS AND FILES   65

word processor. Don't worry; these steps will work with whichever program Windows starts.)

Now let's change the Directions memo and save it with a different name so that you will have a couple of documents to play with. Here are the steps:

1. Maximize the Directions document window to make it easier to see the document.

2. In the first instruction, double-click the word **North** to select it, and type *South*.

3. In the second instruction, change the word *right* to *left*.

4. To save the document with a different file name, click the **File** menu, and then click **Save As** to display the Save As dialog box.

5. In the **File name** text box, type *North Directions*.

6. Leave all the other settings as they are, and click **Save** to save this new version of the document with a different name.

7. Click the **Start** button, and click **Documents** to display its submenu, which now includes North Directions as well as the original Directions.

   Notice that you don't have to close or minimize the document window in order to access the Start menu and do other types of work.

8. Click anywhere away from the menus to close them.

9. Now click the **Close** button to close the North Directions window.

SEARCHING FOR FILES

You've just seen how to open a document you have recently worked on. But what if you need to retrieve a document that you worked on a while ago? If you know the document's name and the drive and folder where it is stored, you can use My Computer or My Network Places to locate and open it. If you're hazy about the document's name or location, you can use the Search feature to track it down. As you'll see, you can also use this feature to find and start programs.

HOW DOES WINDOWS KNOW WHICH PROGRAM TO START?
When you save a file, Windows adds an *extension* to the file name to identify the file type. File types are associated with programs. For example, if you double-click a file with a *.xls* extension, Windows knows to open the file in Microsoft Excel because the *.xls* file type is associated with Excel. However, the associations might change as you install new programs. For example, the *.rtf* extension is associated with WordPad unless you install Word, which takes over the association. To view or edit associations, open My Computer, and on the Tools menu, click Folder Options to display the Folder Options dialog box. Click the File Types tab to see the list of file type extensions on your computer.

Using My Computer

My Computer is represented by an icon directly on the desktop because it is frequently used for basic file management. The quickest way to become familiar with My Computer is to start using it. To find the Directions document, which is stored in the Staff Party folder on drive C, follow these steps:

1. On the desktop, double-click the **My Computer** icon.

   Windows opens the My Computer window and displays the window's button on the taskbar.

2. Maximize the window if it is not already maximized.

3. On the **View** menu, click **Arrange Icons**, and then click **by Drive Letter**.

   Your My Computer window should now look something like the one shown in this graphic:

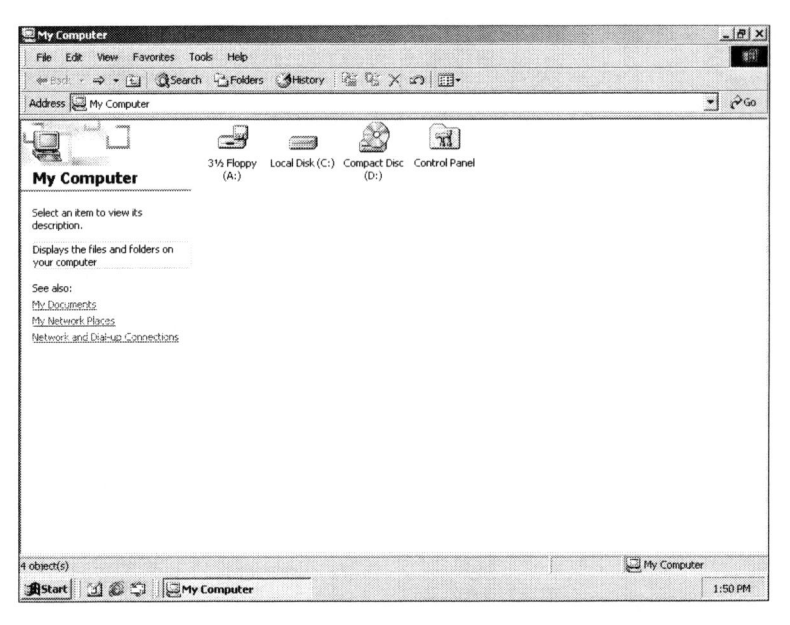

   Don't worry if your window contains different icons than our window does. Your icons represent the setup of your particular computer, and some of your icons might have different names.

We'll now take a short detour to show you how to display information about the various drives in your computer. Follow these steps:

1. Click the **Local Disk (C:)** icon, which represents your computer's drive C.

HARD DISK OR HARD DRIVE?

The terms "hard disk" and "hard drive" are often used interchangeably and can sometimes be confusing. The hard *disk* is the physical object on which data is stored. The hard *drive* controls the hard disk. For all practical purposes, you can think of them as the same thing.

CHAPTER 3 MANAGING FOLDERS AND FILES 67

On the left side of the My Computer window, Windows displays the capacity and the amount of used and free space on drive C, as shown in this graphic:

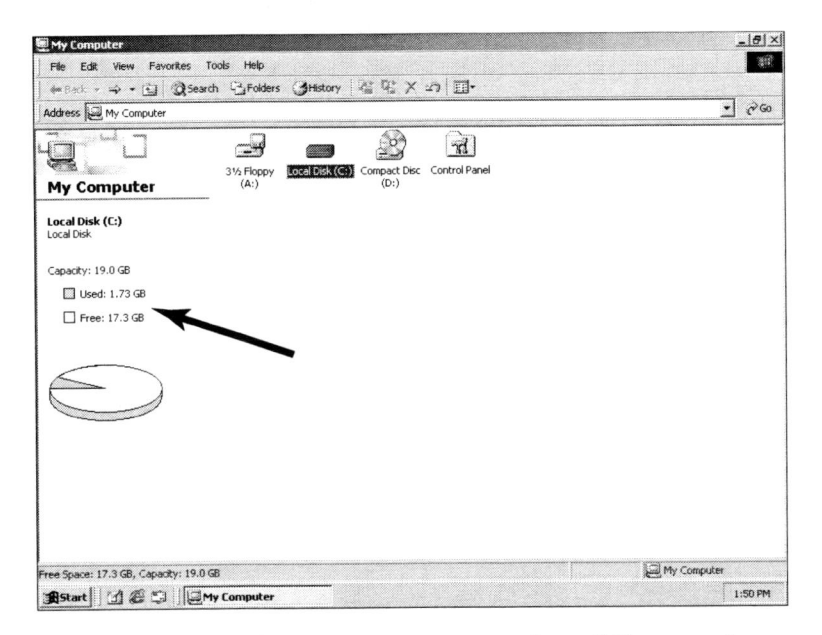

If you use a lot of programs or store a lot of files, or if you have a relatively small hard disk, you might have considerably less free space available.

2. Now right-click the **Local Disk** (C:) icon, and click **Properties** on the shortcut menu.

   Windows displays the dialog box shown in this graphic:

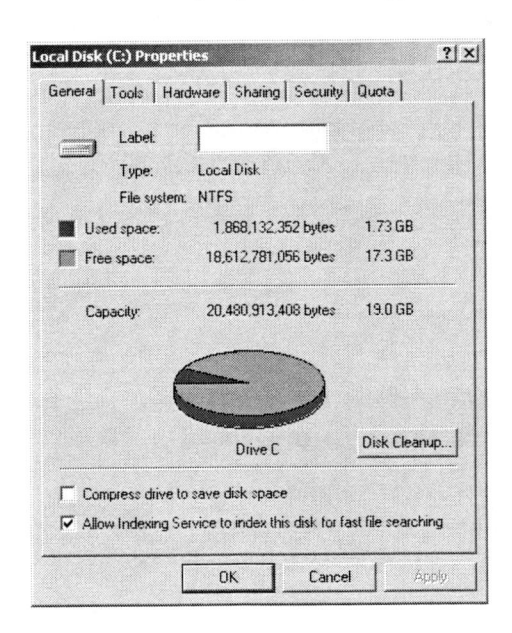

DISPLAYING FILE PROPERTIES

If you right-click a file icon and click Properties on the shortcut menu, the Properties dialog box for the file tells you about the file, including which program will be used to open the file if you double-click its icon. You can change the file type association for this file by clicking the Change button, selecting the desired program, and clicking OK. The dialog box also summarizes the information about the file that is available in Details view in the My Computer window. You can use the dialog box's Help button (the question mark at the right end of the title bar) to find out more about each specific item.

MORE ABOUT...
Disk Cleanup , page 204

MORE ABOUT...
Defragmenting, page 205
Backing up, page 192

On the General tab, Windows displays the capacity and the amount of used and free space on the hard disk in the drive. You can assign a label, or name, to the hard disk. You can also free up space by clicking the Disk Cleanup button and following instructions.

On the Tools tab, you can check your disk for errors and defragment or back up your hard drive.

If you are connected to a network, you can use options on the Sharing tab to set access rights and passwords so that specific people can work with the files on your computer.

3. Take some time to explore the various options in the Properties dialog box, and then click **Cancel** to close it.

4. One at a time, right-click the other drive icons in the window, click **Properties**, and check out the drive descriptions.

Now let's track down the Directions document:

1. Double-click the icon for **drive C** to display its contents in the window.

   In the window's title bar, the name of the drive replaces My Computer.

2. Double-click the **Staff Party** icon folder to display its contents.

   Notice that double-clicking an icon does not open a new window, but instead changes the contents of the window and the name in the title bar.

3. Click the **Up** button.

4. Double-click **Staff Party** again.

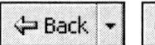

   You can also click the Back and Forward buttons to move back and forth between windows you have already displayed.

Having located the Directions document, you need to open it. Here are the steps:

USING MULTIPLE WINDOWS
To look at files stored in several folders simultaneously, you can display multiple My Computer windows. On the Tools menu in the My Computer window (or any window), click Folder Options. In the Browse Folders area, select the "Open each folder in its own window" option, and click OK.

1. Double-click the **Directions** icon to both start the associated program and open the document.

2. Use the **Save As** command to save a copy of the document in *Rich Text Format* with the name *South Directions*.

3. Click the **Close** button to close the document and quit the program, but leave the Staff Party folder window open.

CHAPTER 3   MANAGING FOLDERS AND FILES   69

Now let's change the way the contents of the active folder are displayed in the window:

1. Click the **Views** button on the toolbar.
2. In the drop-down list, click **Details**.

   Your view of the documents in the Staff Party folder changes to look like the one shown in this graphic:

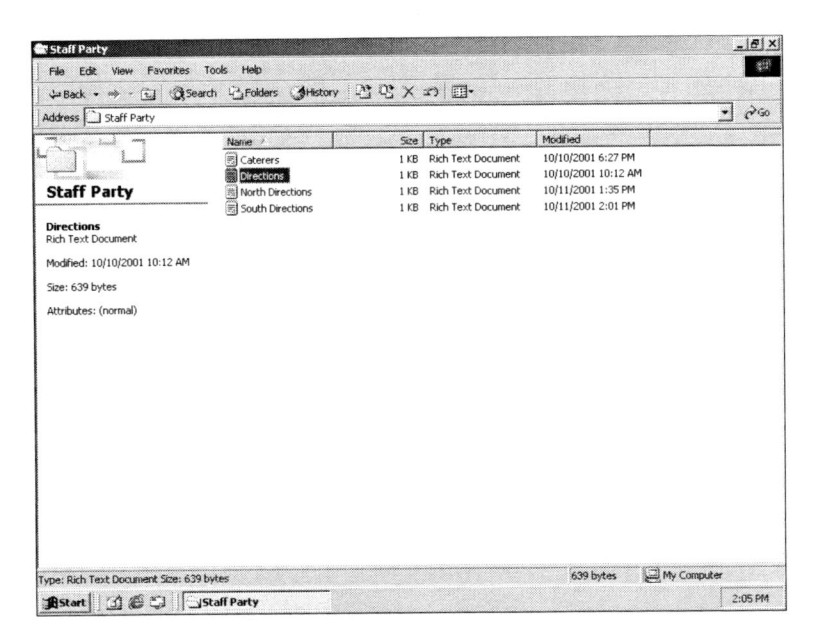

   [screenshot of Staff Party folder in Details view]

   Now you can see each file's size and type, as well as the date and time it was last modified.

3. Click the **Up** button on the toolbar to move up one folder level.

   Notice that changing the view for one folder does not affect the view for other folders.

4. Click the **Back** button on the taskbar to redisplay the contents of the Staff Party folder.

5. Click the **Views** button again, and click **List**.

   The window now lists the files but not their details.

6. To open the Directions memo from this view, simply double-click *Directions*. Then close the document again.

USING THE EXPLORER BAR

By default, the My Computer window displays the contents of a specific folder on the right and instructions, links, and useful information on the left. You can open a pane, called the

---

TURNING BUTTON LABELS ON AND OFF

By default, the toolbar displays labels on some of the toolbar buttons but not all of them. If you want to hide these labels, on the View menu click Toolbars, and then click Customize. In the Customize Toolbar dialog box, select "No Text Labels" in the Text Options drop-down list, and then click Close. If you want to display labels for all the toolbar buttons, in the Customize Toolbar dialog box, select "Show text labels" in the Text Options drop-down list, and click Close.

Explorer bar, within the window so that you can view and access your computer's storage locations in ways that fit your work habits. After you get used to the power and efficiency of the Explorer bar, you might want to keep its pane open permanently. Here's how to display your computer's storage using the Explorer bar:

1. On the **View** menu, click **Explorer Bar** to display the submenu shown in this graphic:

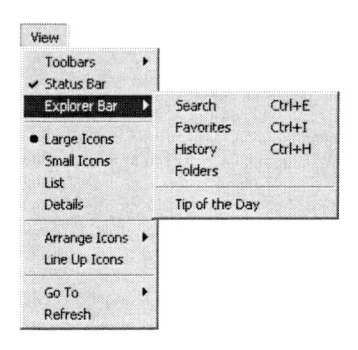

Clicking the Tip of the Day command opens a pane at the bottom of the window and displays some tidbit of information that might be new to you. The Search, Favorites, History, and Folders commands each open a pane on the left side of the window. In this section, we concentrate on the Folders pane.

2. Click **Folders**.

The window now looks like the one shown in this graphic:

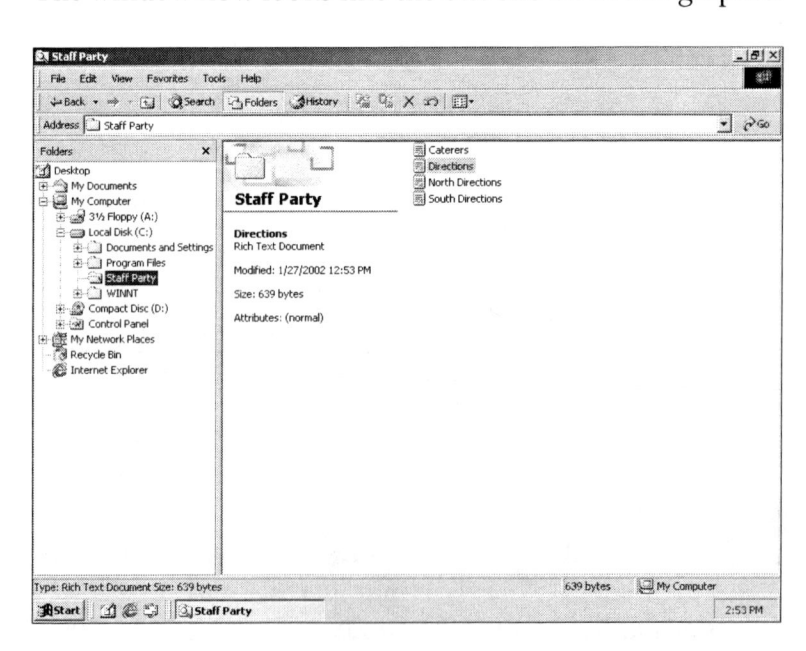

SEE ALSO...
Search pane, page 78
Favorites and History panes, page 73

SORTING
To quickly sort items in Details view, click a column header. For example, if you click the Modified header, the items are sorted to display folders before files and the most recently updated item first. Click the header again to reverse the sort order with files before folders and the oldest item listed first.

CHAPTER 3 MANAGING FOLDERS AND FILES   71

You could also change to this view by clicking the Folders button on the toolbar.

🗁 Folders

The Folders pane displays a hierarchical diagram, called a *tree*, of all your available storage space. The tree in the left pane is arranged like this:

- **Level one.** At the top is the desktop.

- **Level two.** One level down from the desktop are My Documents, My Computer, My Network Places, Recycle Bin, and Internet Explorer.

- **Level three.** One level down from My Computer are your computer's drives and Control Panel.

- **Level four.** One level down from your computer's drives are all the folders stored on each drive.

- **Level five.** The next level is the files or folders contained in the folder selected in the left pane, which are displayed in the right pane.

You can expand and collapse the tree, displaying only the highest levels or zooming in for a closer look at folders and subfolders. Let's experiment in the left pane:

1. Click **Local Disk (C:)**.

   The folders and files contained on drive C are displayed in the right pane, as shown in this graphic:

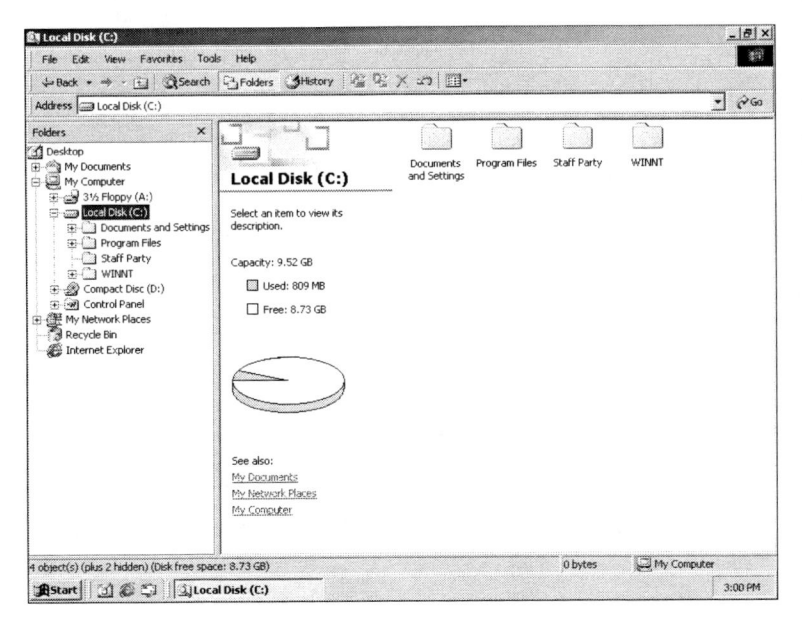

DISPLAYING ALL FILES

When you open some folder windows, Windows might not display files that are critical to its own or a program's operation, because deleting or moving these files would create havoc. To display these files, on the Tools menu click Folder Options, and in the Folder Options dialog box, click the View tab. In the Advanced Settings list, select the "Show hidden files and folders" option, and click OK. For safety, you should work with the "Do not show hidden files and folders" option selected, and select the Show hidden files and folders option only on the rare occasion when you absolutely need to manipulate these important files.

The minus symbol to the left of the drive indicates that the drive's folders are expanded.

2. In the left pane, click the minus symbol next to **Local Disk (C:)**.

   Windows contracts the tree. The minus symbol to the left of the disk name changes to a plus symbol, indicating that the drive contains folders that are not displayed in the left pane.

3. In the left pane, click the plus symbol next to **Local Disk (C:)** to redisplay its folders.

4. In the left pane, click the **Program Files** folder icon once.

   Notice that the folder's icon changes to an open folder without expanding the tree to display its contents in the left pane. This single-click technique is useful when you want to keep the "big picture" in view in the left pane as well as see the contents and details of a particular folder in the right pane. (Actually, you can't see the contents of the Program Files folder unless you click the Show Files link in the right pane. Windows doesn't want you to accidentally delete or move any of these critical files.)

You can also change the display by double-clicking icons in the right pane. Try this:

1. In the right pane, click the **Show Files** link.

2. In the right pane, double-click the **Accessories** folder.

   Windows expands the tree in the left pane to display the Program Files folder's contents, opens the Accessories folder, and displays its contents in the right pane.

3. Click the **Up** button on the toolbar.

   Windows closes the Accessories folder in the tree in the left pane and then opens the Program Files folder, displaying the contents of that folder in the right pane. (Notice that clicking the Up button does not collapse the tree in the left pane.)

4. Click the **Up** button again to display the contents of drive C.

5. Double-click the **WINNT** folder icon in the right pane, and click the **Show Files** link to reveal the folder's contents.

   As with the Program Files folder, Windows initially hides the contents of this folder so you don't accidentally delete a crucial file.

CHAPTER 3 MANAGING FOLDERS AND FILES 73

6. Click the **Views** button, and click **Details** in the drop-down list.

7. Using the vertical scroll bar, scroll all the way to the bottom of the right pane to check out its contents.

Now you can see more file details, as shown in this graphic:

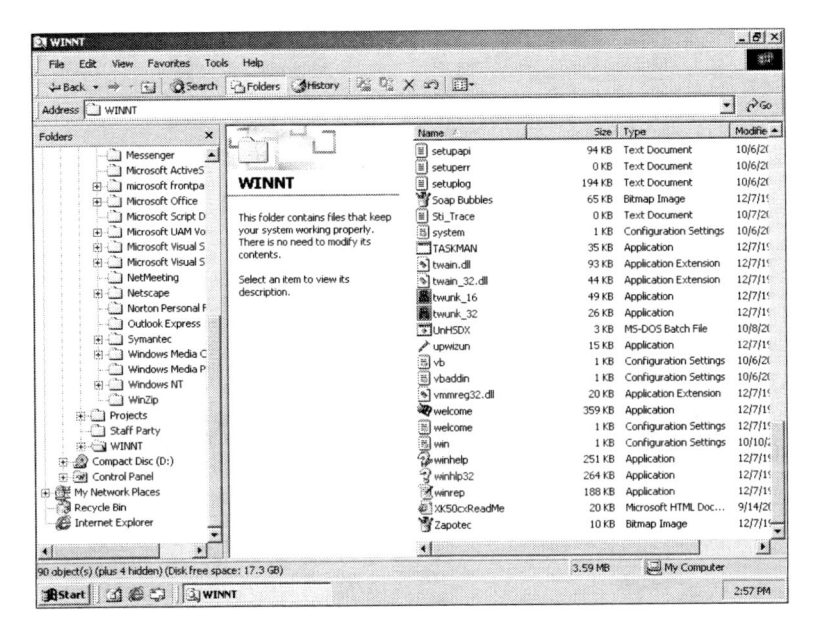

Notice the descriptions in the Type column and the various icons to the left of the file names. You can start any program by double-clicking its icon in the right pane.

MORE MY COMPUTER TRICKS

To move up one folder level, press Backspace. To display a different folder in the active window, type the folder's path in the Address bar. For example, you can type C:\Staff Party and press Enter to display the Staff Party folder. To close multiple folders, hold down Shift and click the Close button of the lowest-level folder window. For example, if the drive C and Staff Party windows are open, you can close them both by holding down Shift and clicking the Close button of the Staff Party window. However, using Shift+Close in the drive C window closes the drive C window, but not Staff Party.

FAVORITES AND HISTORY

If you click Explorer bar and then click Favorites on the View menu, the Explorer bar opens with your list of favorite files, folders, and Web sites displayed. You can click any favorite to go directly to that location. If you point to Explorer bar and then click History, the Explorer bar opens with buttons for 3 Weeks Ago, 2 Weeks Ago, Last Week, each individual day of the current week, and Today. If you know you worked on a file or visited a Web site during a specific period of time, you can often quickly locate it by clicking the appropriate button.

INSTANT EXPLORER BAR

You can open My Computer with the Folders pane already open in one of three ways: Right-click the My Computer icon on the desktop, and click Explore on the shortcut menu; or right-click the Start button, and click Explore; or click the Start button, display the Programs and Accessories menus, and then click Windows Explorer. (If you are familiar with earlier versions of Windows, you will recognize that Windows 2000 incorporates the functionality of Windows Explorer into My Computer, making the need for a separate program obsolete.)

8. Experiment with expanding and contracting folders in the left pane and displaying files in the right pane until you are familiar with the various techniques for displaying the contents of folders. Then close the window.

Using My Network Places

If you are working on a network, you might want to make your documents available to other people by sharing the drive or folder where you have stored the documents. You might also want to be able to find files on other networked computers. In this section, we discuss techniques for using Windows 2000 to make the documents on your computer available to others and to locate other people's documents. If you are not working on a network, you can skip this section.

Sharing Folders

Sharing a folder is easy, and because you are able to share individual folders rather than an entire drive, you can structure your folders so that only the information you want to share is accessible across the network.

As a demonstration, suppose other people need to access the documents related to the staff party, which are stored on your computer. You could have stored the staff party directions in the ready-made My Documents folder, but you didn't want other people to access other files in that folder. Here's how to share the Staff Party folder:

1. Open My Computer, and display the contents of **drive** C.
2. Right-click **Staff Party**, and then click **Sharing**.

    Windows displays the Staff Party Properties dialog box, with these options:

MAPPING NETWORK DRIVES

To avoid having to work through My Network Places every time you want to access a folder, you can "map" the folder to a drive letter. Open My Computer, and on the Tools menu, click Map Network Drive. (You can also right-click the My Computer or My Network Places icon, and then click Map Network Drive on the shortcut menu.) In the Map Network Drive dialog box, select a letter for the shared folder in the Drive drop-down list, and enter the folder's path in the Folder box. If you want Windows to reconnect to this folder each time you turn on your computer, select the Reconnect at logon check box, and then click Finish. When the dialog box closes, the shared folder's contents are displayed in a new window. You can then work with the documents in the folder just as you would work with the documents on your own computer. From then on, the folder will appear as a drive in My Computer so that you can access its contents with just a couple of mouse clicks. To cancel the mapping, use the Disconnect Network Drive command on the Tools menu.

Chapter 3 Managing Folders and Files

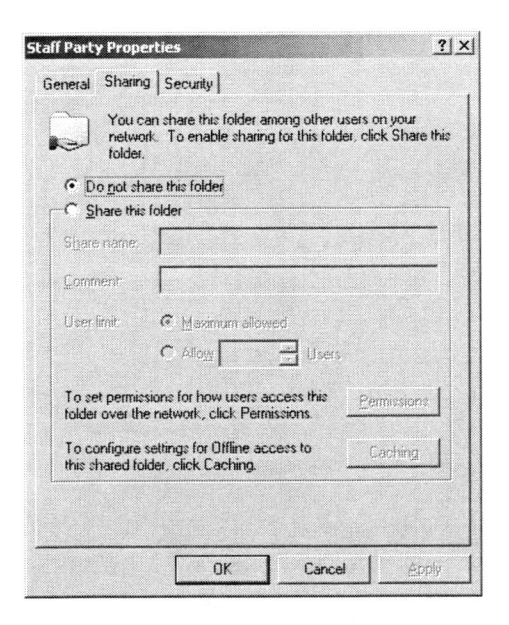

3. Select the **Share this folder** option.

4. If you want to give this folder a different name for sharing purposes, you can enter a new name in the Share name text box. We'll stick with the name *Staff Party*.

5. Click in the **Comment** text box, and type *Annual staff party information*.

6. Click **OK** to complete the sharing procedure.

   Back in the folder window, Windows indicates that the Staff Party folder is shared by adding a hand to the folder icon, so it looks like this:

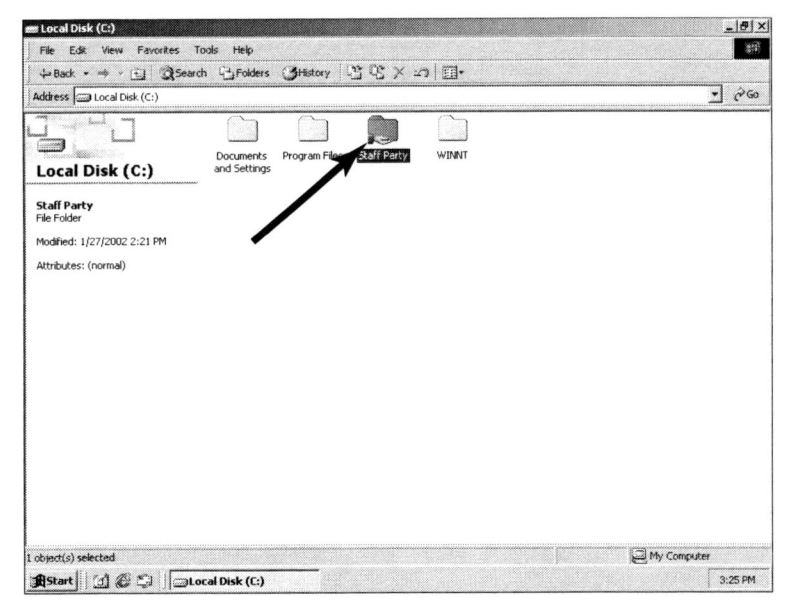

Can't share or access documents?

The way the person who administers your network has set it up might limit the computers and files you can access and what you can do with them. If you see a message while following our examples telling you that you don't have this right or that privilege, don't worry. The message just means your computer is not allowed to do what you just asked it to do.

7. Click the **Minimize** button to minimize the window and display the desktop.

Now we'll move to another computer to show you how to access this shared folder across the network.

Connecting to Shared Folders

To use a document that is stored in a shared folder on another computer, you use My Network Places to locate the folder and then, if you have permission to access the folder, you can open its documents by double-clicking them in the usual way. Here's how you would access the files in the Staff Party folder if they were stored on another computer on your network:

1. On the desktop, double-click the **My Network Places** icon.

2. If you are working on a network domain, double-click **Entire Network**. If you're not on a network domain, you can double-click **Computers Near Me**.

3. If the computer you are looking for belongs to a workgroup, double-click that workgroup's icon.

    The window displays icons for each of the computers in the workgroup.

4. Double-click the icon for the computer on which the shared Staff Party folder is stored.

    The window now displays the storage locations that you have the right to access on that computer, similar to those shown in this graphic:

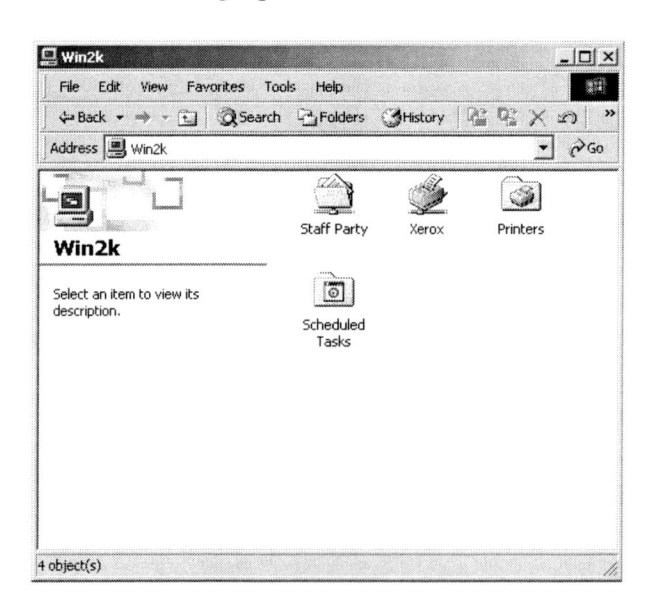

Moving or renaming shared folders

If you try to move or rename a shared folder, Windows warns you that the folder will no longer be shared after the move or re-naming operation. Click Yes in the message box if you really do want to move or rename the folder. Then, if you want to share the folder again, you will have to repeat the steps to share it.

Chapter 3 Managing Folders and Files

5. Double-click the shared **Staff Party** folder.

   Windows opens the Staff Party folder and displays its documents, as shown in this graphic:

   ![Staff Party on Win2k window screenshot]

6. Close the window.

Stopping Sharing

If you no longer want to share a folder, you can discontinue sharing by following these steps:

1. In the interest of good working relationships, warn colleagues ahead of time—perhaps by sending a quick e-mail message—that you are going to stop sharing a folder.

2. Click the **Local Disk** (C:) button on the taskbar to display its window.

3. Right-click the shared **Staff Party** folder, and click **Sharing** on the shortcut menu to display the Sharing tab of the Staff Party Properties dialog box.

4. Select the **Do not share this folder** option, and click OK.

   Because the folder is no longer shared, the hand disappears from the folder icon.

As you have seen, Windows 2000 makes using documents on networked computers as easy as using those on your own computer, hiding all the intricacies of the network so that you can focus on your work.

VIEWING CONNECTIONS TO YOUR COMPUTER

Using a simple MS-DOS command, you can view a list of all the network computers currently connected to your computer and which resources they are using. On the Start menu, click Programs, Accessories, and Command Prompt. In the Command Prompt window, type *net use*, and press Enter. See the tip on page 30 for more information about MS-DOS.

SEARCHING FOR DOCUMENTS

If you don't know where to begin looking for a document or a program, your best bet is to search for it. The vast majority of searches are simple attempts to locate a file based on all or part of its name, so in this section we'll show you how to conduct this type of search using the Explorer bar's Search pane. Follow these steps:

1. Click the **Search** button on the Local Disk (C:) window's toolbar.

   Clicking this button is the equivalent of clicking Explorer bar and then Search on the View menu. The window now looks like the one shown in this graphic:

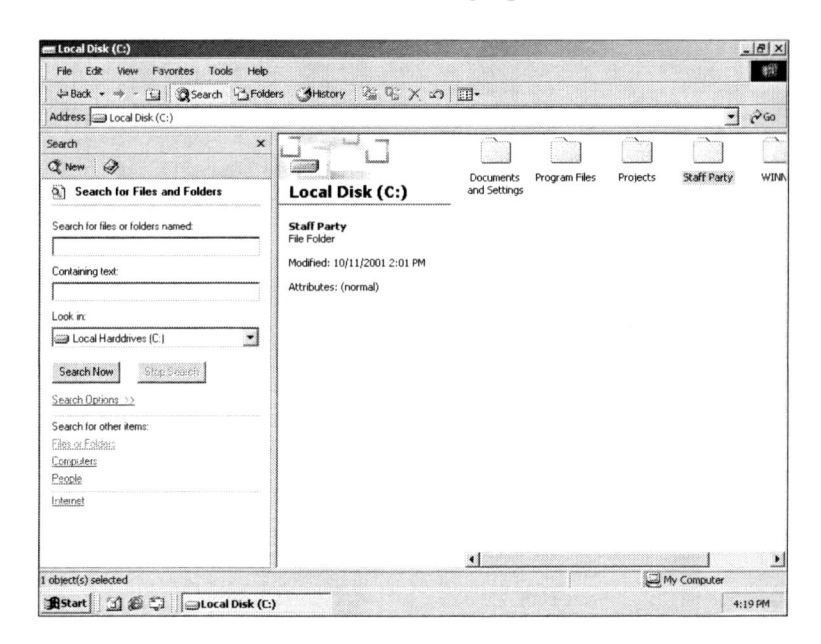

SEARCHING FOR OTHER THINGS

At the bottom of the Search pane are links you can use to search for computers, people, and Internet information. To search for a computer, click the Computers link. The Explorer bar changes to enable you to enter a computer name, and after you click the Search Now button, the shared files on that computer are displayed in the right pane. To search for a person, click the People link. The Find People dialog box appears, and you can then search your address book or a variety of Internet directory services. To search for information on the Internet, click the Internet link. The Explorer bar changes so that you can specify what you want to find and then click a Search button to open Internet Explorer and display the search results. (Obviously, you won't find anything unless you are connected to the Internet.) When the My Computer window is not open, you can open the Search pane to search by clicking Start, clicking Search, and clicking what you want to search for in the Search submenu.

2. In the **Search for files or folders named** box, type *Directions*.

3. If drive C is not already selected in the Look in box, click **Local Harddrives (C:)** in the **Look in** drop-down list.

4. If the **Search Options** box is not expanded, click the **Search Options** link.

5. Click the **Advanced Options** check box. If the **Search Subfolders** check box is not already selected, click it too.

6. Finally, click the **Search Now** button to start the search.

   Windows searches all the folders and subfolders on drive C, and displays results like those shown in this graphic:

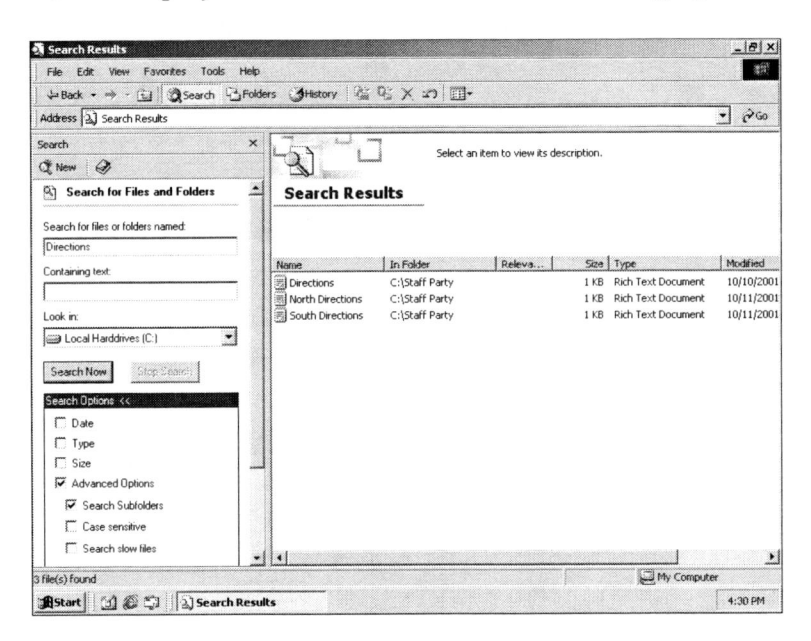

7. Click the **Close** button in the top right corner of the Search pane.

MORE COMPLEX SEARCHES

In addition to searching for a document by name and location, you can search by modification date (when it was last saved), file type, and size. You can search for documents containing a particular word or phrase you type in the "Containing text" box. For example, you could search for a Word document that you saved between June 4 and June 14, 2001 and that contains the words Adventure Works. You can find files containing text with specific capitalization by selecting the "Case sensitive" check box in the Advanced Options section. When you finish one search, you can start a new one by clicking the New button, and you can interrupt a search by clicking the Stop Search button. If you want to save the results of a search, you can click Save Search on the File menu, designate a file name and location for the search in the Save Search dialog box, and click Save. The next time you need to conduct that particular search, you can double-click the file to display the search criteria, rather than having to enter them all over again.

As you can see, Windows finds all the documents with names that include the word *Directions*. You can select a document and use the commands on the window's File menu to manipulate the document in various ways, including opening, printing, and renaming it. (You can also open the document by double-clicking it.)

Organizing Folders and Files

As you work with your computer, you will accumulate more and more files that you want to keep, either because you need the information contained in them as a record of what you did and when, or to use as the basis for new files. If you are systematic about how you name your files, you might have no trouble scrolling through a long list of files to find exactly the one you want. More likely, you will want to create some kind of hierarchical "filing system" of folders and subfolders, which will enable you to easily locate any file on your computer. The real strength of Windows becomes apparent when you want to organize your folders and files by moving, copying, and deleting them to conform to whatever system you come up with. Why? Because you can perform these tasks visually by dragging icons rather than having to type obscure commands.

Deciding on a System

Before you practice creating folders and moving documents, you might want to make a few decisions about what your folder and document structure should look like. When Windows 2000 was installed on your computer, various folders were created on your hard drive to hold all the Windows files. When you install application programs, those programs also create folders. Your concern here is not with these program folders. In fact, unless you really know what you're doing, it is best to leave program folders alone. Your concern is instead with the folders you create to hold your own documents.

Because you can use long folder names and file names with Windows 2000, you might think it would be easy to name documents so that they are readily identifiable. There's no question that being able to use several words helps. Nevertheless, coming up with a few rules for naming files is a must. If you have ever wasted time trying to locate a document, you will probably find that spending a few minutes now deciding how to avoid such incidents in the future will more than repay you in increased efficiency. A folder-naming or file-naming convention is a must if more than one person on your network uses the same set of documents.

However you decide to set up your folder structure, we strongly recommend that you store all the folders and documents you create in your My Documents folder. Using My Documents as an all-purpose storage location greatly simplifies the backing up of your work, because you can back up the folder and all its subfolders in one operation. In Windows 2000, your My Documents folder is stored in your personal profile folder, and is accessible only to you.

Otherwise, there are no hard and fast rules for organizing documents, and the scheme you come up with will depend on your organization's requirements and the nature of your work. For example, if your documents are client-based, it makes sense to identify them by client. You might use the date, followed by the client's name, followed by the type of document. Thus, the file name *05_20_02 Smith Letter* might designate a letter written to Smith Associates on May 20, 2002, and the file name *06_14_02 Smith Invoice* might designate an invoice sent to the same client a few weeks later.

The important thing is to come up with a simple scheme and to apply it consistently. You can then use Windows to manipulate the documents individually and in groups. For example, suppose you have accumulated so many documents in your client folders that you need to subdivide your client documents by type to make them more manageable. You can create a subfolder called *Invoices*, select all the documents that have *Invoice* as part of their file names, and drag all the documents to the new folder. In the next sections, we'll demonstrate how to use My Computer to tackle tasks like this one.

PORTABLE FILE NAMES
Long file names work fine if you do all your work with programs designed to run on Windows operating systems, but if you might need to open a file in a program that runs on a different operating system, think carefully about the file names you assign in Windows programs. For example, suppose you create a Word document called 2000 Product Brochure and you later need to open it in an MS-DOS program. In that program, you'll see the file name *2000PR~1.DOC*. The name now has only eight characters; a tilde (~) indicates that the name is truncated, the spaces are gone, and the three-character file type extension is visible. If you have several documents with long file names that start with the same eight characters (*2000 Product List*, *2000 Product Reviews*, *2000 Product Proposals*, and so on), their short file names are distinguished only by the number after the tilde in each file name (*2000PR~1.DOC*, *2000PR~2.DOC*, and so on). This makes it difficult to know at a glance which document is which. So if you want your documents to be portable from Windows to other operating systems, try to assign file names that work well no matter what the environment.

CREATING NEW FOLDERS

You saw in Chapter 2 how to create a new folder while saving a document. Now we're going to create another folder to organize the documents you've created so far. Follow these steps:

1. Display the contents of the **Staff Party** folder in the open window.

2. On the **File** menu, click **New** and then **Folder** to display a new folder icon within the Staff Party window.

3. With the new folder's name selected, type *Directions* to replace the highlighted text, and press **Enter**.

SELECTING FOLDERS AND FILES

Having created the new folder, you're ready to select the documents you want to move or copy into it. You've already seen how to click an icon to select it. Here, we'll show you a few other methods for selecting:

1. In the Staff Party window, click the first document icon, hold down the **Shift** key, click the last document icon, and release **Shift**.

   The entire set of documents is now selected. The window displays the number of selected documents and their total size, as shown in this graphic:

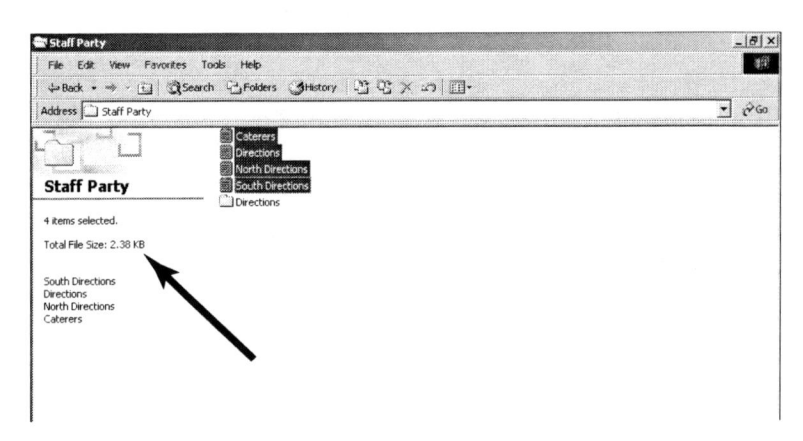

> **DRAGGING TO SELECT**
>
> You can drag a selection rectangle around the icons of the files you want to work with. Point above the top left corner of the first icon, hold down the left mouse button, and drag beyond the bottom right corner of the last icon. (Sometimes it's easier to start at the bottom and drag up.) The rectangle expands as you drag, highlighting each icon it touches. Release the button when everything you want is selected.

2. Hold down the **Ctrl** key, click the **Directions** document, and release **Ctrl**.

   That icon is no longer part of the selection.

3. On the **Edit** menu, click **Select All** to select everything, including the new folder.

4. Click the **Directions** folder icon.

   Only that item is selected.

5. On the **Edit** menu, click **Invert Selection** to deselect the selected item and select the other items in the window.

   This command is convenient when a folder contains many documents and you want to select all but a few of them.

6. Click an empty area of the window to deselect everything.

Moving and Copying Folders and Files

To demonstrate how to rearrange folders and files, we'll move the Staff Party folder into the My Documents folder and copy documents from the Staff Party folder to the new Directions subfolder. Here are the steps:

1. Display the contents of drive C, right-click the **Staff Party** folder, and click **Cut** on the shortcut menu.

   The Staff Party icon is dimmed to show that Windows has put a copy of the folder and its contents on the Clipboard.

2. Click the **Up** button to display My Computer, and click the **My Documents** link to display the contents of that folder.

3. Right-click a blank area of the folder window, and click **Paste** on the shortcut menu.

   Windows removes the Staff Party folder from drive C and pastes the copy on the Clipboard in the My Documents folder, as shown in this graphic:

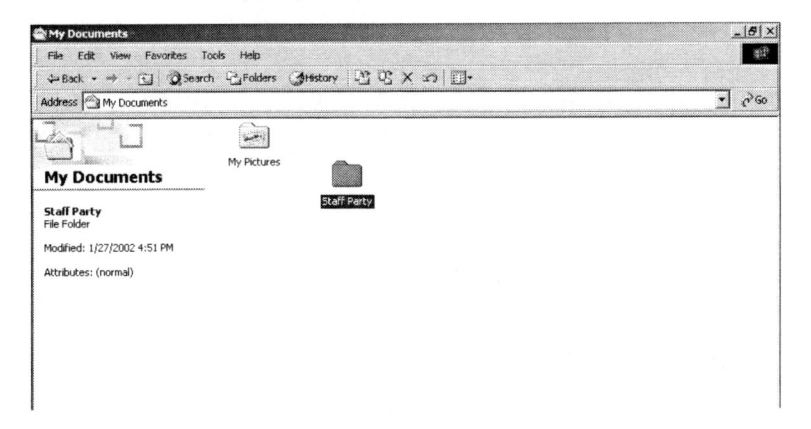

4. Navigate to the drive C folder to verify that it no longer contains the Staff Party folder.

Now we'll use the Explorer bar to move a document to a different folder, and then we'll copy another document. The secret to efficient moving and copying with the Explorer bar is to make sure the destination folder is visible before you select the folder or document you want to move or copy. Try this:

1. Click the **Folders** button to open the Folder pane in the Explorer bar.

2. In the Folders pane, click the plus symbol next to **My Documents**, and then click the plus symbol next to the **Staff Party** folder.

3. Switch to **Details** view if you aren't already there.

   We like to rearrange files in the Details view so that we can check dates and times and be sure we are moving or copying the correct files or versions of files.

4. Click **North Directions** in the right pane.

5. Using the left mouse button, drag the image of the selected document from the right pane over the **Directions** folder in the left pane.

   When you release the mouse button, the North Directions icon disappears from the right pane.

6. Click **South Directions** in the right pane. Hold down the **Ctrl** key, and drag the image of the selected document over the **Directions** folder in the left pane. Release the mouse button, and then release the **Ctrl** key.

   As you drag, a plus symbol is displayed below the pointer to indicate that you are copying the document, not moving it. When you release the mouse button, the selected document's icon remains in the right pane. (If you release the Ctrl key before the mouse button, the plus symbol disappears, and Windows moves the document instead.)

7. Click the **Directions** folder in the left pane to display its contents in the right pane.

   The moved and copied documents are safely stored in their new folder.

MORE ABOUT...
Switching views, page 69

Chapter 3 Managing Folders and Files

Follow these steps to create a copy of a document within the same folder:

1. Right-click the **North Directions** icon in the right pane, and click **Copy** on the shortcut menu.

2. Right-click an empty area of the right pane, and click **Paste** on the shortcut menu.

   Windows pastes a copy of the Clipboard's contents in the Directions folder, assigning the new document the name *Copy of North Directions*.

You can use the same technique to copy documents from one folder to another, but let's try another way:

1. Click the **Staff Party** folder in the left pane, and click the **Directions** document in the right pane to select it.

2. Click the **Copy To** button on the toolbar.

   Windows displays the Browse For Folder dialog box shown in this graphic:

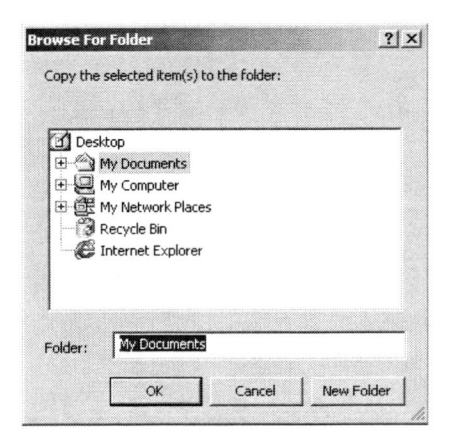

3. Click the plus symbols next to **My Documents** and then **Staff Party**.

4. Click the **Directions** folder, and click **OK**.

5. Click the **Directions** folder in the left pane to see the results of the copy procedure in the right pane.

> **DOES WINDOWS COPY OR MOVE BY DEFAULT?**
>
> When you use the left mouse button to drag a folder or document to a new location on the same drive, Windows moves the object unless you hold down the Ctrl key, in which case it copies the object. When you use the left mouse button to drag between drives, Windows copies the object, unless you hold down the Shift key, in which case it moves the object. If you find this logic confusing, use the right mouse button to drag. When you release the mouse button, Windows displays a shortcut menu, from which you can select the action you want.

As you can see in this graphic, the Directions folder now contains four documents:

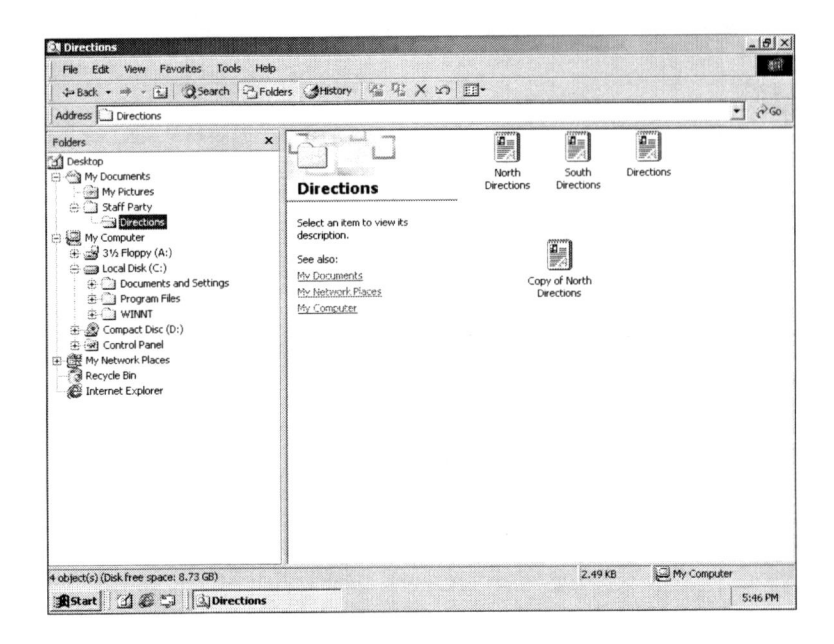

RENAMING FOLDERS AND FILES

During the course of your work, you will sometimes want to change a file name. For example, suppose you want all the file names of the documents in the Directions folder to start with a unique word. Try these four renaming methods:

1. In the Directions folder, right-click the **Directions** document, and click **Rename** on the shortcut menu.

2. Press the **Home** key to move to the beginning of the name, type *West* and a space, and press **Enter**.

3. Click the **Copy of North Directions** document, and on the **File** menu, click **Rename**.

4. Type *East Directions*, and press **Enter**.

5. Click the **North Directions** document, and press the F2 key.

    Notice that the name is now selected, ready for you to type a new name.

6. You don't want to change this name after all, so simply press **Enter** to retain the original name.

7. Click the **South Directions** document, wait a second, and then click the icon again to select the name.

    If you click too soon, the document will open.

Chapter 3 Managing Folders and Files

8. As you did with North Directions, press **Enter** to retain the original name.

9. Right-click a blank area of the window, and click **Arrange Icons** and **by Name**.

   The results are shown in this graphic:

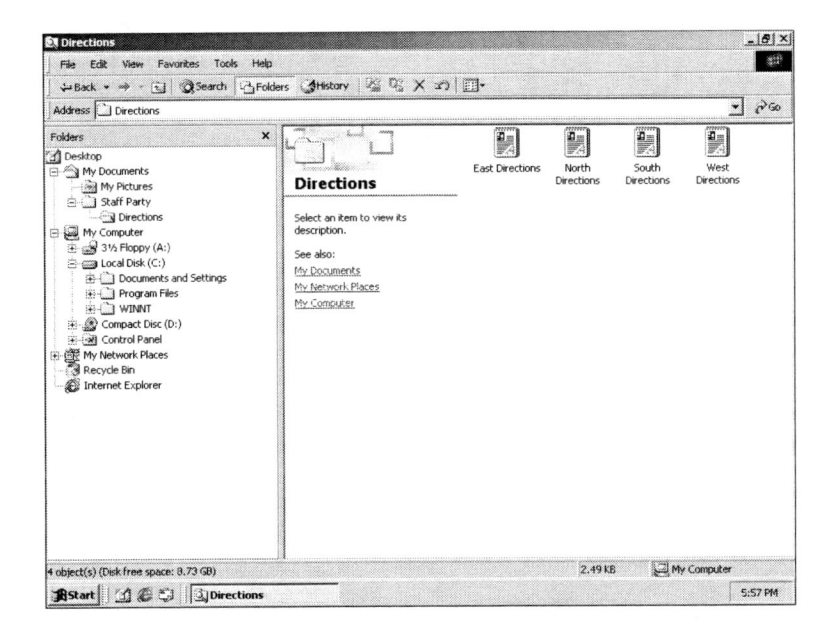

Deleting and Undeleting Folders and Files

If you followed along with the previous examples, you now have two extraneous documents in the Staff Party folder. The potential for confusion is obvious, so let's throw out these duplicates:

1. Display the **Staff Party** folder, and click the **Directions** document.

2. Click the **Delete** button on the toolbar.

   Alternatively, you can press the Delete key on the keyboard.

3. When Windows displays a message box asking you to confirm the deletion, click **Yes** to send the document to the Recycle Bin.

4. Next right-click the **South Directions** document, and click **Delete** on the shortcut menu.

5. Again, confirm the deletion when prompted.

These techniques can be used to delete folders, subfolders, and documents with just a couple of mouse clicks. A great shortcut, you might think. But it's wise to inspect the contents of the folder you are considering deleting (and all its subfolders) before carrying out this type of wholesale destruction.

Fortunately, Windows provides a safeguard against the nightmare of inadvertently deleting vital documents. When you delete objects from your hard disk, Windows doesn't really erase them. As you have already seen, it moves them to the Recycle Bin, which is really just a folder on your hard disk. Until you empty the Recycle Bin folder, you can retrieve objects you have deleted by mistake. Try this:

- Click the **Undo** button on the toolbar to restore South Directions to the Staff Party folder.

You could repeat this step to undelete Directions, but instead let's go rummaging in the Recycle Bin:

1. Minimize the open window, and take a look at the **Recycle Bin** icon on the desktop, which has changed to show that it has something in it, like this:

2. Double-click the **Recycle Bin** icon, and if necessary, resize the window so that you can see all its contents.

   The Recycle Bin looks like the one shown in this graphic:

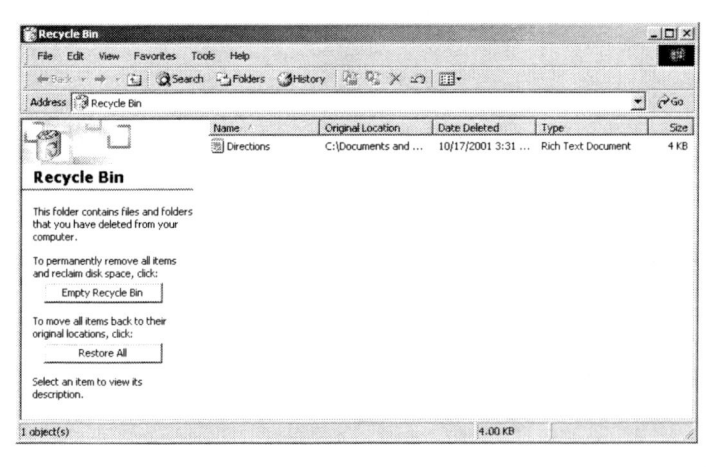

3. Right-click **Directions**, and then click **Restore** on the shortcut menu.

   You can also click the Restore All button in the left pane without selecting Directions.

HOW BIG IS THE RECYCLE BIN?

To check the size of your computer's Recycle Bin, right-click its desktop icon, and click Properties on the shortcut menu. By default, 10 percent of the space on your hard drive is reserved for the Recycle Bin. You can adjust the size by moving the slider to the left (smaller) or right (bigger). If you have more than one hard drive, Windows maintains a bin on each one. Click the drives tab to see how big the bin is on a particular drive. To set different bin sizes for each drive, click the Global tab and select the "Configure drives independently" option before you adjust the slider on each of the drive tabs.

CHAPTER 3   MANAGING FOLDERS AND FILES

4. Close the Recycle Bin window.
5. Back on the desktop, notice that the **Recycle Bin** icon has changed to an empty bin, like this:

Now let's delete both documents again:

1. Click the **Staff Party** button on the taskbar, click the **Restore** button, and if necessary, move the window so that you can see the Recycle Bin icon on the desktop.
2. Click **South Directions** in the Staff Party folder (not the one in the Directions folder), hold down the **Shift** key, and click **Directions** to add it to the selection.
3. Drag the selection over the **Recycle Bin** icon on the desktop, and release the mouse button to drop the files into the Recycle Bin.

   Windows removes the files from the Staff Party window.

If the reason you are deleting files is to free up drive space, keep in mind that your efforts won't yield results until you empty the Recycle Bin. Follow these steps to remove documents from the Recycle Bin and completely erase them from your hard disk:

1. Double-click the **Recycle Bin** icon to open its window.
2. Select **Directions**, press the **Delete** key, and then click **Yes** to confirm that you want to permanently remove the document.
3. Click the **Empty Recycle Bin** button on the left side of the window to erase the remaining contents of the bin, and then click **Yes** to confirm your command.
4. Close the Recycle Bin window.
5. Back in the Staff Party window, click the **Recycle Bin** in the Folders pane to confirm that it is empty.

If you are sure you won't need to restore any of the documents in the Recycle Bin, you can empty it without checking it by right-clicking its icon on the desktop and clicking Empty Recycle Bin on the shortcut menu. Click Yes to confirm your command.

DELETING WITHOUT RECYCLING
If you are certain that you will never need a particular document, file, or folder, you can delete it permanently by holding down the Shift key while pressing the Delete key. This action is not reversible, so you should always think carefully before using this method.

By the way, Windows doesn't move objects deleted from floppy disks and the hard disks of other computers to the Recycle Bin; it actually deletes them. Always pause before clicking Yes in the Confirm File Delete message box when deleting files from anywhere but your hard disk, because this type of deletion is irreversible.

Customizing the My Computer Window

More About...
Displaying file types, page 162

As you create more and more files and folders, you might want to see more information in the My Computer window at one time. Windows helps reduce clutter by not displaying some file types. (Usually you wouldn't want to touch these files anyway.) But to see more information, you can also simplify the display. Here's how:

1. Display the **Directions** folder, and then on the **Tools** menu, click **Folder Options**.

   Windows displays the dialog box shown in this graphic:

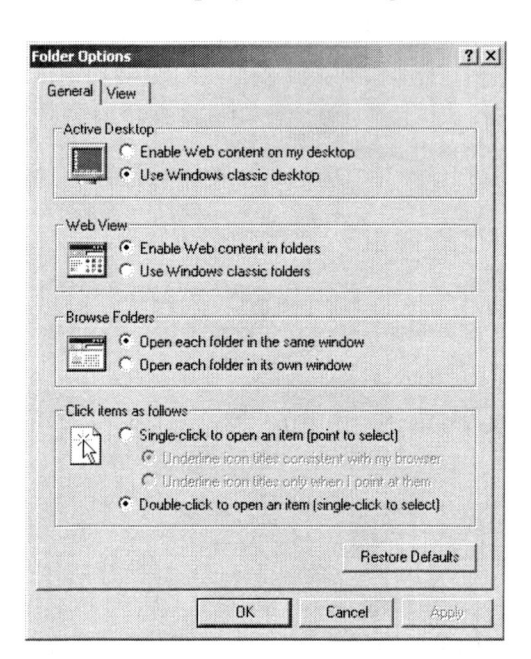

2. In the Web View area, select the **Use Windows classic folders** option, and then click **OK**.

   The window's right pane now contains nothing but the document icons.

Chapter 3 Managing Folders and Files

3. On the **View** menu, click **Toolbars**, and then click **Address bar**.

   The Address bar disappears, leaving more room in the window for folder and file information.

Now let's adjust the width of the panes and columns. Follow these steps:

1. Switch to **Details** view.

   The Directions folder window now looks like the one shown in this graphic:

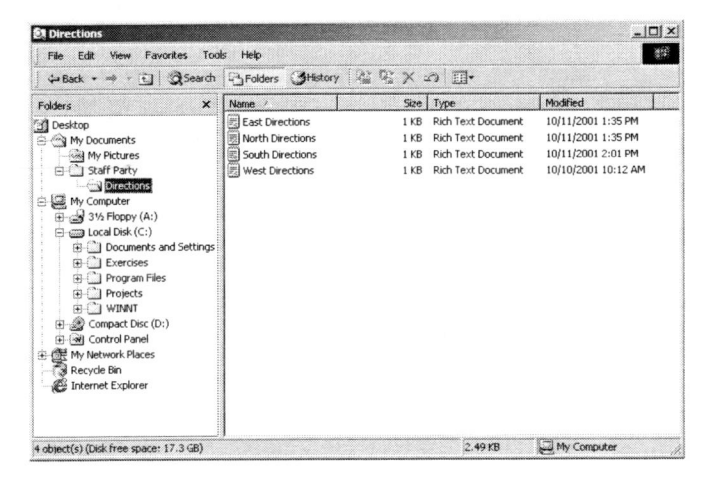

2. Point to the right border of the Explorer bar, and when the pointer changes to a double-headed arrow, drag to resize the pane.

3. Point to the right border of any of the column headings, and drag to resize the column.

4. Close the Directions folder.

Keep in mind that most of these customization techniques also work in other windows and Windows-based applications, such as the Recycle Bin and Microsoft Outlook Express.

In this chapter, we have given you an overview of the tools Windows 2000 provides to help you organize your documents so that you can quickly find them. Now it's up to you!

Moving the Address bar

To reclaim the space occupied by the Address bar without turning it off, you can move the Address bar to the right of the toolbar or menu bar. Point to the word *Address* at the left end of the bar. Hold down the left mouse button and, when the pointer changes to a four-headed arrow, drag the Address bar up into the blank area to the right of the toolbar or the menu bar.

E-Mail Basics

4

After a discussion of internal and Internet e-mail concepts, we show you how to use Outlook Express to send, reply to, and forward messages. You also learn how to use the Address Book, attach files, and organize messages.

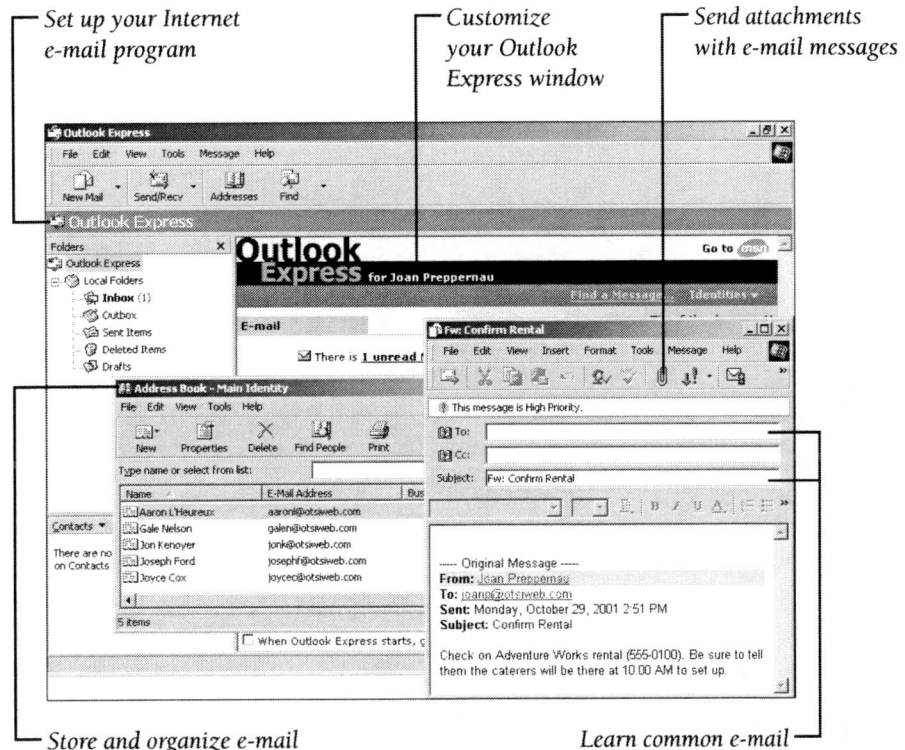

- Set up your Internet e-mail program
- Customize your Outlook Express window
- Send attachments with e-mail messages
- Store and organize e-mail addresses in the Address Book
- Learn common e-mail etiquette and practices

People don't usually work in isolation. Whether you are using Windows 2000 on a computer connected to your organization's network or on a stand-alone computer, you will probably use your computer to communicate with other people via electronic mail, or *e-mail*. You might also use instant messaging, or *IM*. Windows 2000 includes Microsoft Outlook Express, a simple yet powerful e-mail program. MSN Messenger, an instant messaging program that enables you to chat with friends and coworkers and monitor their online status, is not installed with Windows 2000 but is easy to install from the Web.

In the first section of this chapter, we set the stage by exploring a few e-mail concepts. We look at how to send and receive e-mail using Outlook Express. Then we briefly discuss instant messaging and MSN Messenger.

LEARNING E-MAIL CONCEPTS

There's nothing difficult about the concept of e-mail. E-mail within an organization (internal e-mail) is simply a way of sending messages that bypass the traditional mail room. E-mail to the outside world (Internet e-mail) is a way of sending messages that bypass the post office. The beauty of e-mail is that it doesn't use paper resources, it's fast, and it costs nothing (at least nothing more than is already being spent on network resources and/or Internet access). Many people prefer e-mail to talking on the phone because each person can send and respond to e-mail messages in their own time frame. E-mail also makes it easier for people in different time zones to take care of important business. You can include files, programs, and other attachments with messages, and the same message can be sent to several people without any additional effort. Because of all these factors, it's easy to understand why even people with abysmal letter-writing habits become staunch advocates of e-mail as a means of communication. Using e-mail, you can fire off a note to the person across the hall or to someone living on the other side of the world. You can share ideas with your organization's president or communicate with politicians and celebrities. (Of course, there's no guarantee that the recipients of your messages will actually read them, let alone respond to them!)

Like any other good thing, it's possible to have too much e-mail. Used wisely, e-mail can increase efficiency and reduce the amount of paper you use, but without a little restraint, e-mail can add unnecessarily to the burden of information overload. For example, if you get in the habit of copying messages to your entire department, everyone will feel obliged to spend time reading your messages whether or not they actually need to. Keep this potential for misuse in mind as you begin integrating e-mail into your daily routine.

Knowing the Difference between Internal E-Mail and Internet E-Mail

Sometimes people confuse internal e-mail with Internet e-mail, and it's easy to understand why—they are similar in many ways. However, having internal e-mail doesn't necessarily mean you have Internet e-mail, and vice versa. To be able to send e-mail to a colleague down the hall via internal e-mail, both your computer and your colleague's computer have to be connected to the company's network. To be able to send e-mail to a customer in another state via the Internet, both your computer and your customer's computer have to be able to access the Internet.

Let's briefly look at an example of internal e-mail. Suppose you want to tell an engineer in the product design department about a minor change in a product's specifications. You create a new e-mail message, address it to the engineer, specify the topic, type the message, and send it. Your e-mail program adds information such as the current date and time, and your e-mail address, and sends the message from your computer to your company's mail server. The mail server then holds the message in the engineer's mailbox until she turns on her computer, at which time she can use her e-mail program to read the message and reply to it at her convenience. The reply makes the same journey in reverse: From the engineer's computer, it travels to the

---

Inappropriate uses of e-mail

Just as there are inappropriate, and even illegal, uses of traditional mail services, there are also inappropriate uses of e-mail. Harassment and fraud through e-mail are just as illegal as they are through regular mail. Mass e-mailing (junk e-mail, also called *spam*) and chain e-mailing are both frowned on by the Internet community. With junk paper mail, the recipient can decide at a glance whether to spend time and energy opening it. But with junk e-mail, the recipient is forced to spend time and resources (connect charges and hard disk space) before he or she can make that decision. Because of this intrusion, junk e-mail messages are sometimes punished vigilante-style. The messages are often globally erased using programs called *cancelbots*, and the hard disks of their senders might be swamped by replies that have huge but useless file attachments.

company mail server, which holds the reply in your mailbox until you use your e-mail program to read the reply.

Now suppose you want to use Internet e-mail to send a note to a customer thanking him for a recent order. Again, you compose and send your message, but this time the process involves a few additional steps. If you are working on a network, the message goes to your mail server as usual, and the mail server forwards it via the Internet to your customer's mail server so he can download it to his computer at his convenience. If you are working on a stand-alone computer, your mail server is maintained by your Internet service provider (ISP), so you must connect to your ISP before you send the message. Your ISP's mail server then sends the message to your customer's mail server, which might be maintained by his company or by another ISP.

Obviously, for such a seemingly simple process to succeed as well as it does, some pretty complex things have to happen behind the scenes. We won't delve into the technology that makes each type of e-mail possible in this course. Instead, our goal is to give you enough information to take advantage of these powerful communication tools.

Understanding E-Mail Addresses

E-mail addresses are like postal addresses, but instead of the five or six items of information needed to send a letter, only one or two items are needed to send an e-mail message.

Before an organization implements an e-mail system, someone usually decides on a policy for assigning a unique e-mail address, or *alias*, to each person's mailbox. In small organizations, the addresses might be the first names of the mailbox users. In larger organizations, the addresses might be the first names plus the first initial of the last names, or some other scheme that is intuitive but avoids duplicates. For example, a typical internal e-mail address for a person named Christopher Dooley might be *christopher* or *chrisd*.

Instant e-mail
If you're simply trading quick bits of information with a colleague (down the hall or around the world) and you're both online at the same time, you can use MSN Messenger to send instant real-time messages instead of sending e-mail messages.

A typical Internet e-mail address is more complicated. For example, the address for Christopher Dooley might look something like this:

chrisd@example.dom

CHAPTER 4 E-MAIL BASICS

If you had to say this e-mail address out loud, you'd say *chris dee at example dot dom*.

The part of the address to the left of the @ sign is the name that identifies the user, and the part to the right of the @ sign is a *domain name* that identifies the e-mail server where the user's mailbox is located. In our example, *chrisd* is the user name and *example.dom* is the domain name. (Our example uses a fake domain name. Usually, the last part of the domain name identifies the type of domain.)

In the universe of e-mail, many users can have the name *chrisd* and many users can have mailboxes at *example.dom*. But only one user named *chrisd* can have a mailbox at *example.dom*. In other words, *chrisd@example.dom* must be a unique address. If a user named Christine Doe wants a mailbox at *example.dom* and *chrisd* already exists, she cannot choose *chrisd* as her user name. She must either choose a name like *chrisdoe* so that her e-mail address is *chrisdoe@example.dom*, or she must move her mailbox to a different e-mail server so that her e-mail address is something like *chrisd@secondexample.dom*.

Obviously, to send e-mail to someone, you must know his or her correct e-mail address. If you send e-mail to a nonexistent address, you usually get a *bounce back* message, the equivalent of a return-to-sender stamp from the postal service (but you'll get it much faster). If you send it to the wrong address, the

MORE ABOUT...
Finding e-mail addresses, page 104

TOP-LEVEL DOMAIN NAMES
Domain names in the U.S. were originally organized into six top-level categories: *com* (companies), *edu* (educational institutions), *gov* (government agencies), *mil* (military agencies), *net* (network administration support), and *org* (nonprofit organizations). Because almost every company, large and small, has its own domain name, the com category quickly became overcrowded. The domain name categories have been expanded to include several more options, such as *info* and *biz*. Domain names outside of the U.S. often end in a two-letter abbreviation that signifies the country in which the company or person using the domain name is located—for example, *ch* (Switzerland), *de* (Germany), *no* (Norway), *se* (Sweden), and *uk* (United Kingdom). Some countries have strict guidelines for qualification for one of these domain identifiers; others are available to anyone who asks. For example, in Sweden, a company must prove that it operates a licensed business with a unique name in order to qualify for a domain name ending in *se*. Many Swedish businesses instead apply for domain names ending in *nu*, from the small Polynesian country of Niue, which means *now* in Swedish. These domain names are used as marketing tools, so that their URL tells people to buy.now, shop.now, or come.in.now. The *tv* domain identifier, which belongs to the country of Tuvalu, is available to anyone wanting to indicate that their site is a television station. Western Samoa's domain identifier, *ws*, is available for those wanting to indicate that their site is merely a Web site.

results can range from negligible to disastrous. For example, suppose you send a message inviting Christine Doe to lunch but mistakenly address it to *chrisd@example.dom* instead of to *chrisdoe@example.dom*. You might end up having lunch with the wrong Chris! More importantly, you might send a critical, time-sensitive message to the wrong address and never know why you didn't get a reply. The moral: Double-check the address of the person you want to correspond with before you send a message on its way.

Setting Up Internet E-Mail

For people on a network to send and receive e-mail, the network administrator has to do all kinds of work behind the scenes to set up the e-mail server, establish user accounts, arrange for Internet access, and manage the whole system. If your network administrator has already configured Outlook Express as your e-mail program, you can jump ahead to "Starting Outlook Express for the First Time" on page 101. If you are using a different e-mail program, you can read along to get an idea of how things work.

If you are working on a stand-alone computer, Internet e-mail might not be set up, and you can't send or receive e-mail until you give Windows some information. Here are the steps for accomplishing this task:

1. Double-click the **Connect to the Internet** icon on your desktop.

    If you don't have a Connect to the Internet icon, you can click the Start button to display its menu. Then point to Programs, then Accessories, and then Communications to display each of those submenus, and click Internet Connection Wizard. (You might have to click the *double chevrons*, the two arrows at the bottom of the submenus, to see all your choices.)

SEARCHING FOR E-MAIL ADDRESSES

If you are working on a networked computer, your organization might provide an address book you can use to look up the e-mail addresses of your coworkers. If you need to locate an Internet e-mail address, on the Start menu click Search, and then click For People; or on the Outlook Express toolbar, click the down arrow to the right of the Find button, and then click People in the drop-down list. Next select a directory service from the Look In drop-down list. (A directory service is like a telephone directory, except that it records names, e-mail addresses, and postal addresses, as well as telephone numbers and web sites, all organized by location or category.) Enter the requested information and click Find Now. If you are prompted to connect to your ISP, do so. After a few seconds, the results of the search are displayed in the list box at the bottom of the Find People dialog box.

The Internet Connection Wizard starts and displays its first page, which is shown in this graphic:

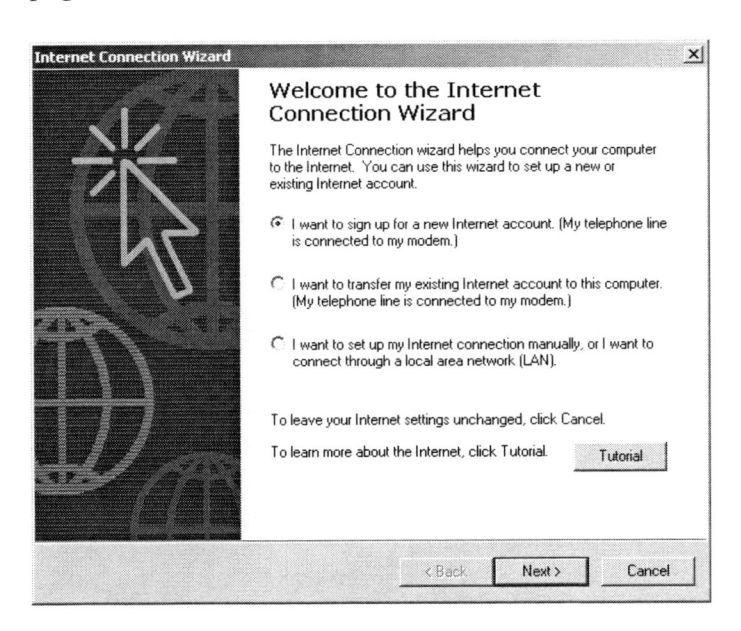

2. You now have three choices:

  - If you do not have an ISP, select the first option, and click **Next**.

  - If you have an ISP but need to set up your computer to connect to the ISP's server, select the second option, and click **Next**.

  - If your computer is connected to a network but is not set up for the Internet, or if you want to configure your settings manually, select the third option, and then click **Next**.

3. On the wizard's next page, enter the requested information, clicking **Next** to move to each successive wizard page.

    If you selected the second option, and you don't have all the necessary information, ask your ISP to provide it. If you are unsure about any of the information, click the Help button to get assistance.

    If you have never used e-mail on your computer before, you will need to enter the following:

    - Your first and last name; for example, *Christopher Dooley*.
    - Your e-mail address; for example, *chrisd@example.dom*.

- Two mail server names: an incoming (*POP3* or *IMAP*) name and an outgoing (*SMTP*) name—probably the name you use when you connect to your ISP; for example, *mail.example.dom*.

- Your logon name—probably the name you use when you connect to your ISP; for example, *chrisd*. (If your ISP uses Secure Password Authentication, it might give you other instructions.)

- Your password.

- A friendly name that Outlook Express will use for your e-mail settings; for example, *My Connection*.

You will also be given the opportunity to set up and join Internet newsgroups. This course doesn't cover the newsgroup capabilities of Outlook Express, but you can find out more by using the Outlook Express Help system.

If you chose the third option on the wizard's first page, you will need to enter the following information:

- Your connection method.

- Whether you want to use a proxy server or automatic configuration script.

- Whether you want to set up an Internet e-mail account.

4. On the wizard's final page, deselect the option to connect to the Internet immediately, and click **Finish**.

The wizard closes, and the Connect to the Internet icon disappears from your desktop. (The Internet Connection Wizard is always available through the Start, Programs, Accessories, and Communications menus if you need it again.)

If you are connecting to the Internet via a modem, the next step is to check that everything is working properly:

1. If you have an external modem, make sure your modem is connected to your computer and turned on.

2. Open My Computer, and if no links appear of the left side of the window, on the **Tools** menu, click **Folder Options**, select the **Enable Web content in folders** option, and click **OK**.

ABOUT PASSWORDS

A password is a security device designed to let authorized users into an account and keep unauthorized users out. Passwords can't serve this function unless they are secret. If you use a stand-alone computer to exchange personal e-mail with friends and family, the secrecy of your password might be a low priority. Otherwise, you will want to ensure that your password is complicated enough that it is too hard to guess. (Combinations that include uppercase and lowercase letters, punctuation, and numbers are the best.) Be careful, however, not to make it so complicated that it's hard to remember without writing it down. You should change your password regularly. (Your organization might alert you when it is time for a change.)

Chapter 4   E-Mail Basics

3. Click the **Network and Dial-up Connections** link on the left side of the window.

4. In the Network and Dial-Up Connections window, if your modem is not already installed, double-click the **Make New Connection** icon.

   The Network Connection Wizard's first page appears so that you can set up the connection to your ISP.

5. Enter the required information on the Network Connection Wizard's pages, clicking **Next** to move from page to page.

6. On the final page, click **Finish**.

   An icon for your new connection is now displayed in the Network and Dial-Up Connections window.

7. Close the window.

If you have any difficulty making the connection, contact your ISP for troubleshooting assistance.

Starting Outlook Express for the First Time

Assuming that you have a working e-mail connection, here are the steps for starting Outlook Express so that you can take a closer look at the program:

1. Click the **Launch Outlook Express** button on the Quick Launch toolbar.

   You can also display the Start and Programs menus, and click Outlook Express.

2. If Outlook Express prompts you to select the connection you want to use, select the connection for your ISP, and click **OK**.

Working offline

If your computer connects to the Internet via a modem, you can work with e-mail without connecting to your ISP. This method, called *working offline*, enables you to compose messages and responses and store them in your Outbox. You can then go online and send all the messages at once. Knowing how to work offline is handy if you are away from your desk and want to compose messages on a laptop or if you are using an Internet service computer (in an airport or Internet café, for example) and are being charged by the minute for connection to the Internet.

Microsoft Outlook

Outlook Express is a scaled-down version of Microsoft Outlook. In addition to e-mail, Outlook includes a calendar, a contacts manager, a to-do list, a journal, and a notes feature. For more information, check out *Quick Course in Microsoft Outlook*, another course in this series.

3. If you see a logon dialog box, enter your user name and password (if it's not already entered), and click **OK**.

4. If you did not previously enter your user information, the Internet Connection Wizard prompts you to do so now. You will need to enter the following, clicking **Next** on each page of the wizard:

    - Your first and last name; for example, *Christopher Dooley*.
    - Your e-mail address; for example, *chrisd@example.dom*.
    - Two mail server names: an incoming (*POP3* or *IMAP*) name and an outgoing (*SMTP*) name—probably the name you use when you connect to your ISP; for example, *mail.example.dom*.
    - Your logon name—probably the name you use when you connect to your ISP; for example, *chrisd*. (If your ISP uses Secure Password Authentication, it might give you other instructions).
    - Your password.

    On the wizard's final page, click **Finish**.

5. Maximize the Outlook Express window, which looks like the one shown in this graphic:

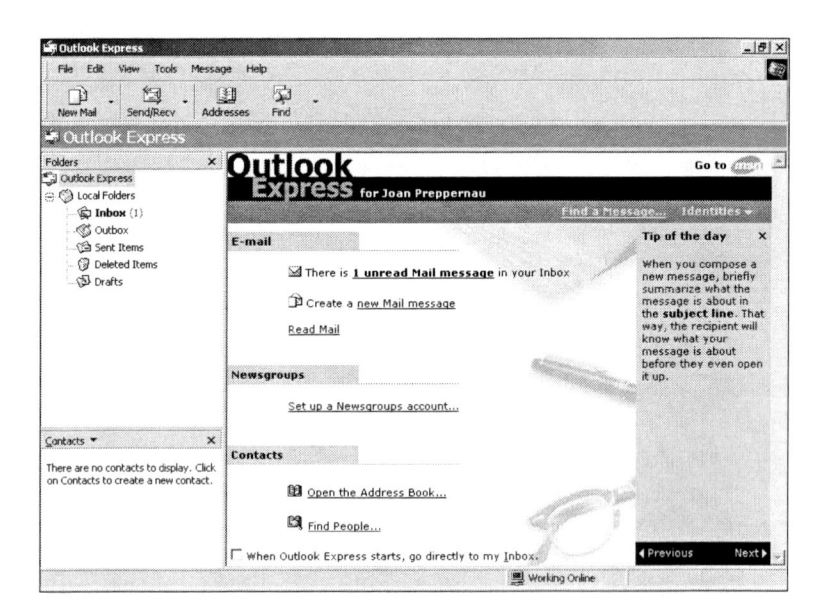

As you can see, the Outlook Express window is divided into three panes. The top left pane, called the *Folders list,* displays a tree diagram of the predefined Outlook Express folders. The bottom left pane, called the *Contacts pane,* displays your contact list, which is currently empty. (Your contact list is an electronic address book where you can store the names, e-mail addresses, postal addresses, telephone numbers, and additional pertinent information about the people with whom you frequently correspond. You'll soon learn more about how to set up contacts.) The right pane provides easy access to e-mail, newsgroup, and contact information, as well as a panel with tips for using Outlook Express. If you are connected to the Internet, you can click the Go to MSN button in the top right corner of the pane to go directly to the Web through the Microsoft Network (MSN) Web site.

6. Click the check box at the bottom of the right pane so that Outlook Express will go directly to your Inbox when it starts (or leave it deselected if you prefer).

7. Click **Inbox** in the Folders list.

The right pane changes to display the contents of the Inbox, as shown in this graphic:

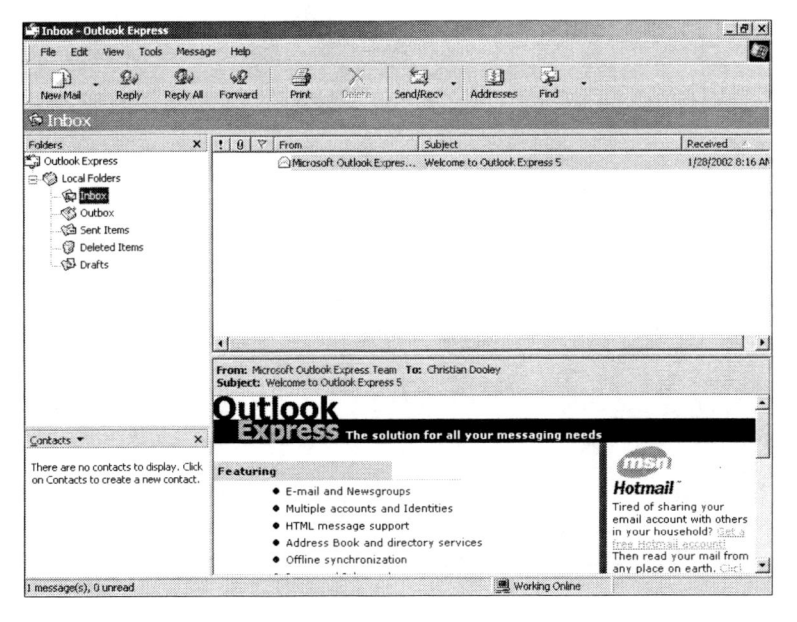

Outlook Express handles all e-mail messages through the Inbox, whether they come from a colleague down the hall or a client in another country.

WHICH FOLDERS SHOULD I USE?

Depending on how your e-mail account is set up, you might see more than one set of folders in the Folders list. If a secondary set of folders is specifically set up for your e-mail account, use those folders rather than the ones we specify here.

In the preceding graphic, the Inbox folder is selected in the Folders list in the left pane, and its contents are summarized as a list of message headers in the top right pane. The text of the message whose header is highlighted is displayed in the bottom right pane, called the *preview pane*.

CUSTOMIZING THE OUTLOOK EXPRESS WINDOW

The default layout of the Outlook Express window might suit your needs as long as you have only a few messages in your Inbox. But after a while, your message header list might get too long to fit in its allotted space. Let's take a look at some of the ways you can customize the window:

1. On the **View** menu, click **Layout**.

    Outlook Express displays the dialog box shown here:

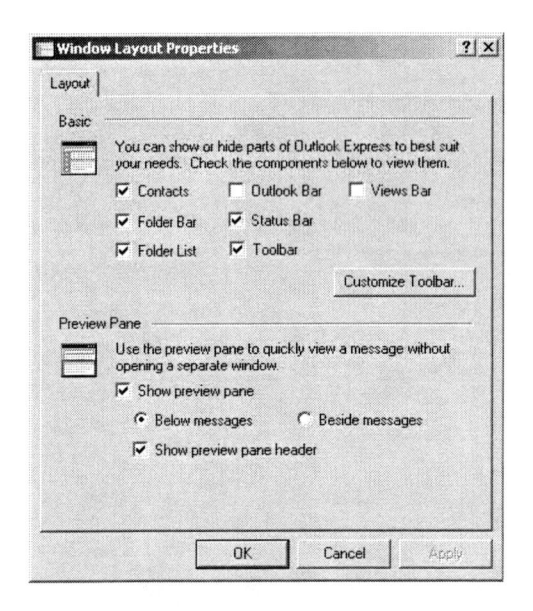

2. Drag the dialog box by its title bar to the top right corner of the screen.

CHANGING THE OUTLOOK BAR ICONS

You can view only eight large items at a time on the Outlook bar. If you want to view more than eight, you can switch to small icons by right-clicking a blank area of the Outlook bar and clicking Small Icons on the shortcut menu.

3. In the **Basic** area, select only the **Folder Bar**, **Outlook Bar**, **Status Bar**, and **Toolbar** check boxes. (Deselect the other check boxes.)

4. In the **Preview Pane** area, deselect the **Show preview pane** check box.

CHAPTER 4   E-MAIL BASICS

5. Click **Apply** to apply the changes without closing the dialog box.

6. Click the **Customize Toolbar** button. Click the down arrow to the right of the **Text Options** box, click **No text labels** in the drop-down list, and then click **Close**.

7. Click **OK** to close the Window Layout Properties dialog box.

   The results are shown in this graphic:

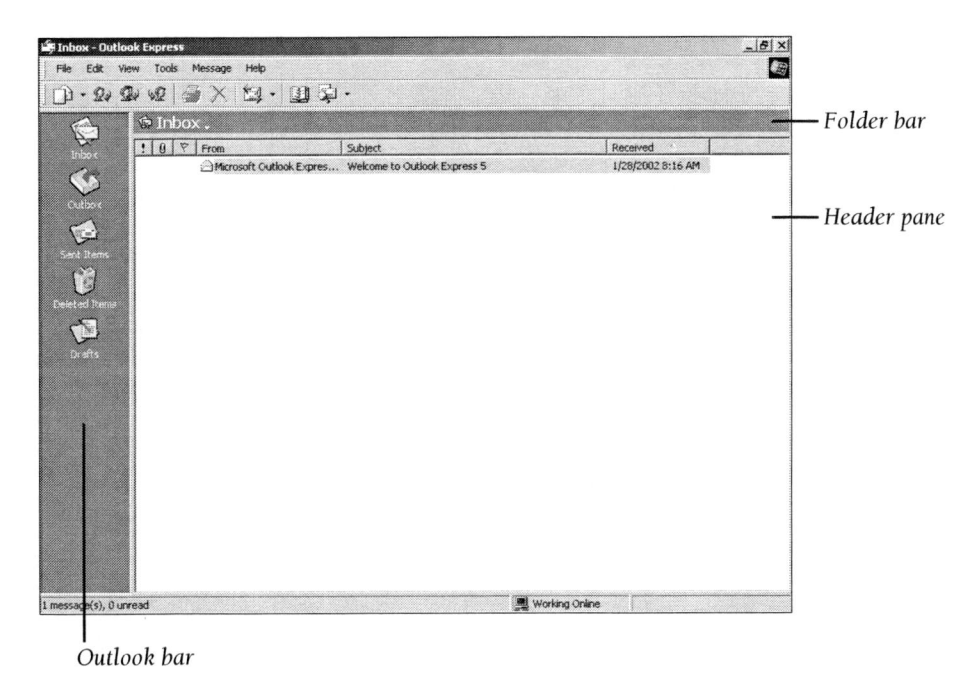

   Folder bar

   Header pane

   Outlook bar

Let's see how to move around Outlook Express in this view:

1. On the Folder bar above the right pane, click the word **Inbox**.

   The Folders list drops down.

2. Click **Outlook Express** in the Folders list.

   The contents of the right pane change to display the options shown earlier, and the Folder bar indicates that you are looking at the Outlook Express folder.

3. Click **Outlook Express** on the Folder bar to display the Folders list again, and then click the **pushpin** at the top of the list.

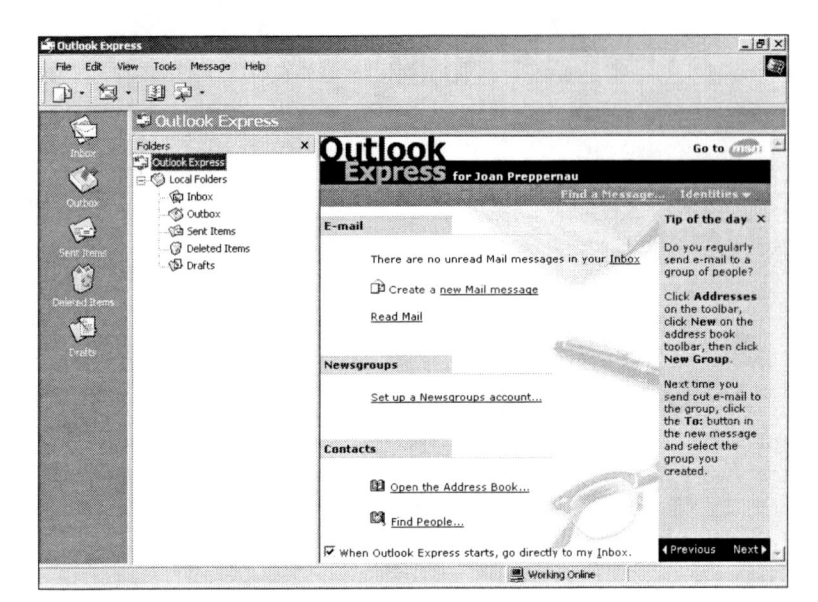

The Folders list stays open, as shown in this graphic:

Notice that the icons on the Outlook bar represent the same folders as those in the Folders list.

4. To close the Folders list, click its **Close** button.

5. Click the **Inbox** icon on the Outlook bar to redisplay the message header list.

After you have worked your way through this chapter, you might want to experiment with various layouts to find the one that best suits the way you work. But for now, let's move on to see how to send and receive messages.

Sending Messages

At its simplest, e-mailing involves the sending and receiving of messages. We'll look at the sending side of the process first. For this example, suppose you are arranging the facilities for the staff party we have been using as our example, and you want to remind yourself to confirm the rental of the Adventure Works facilities first thing tomorrow morning. Follow these steps to compose your first message.

1. On the toolbar, click the **New Message** button, (not its down arrow).

Chapter 4 E-Mail Basics

This button's label (when it's visible) is *New Mail*. In our instructions, however, we'll refer to buttons by the names ScreenTips uses.

2. When Outlook Express opens the New Message window, drag the side of the frame until you can see all the buttons on the toolbar at the top of the window, as shown here:

More About...
Sizing windows, page 17

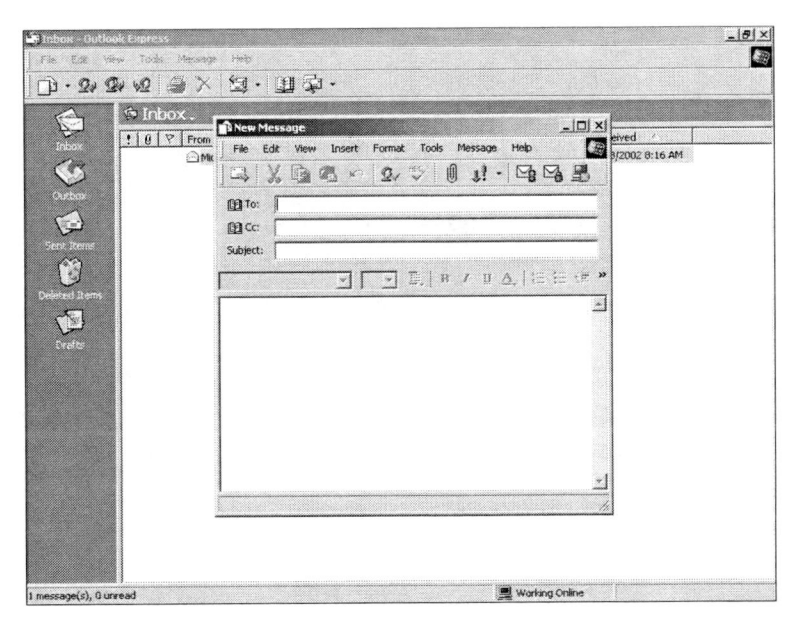

3. Type your own e-mail address in the **To** box, and press **Tab** to move to the Cc box.

   For practice, you are just sending a message to yourself. Obviously, if you were sending a message to someone else, you would type his or her e-mail address in the To box.

   To send a message to several people, you type their addresses one after the other, separated by commas or semicolons.

   To send a courtesy copy of a message, you type the address of the copy recipient in the Cc box.

More About...
Sending copies, page 115

4. For this message, leave the **Cc** box blank, and press **Tab** to move to the **Subject** box.

5. In the **Subject** box, type *Confirm Rental*, and press **Tab** to move to the message area.

6. In the message area, type this:

   Check on Adventure Works rental (555-0100). Be sure to tell them the caterers will be there at 10:00 AM to set up.

7. On the **Message** menu, click **Set Priority**, and then click **High** to designate this message as important.

More About...
Message priority, page 116

Alternatively, you can click the **Set Priority** button on the window's toolbar. The message window now looks like the one shown in this graphic:

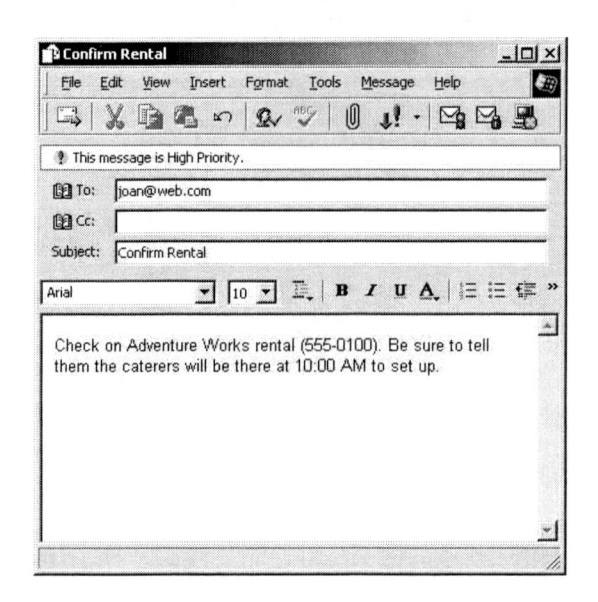

E-mail etiquette

Some general rules apply when composing e-mail messages:

- **Use standard capitalization.** All lowercase is hard to read, and all uppercase—which conveys shouting—is considered rude. (Sending rude messages is called *flaming*.)
- **Use emoticons judiciously.** Emoticons (or "smileys")—combinations of characters that look like faces or symbols when viewed sideways—can be entertaining, but overusing them can become tiresome. In some programs, these combinations are automatically converted to graphic icons.
- **Use descriptive subject headings.** People often need to be able to spot a message easily. For example, a general subject line, like "A New Idea" says little about the message, whereas "Slogan for New Product" describes more precisely what the message content is about.
- **Identify priority messages for busy people.** If a message is time-sensitive, start the subject line with the word "Urgent." If the message does not require any action on the part of the recipient, start the line with FYI (for your information).
- **Be concise.** Avoid long paragraphs, which are hard to read on the screen. Try to limit the message length to one screenful of information, so that the recipient can see the entire message at a glance.

8. If you want, use the buttons on the Formatting toolbar above the message area to format the message.

9. Send the message by clicking the **Send** button.

    If you are connected to a network or to your ISP, clicking Send sends the message to your mail server.

    If you are working offline, clicking Send transfers the message to your Outbox, and the Outbox icon on the Outlook bar indicates that you have one message waiting to be sent.

10. If you are working offline and the program displays a message telling you that you can send the message later by choosing the **Send and Receive** commands, select the **Don't show me this again** check box, and click **OK**.

USING CONTACTS

After a while, you'll probably find yourself e-mailing a few people frequently. You can store their names and addresses in the Address Book so that you don't have to type them every time. Here's how:

1. Click the **Address Book** button on the toolbar.

    This button's label (when it's visible) is *Addresses*, but we'll refer to it by its more descriptive ScreenTip.

    Outlook Express displays the window shown in the graphic on the next page.

SENDING COPIES OF MESSAGES

The Cc and Bcc lines an e-mail message allow you to send two types of copies:

- **Carbon copies.** When you "Cc" one or more people on an e-mail message, they receive the same message as the recipients on the To line. The recipients listed on the To and Cc lines are all visible to each other, and if any of them uses "Reply All" to respond to the message, their reply goes to the sender and anyone else listed on the Cc line. If they use "Reply," the reply goes only to the sender. It is generally accepted that some kind of action is required of the recipients on the To line, but the recipients on the Cc line are receiving a copy of the e-mail only for their own information. For that reason, carbon copies are also referred to as *courtesy copies*.

- **Blind carbon copies.** To hide recipients' names and addresses, use the Bcc line, which is not displayed by default. Any name on the Bcc line is hidden from other recipients on the Bcc, Cc, or To lines. A Bcc recipient can send a reply to an e-mail message but will not receive a reply sent by the primary recipients. To send a blind carbon copy, click the Cc button, select the blind copy recipient from your contact list, click Bcc, and click OK. (If the intended recipients are not on the list, you can add them to it.) In some organizations, blind copies are considered sneaky and are frowned on because they create an atmosphere of mistrust, so use them rarely and judiciously, or not at all.

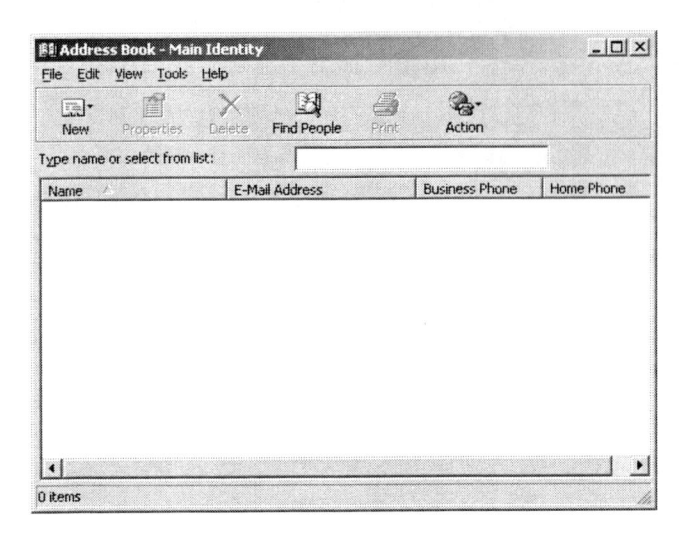

2. Click the New button on the Address Book window's toolbar, and click **New Contact** in the drop-down list.

   The dialog box shown in this graphic appears:

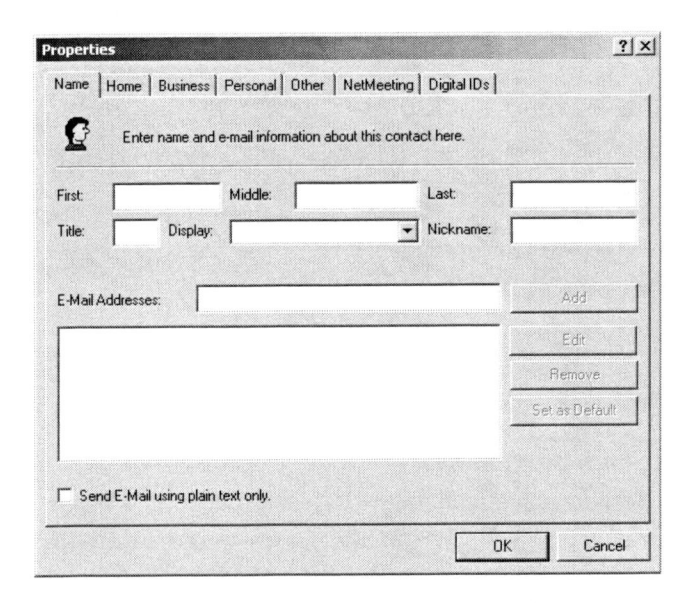

MESSAGE PRIORITY

By default, all messages are assigned Normal Priority. Designating a message as High Priority places an exclamation mark next to the message header, along with the notation "This message is High Priority." Designating a message as Low Priority places a down arrow and the notation "This message is Low Priority."

CREATING GROUPS

If you frequently send messages to the same set of people, you can create a group in the Address Book. On the Address Book's toolbar, click the New button, select New Group from the drop-down list, and assign the group a name. Next assign people to the group. To add someone new to both the group and the Address Book, click New Contact. To add an existing contact, click Select Members. To add someone new to the group only, type the name and e-mail address in the respective Name and E-Mail boxes, click the Add button, and then click OK. In the New Message window, type the name of the group in the To box to address the message to everyone in the group.

The Properties dialog box provides a template for adding Internet addresses to your Address Book.

3. On the **Name** tab, type your own first and last names in the appropriate fields.

   The names you type in the First, Middle, and Last boxes of the Properties dialog box are transferred to the Display box in the same order: first/middle/last. You can switch the display order of the name to last/first/middle by clicking the arrow to the right of the Display box and making a selection from the drop-down list.

4. In the **Nickname** box, type *myself* (or any short, memorable word that strikes your fancy).

5. In the **E-Mail Addresses** box, type your own e-mail address. Then click the **Add** button to transfer the address to the list box.

6. On the other tabs of the dialog box, type any other information you want to store.

7. Click **OK** to add this contact to the Address Book.

8. Click the **New** button on the toolbar, click **New Contact**, and repeat steps 4 through 8 to create another Address Book entry for yourself. This time, add a middle name or initial to your name, and assign *me* as the nickname.

Now let's try sending another message, this time using the Address Book to see how it speeds up the addressing process:

1. With the Address Book window open, right-click your own name, click **Action**, and then click **Send Mail** on the shortcut menu.

MORE ABOUT THE ADDRESS BOOK

When you respond to a message, by default the recipient's address is automatically added to your Address Book. To turn off this feature, on the Tools menu, click Options. Then deselect the "Automatically put people I reply to in my Address Book" check box on the Send tab of the Options dialog box. You can enter a partial address in the To box and then click the Check Names button on the message window's toolbar to have Outlook Express check the partial entry against the Address Book; Outlook Express then displays potential complete addresses. You can sort the entries in the Address Book by first or last name, e-mail address, or phone number by clicking the respective column header. Clicking again reverses the sort order. You can erase a contact or group by selecting the entry, clicking the Delete button, and then confirming the deletion. You can print Address Book information by selecting entries, clicking the Print button, and choosing a print style: Memo (all data), Business Card, or Phone List.

Outlook Express opens the New Message window with your display name (the more readable version of your address) already in the To box.

2. Fill in the **Subject** box, type a message, and then click **Send**.
3. Close the Address Book window.

If you are working offline, notice that the Outbox folder now contains two messages waiting for transmission.

ATTACHING ITEMS TO MESSAGES

With Outlook Express, you can attach several types of items to a message. In this section, we'll look at a couple of them.

ATTACHING STATIONERY

On special occasions, you might want to jazz up the appearance of your e-mail messages by adding sets of predefined formatting called *stationery*. (Bear in mind that recipients of your messages might not be able to see this formatting if they are not using an e-mail program that supports it.) Try this:

1. Click the **New Message** button to open a New Message window.
2. In the **To** box, Type *me*, and click the **Check Names** Button.

   Although this button is officially labeled *Check*, we use its more descriptive ScreenTip name.

   Outlook Express finds the nickname in the Address Book and inserts the corresponding display name.

3. Press **Tab** twice, type *Party Time!* in the **Subject** box, and then press **Tab** again.
4. On the message window's **Format** menu, click **Apply Stationery**.

AUTOMATIC STATIONERY

Outlook Express provides several stationery patterns. If you want to open a new message window with a stationery pattern already applied, you can click the down arrow to the right of the New Message button to see a list of commonly used stationery types.

ATTACHING A SIGNATURE

To create a signature (such as your name, company, and phone number) that appears at the bottom of your e-mail messages, click Options on the Tools menu, and click the Signatures tab in the Options dialog box. In the Signatures area, click New, and then type the text of the signature in the Edit Signature box. (We recommend that you keep it short and avoid being cute.) Select the "Add signatures to all outgoing messages" check box, and click OK. To add the signature to messages on a case-by-case basis, leave this check box deselected. When you want, click Signature on the Insert menu to add the signature to your message.

CHAPTER 4 E-MAIL BASICS   113

5. You don't want any of the patterns listed on the submenu, so click **More Stationery**.

    Outlook Express displays the dialog box shown here:

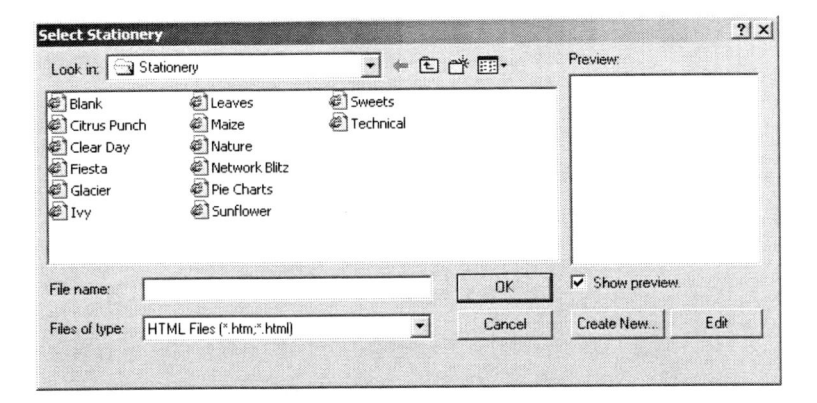

6. Preview the different types of stationery by clicking each option and viewing it in the Preview box.

7. Click **Fiesta**, and click **OK**.

    The background of the message area is now filled with a festive pattern.

ATTACHING FILES

You might not want to attach stationery to messages very often, but you will probably need to attach files. As an example, let's attach one of the Directions memos to a message:

1. In the message area of the open message window, type *Here are the directions* followed by a colon (:), and press **Enter**.

2. Click the **Attach File** button on the window's toolbar.

    Although this button is officially labeled *Attach*, we use its more descriptive ScreenTip name.

ATTACHING WEB PAGES

If you want to send a hyperlink to a Web page with a message, first make sure Rich Text (HTML) is chosen on the New Message window's Format menu. Then in the body of the message, you can simply type any Web page's URL (Internet address) to create an active link to that site. To have text in a message (such as *click here*) act as a link to a Web page, you simply select the text, click Hyperlink on the Insert menu, select the resource type (usually http:), enter the Web page's URL (such as *www.microsoft.com*), and click OK. Then send the message the way you usually do.

ATTACHING A SHORTCUT

If you are working on a network and want someone to read a file, you can send them a shortcut to the file instead of sending the file itself. Select the "Make Shortcut to this file" check box at the bottom of the Insert Attachment dialog box before specifying the file.

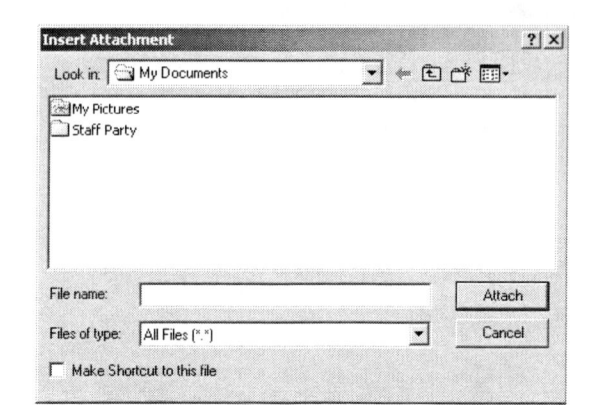

Outlook Express displays the dialog box shown in this graphic:

3. Double-click the **Staff Party** folder, then the **Directions** subfolder, and then the **East Directions** document.

   Outlook Express inserts an icon for the document in the message window's Attach box, as shown in this graphic:

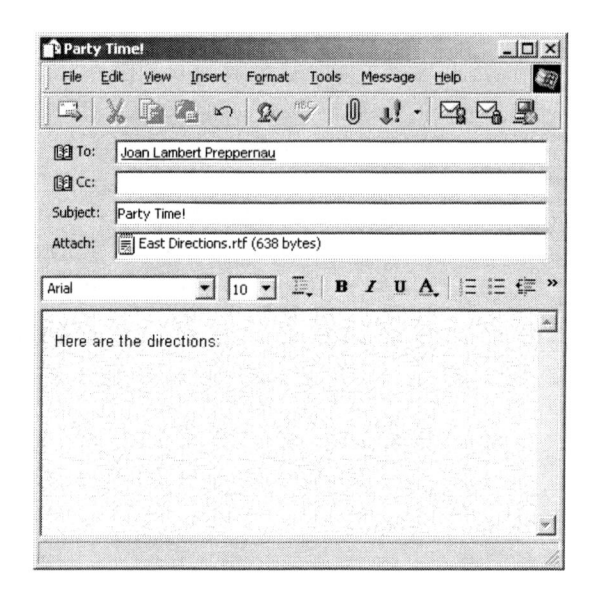

4. Click **Send**.

SENDING OR RECEIVING
Click the down arrow to the right of the Send and Receive All button to see a drop-down list of sending and receiving options. The Send and Receive All option appears in bold, indicating that this option is carried out by default when you click the button.

You can attach more than one file to the same message, but be aware that some mail servers have difficulty handling messages with large amounts of data attached to them.

SENDING MESSAGES STORED IN THE OUTBOX

If you are working offline, you now have several messages stored in the Outbox, waiting for you to connect to the Internet

Chapter 4 E-Mail Basics

so that Outlook Express can send them on their way. (If you are working online, the messages have already been sent, and you can skip this section.)

The messages will be sent automatically the next time you connect to the Internet. Here's how to send the messages when you are working in Outlook Express:

1. On the Outlook bar, click the **Outbox** icon to see your list of messages.

   You don't have to move to the Outbox to send the messages, but if you do, you can watch them disappear.

2. On the toolbar, click the **Send and Receive All** button (not its down arrow).

   When the button labels are visible, the button is called *Send/Recv*.

3. Follow the prompts to establish your connection.

   Outlook Express initiates the connection, sends the messages, and checks for any new messages. (You might need to enter your password during this process.)

4. If necessary, on the **File** menu, click **Work Offline** to disconnect from your ISP.

5. Click the **Inbox** icon on the Outlook bar to see the header of any new messages.

Receiving and Handling Messages

If you are working on a network, your mail server probably automatically routes messages from your mailbox on the server to your computer. Outlook Express notifies you when you receive a new message by displaying an envelope icon in the status area of the taskbar and playing a sound. (Usually, you will want to keep Outlook Express open while you work so that you can receive new messages right away.)

If you are working on a stand-alone computer, or if Outlook Express is set up to retrieve messages according to a schedule, you can retrieve messages that are waiting in your mailbox on the server by clicking the Send and Receive All button on the toolbar. (As you've seen, clicking the Send and Receive All button also sends any messages stored in the Outbox.)

SCHEDULING MAIL DELIVERY

If you are connected to your ISP and running Outlook Express, by default the program checks the server every 30 minutes for new messages. To change this schedule, click Options on the Outlook Express Tools menu and adjust the "Check for new messages every" setting on the General tab of the Options dialog box.

Let's take a closer look at the message headers in the Inbox. The headers include the sender's name, the subject, and the date and time you received the message. When you have not yet displayed a message, an unopened envelope is shown next to the sender's name, and the message header is displayed in bold. An exclamation mark in the first column indicates that the message is urgent, and a paper clip in the second column indicates that the message has an attachment.

Here's how to read a message:

1. Double-click the **Party Time!** message.

   Outlook Express displays the message in its own window and changes the message header's unopened envelope to an opened one.

2. Right-click the attachment in the **Attach** box, and click **Save As** on the shortcut menu.

3. In the Save Attachment As dialog box, rename the file as *New Directions*.

4. Navigate to the **My Documents** folder so that it appears in the **Save in** box.

5. Click **Save**.

   You can then scan the file for viruses and read it at your leisure.

Marking messages

If you display a message in the Preview pane for five seconds or more, Outlook Express changes its closed envelope icon to an open one and the bold font to a normal font to indicate that the message has been read. (To change this setting to more or less than five seconds, click Options on the Tools menu, click the Read tab of the Options dialog box, and then adjust the "Mark message read after displaying for" option.) To manually mark a message as read or unread, right-click its header, and click the appropriate command on the shortcut menu.

Viruses

A *virus* is a man-made program that can be installed on your computer without your knowledge, usually through e-mail attachments or other kinds of downloads. Viruses are created deliberately by pranksters (or criminals) just to cause trouble. To keep your computer virus-free, avoid automatically opening an attachment by double-clicking it. Instead, get in the habit of first saving it to a folder and then scanning the folder with a virus detection and elimination program. Viruses, which used to be confined to program files but which now can attack through word processors and spreadsheet programs as well, can wreak havoc on drives and files. If you begin to notice that your computer isn't working as it used to, a virus could be the cause. You can stay abreast of information about new viruses by visiting Web sites designed for that purpose, such as the Symantec website at *http://www.symantec.com/avcenter*, Vmyths.com at *http://vmyths.com*, and the McAfee AvertVirus Information Library at *http://vil.mcafee.com/hoax.asp*.

CHAPTER 4   E-MAIL BASICS   117

REPLYING TO MESSAGES

Suppose the message now on your screen is from a colleague and requires a response. Here's how to send a reply:

1. With the Party Time! message displayed in its window, click the **Reply to Sender** button on the toolbar.

    This button's label is simply *Reply*, but to make a greater distinction between the two options, we refer to the Reply to Sender and Reply All buttons by their more descriptive ScreenTip names.

    Outlook Express opens a window like the one shown in this graphic:

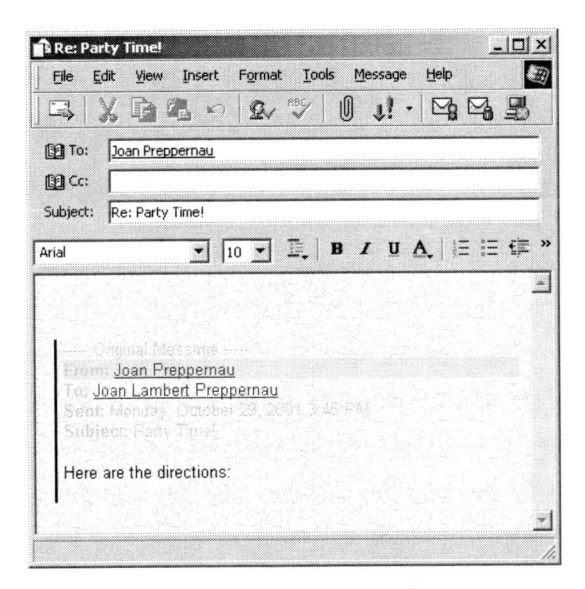

    Notice that the To and Subject boxes are already filled in and that the original message is displayed. (Clicking the Reply to All button displays a similar window, except that the To box contains all recipients' addresses.)

2. Type *Thanks. See you there!*, and then click the **Send** button.

    Outlook Express sends the reply on its way if you are connected to your mail server, or puts it in the Outbox if you are working offline.

3. If necessary, click the **Send and Receive All** button, and read the reply when it arrives.

DRAFTS

If you are working on a message that requires some thought, or if you have to leave a message while you're in the middle of writing it to attend to other business, you can click Save on the File menu to store the incomplete message in the Drafts folder. You can then close the message window. To resume work on the message, you can simply click the message header in the Drafts folder and then proceed just as you would for any other message. After you send the message, it is deleted from the Drafts folder.

Forwarding Messages

You can easily forward messages of interest with just a few mouse clicks. Here's how:

1. Click the **Confirm Rental** header, and then click the **Forward** button on the toolbar.

   Outlook Express displays the message window shown in this graphic:

ORIGINAL MESSAGES

By default, the originating e-mail message (and subsequent additions) will appear at the bottom of the message area of an e-mail reply, preceded by a divider line. It's a good idea to keep these messages in your reply so that conversation participants can keep track of the context. If you want only part of an original message to be displayed, you can make changes to the original text. Click Reply or Forward to open a new message window, and then edit or delete the text as you normally would. If you want only your current message to be displayed, you can change the setting. On the Tools menu, click Options, and deselect the "Include message in reply" option.

2. For demonstration purposes, type *me* in the **To** box.
3. Click an insertion point at the top of the message area, type *Another reminder*, and press **Enter**.
4. Click the **Send** button on the toolbar.
5. If necessary, click the **Send and Receive All** button.

   Outlook Express retrieves the message, and now you can see how a forwarded message looks.

Organizing Messages

When you first start Outlook Express, the program provides five folders: Inbox, Outbox, Sent Items, Deleted Items, and Drafts. In addition to these program-generated folders, you can create your own folders to help organize messages in logical ways.

(Some people prefer to create folders for all their messages so that the Inbox acts only as a temporary receptacle for new messages.)

Let's create a folder and move some messages into it:

1. On the **View** menu, click **Layout**.

2. In the Window Layout Properties dialog box, deselect the **Outlook Bar** and **Folder Bar** check boxes, select the **Folder List** check box, and click **OK**.

3. Right-click **Inbox** in the Folders list, and click **New Folder** on the shortcut menu.

   You see the dialog box shown in this graphic:

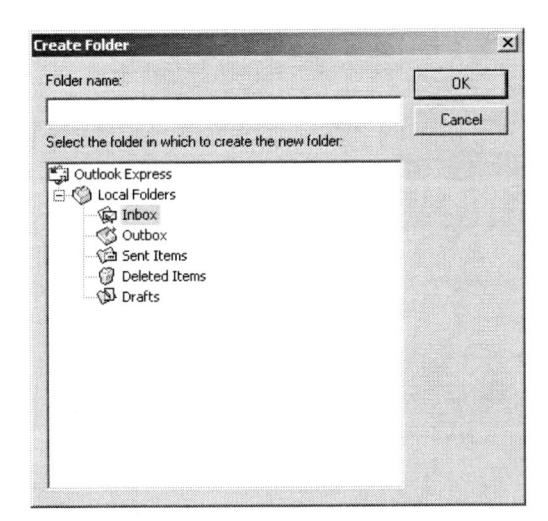

4. In the **Folder name** box, type *Staff Party*, and click **OK**.

5. Click the **Inbox** folder, click the original **Confirm Rental** message, and drag it to the **Staff Party** folder in the Folders list.

Here's another way to move messages:

1. Right-click the **FW: Confirm Rental** message header, click **Move to Folder** on the shortcut menu, make sure the **Staff Party** folder is selected in the Move dialog box, and then click **OK**.

2. Click the **Staff Party** folder in the Folders list.

SORTING MESSAGES

You can quickly sort messages by priority, attachment, sender, subject, or the date received, by clicking the appropriate column header. To reverse the sort order, click the same header again. You can also specify a sort order by clicking the View menu and then clicking Sort By and the option you want.

Outlook Express displays the message headers in their new location, as shown in this graphic:

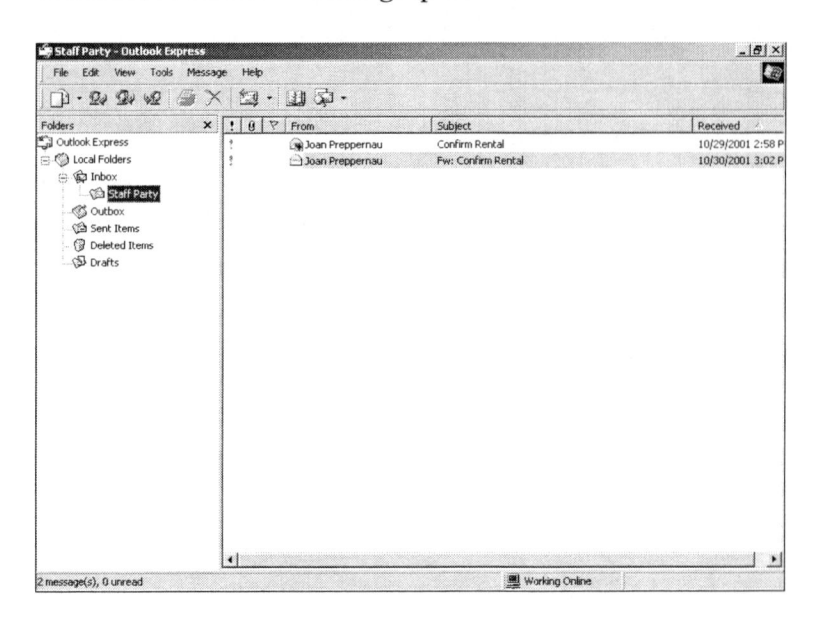

3. Close Outlook Express and, if necessary, disconnect from your ISP.

Deleting Messages

In the early days of e-mail, people would often hang on to old messages so that they had a record of their senders' addresses. Now that it's so easy to add e-mail addresses to the Address Book, keeping old messages is often no longer necessary. Although some companies have policies about keeping e-mail messages for legal reasons, many companies don't, and it's generally considered a good organizational habit to delete messages you no longer need. It's amazing how quickly your message file can grow to gigantic proportions if you don't regularly do some judicious housekeeping.

To demonstrate how to delete messages, we'll clean up the Sent Items folder, but the procedure is the same for any folder. (Caution: if you have any messages in your Sent Items folder that you want to keep for some reason, you can move them to an appropriate folder before emptying the Sent Items folder). This is what you do:

Emptying the Deleted Items folder

It's a good practice to periodically empty the Deleted Items folder so that it doesn't take up too much drive space. However, emptying the Deleted Items folder is irreversible (for all practical purposes), so before you take this step, be sure there's nothing you will need to retrieve. To empty the Deleted Items folder, you can right-click the Deleted Items icon, click Empty 'Deleted Items' Folder on the shortcut menu, and click Yes to confirm that you want to discard its contents.

Chapter 4 E-Mail Basics

1. Click the **Sent Items** icon on the Outlook bar.

   Outlook Express displays the headers of all the messages you have sent. (Outlook Express stores copies of your sent messages in this folder because the "Save copy of sent messages in the 'Sent Items' folder" option is selected by default on the Send tab of the Options dialog box.)

2. On the **Edit** menu, click **Select All**, and then click the **Delete** button on the toolbar.

   In Outlook Express, you can hold down the Shift or Ctrl key and click message headers to select more than one, just as you can in My Computer.

3. Click the **Deleted Items** icon on the Outlook bar.

   Outlook Express has transferred the deleted files to the Deleted Items folder, giving you an opportunity to change your mind about deleting them.

COMMUNICATING WITH INSTANT MESSAGING

Instant messaging—exchanging e-mail in real time—is easy and handy when you want immediate communication. With MSN Messenger, which can be easily installed from the Web site at *http://messenger.msn.com*, you can maintain a list of contacts, see who is currently online, and then have a conversation with one or more of your contacts, either by typing or by setting up a video or audio session. You can send attachments with your instant messages. You can also use cool tools, such as an electronic whiteboard, to help support your messages.

The difference between sending e-mail and sending instant messages is that e-mail provides a permanent record of the messages sent and received. Unless you specifically save an instant messaging session, your conversation is deleted when you close the message window. However if you simply want to trade some quick information with a contact, instant messages are a good way to avoid cluttering up your Inbox.

YOUR PASSPORT TO THE INTERNET

To use MSN Messenger, you must first obtain a Microsoft .NET Passport. This free "electronic passport" contains your identification information, as well as your list of contacts, favorite Web sites, and other information that you choose to store. Your .NET Passport also enables you to sign in to multiple Internet sites and services using one password, and enables you to easily access data you have stored on other computers. To find out more about .NET Passports, go to *http://www.passport.com*.

PART TWO

BUILDING PROFICIENCY

In Part Two, we build on the techniques you learned in Part One to round out your Windows 2000 skills. After completing these chapters, you will know enough to streamline and personalize Windows 2000, as well as troubleshoot common problems. In Chapter 5, you learn several ways to increase your efficiency. In Chapter 6, you learn how to add, remove, and reorganize your Windows setup to suit your own way of working. In Chapter 7, you learn some basic ways to ward off computer mishaps with basic preventive care.

INCREASING YOUR EFFICIENCY

We create shortcut icons on the desktop for programs and folders, and then we add shortcuts to the Start menu, the Programs submenu, and the Startup submenu. Next we display more toolbars at the bottom of the screen and show you some handy techniques for speeding up your everyday tasks. Finally, we use WordPad and Paint to explore linking and embedding files.

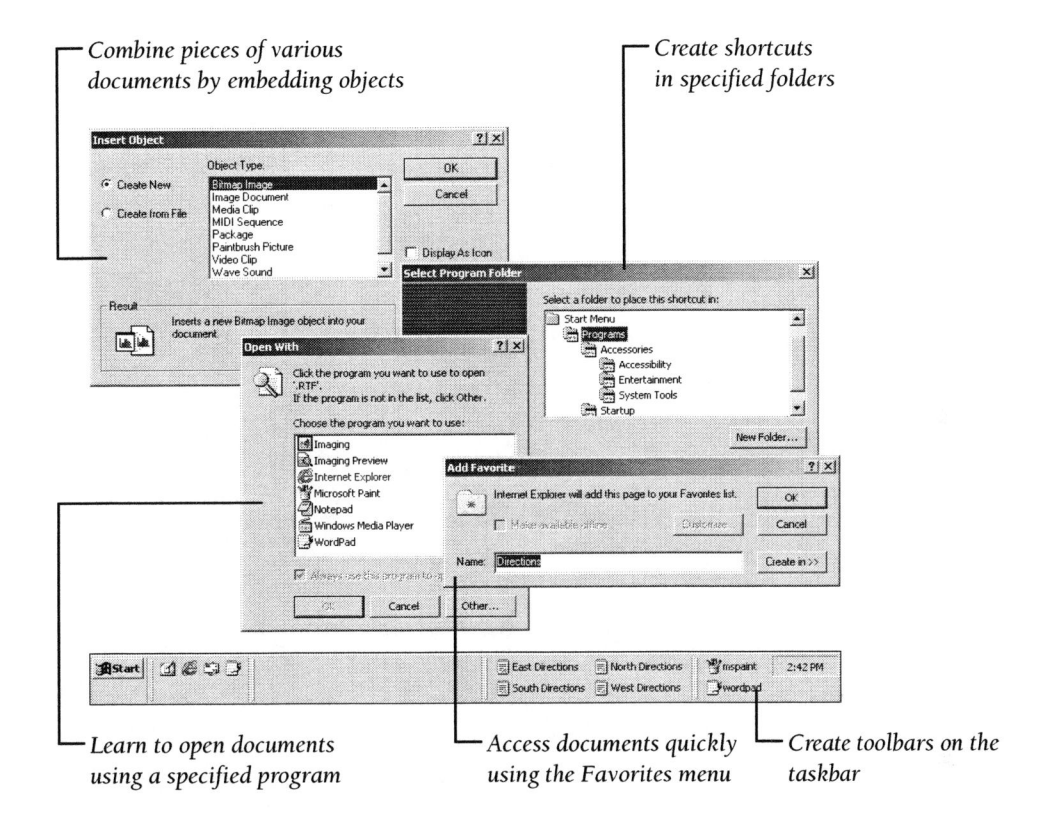

- *Combine pieces of various documents by embedding objects*
- *Create shortcuts in specified folders*
- *Learn to open documents using a specified program*
- *Access documents quickly using the Favorites menu*
- *Create toolbars on the taskbar*

P art One showed you how to accomplish basic Windows tasks and gave you enough information to start working in this environment. By now you've probably experimented a bit, and you're ready to move on to more complex tasks. In this chapter, we focus on how to take advantage of Windows 2000 to get your work done efficiently.

Getting Started Quickly

You've learned how to start a program by choosing it from the Programs submenu of the Start menu. You've also learned how to start a program and open a document at the same time using the following methods:

- **The Documents submenu.** Click the Start button, click Documents, and then click the document you want.

- **The My Computer and My Network Places windows.** Locate the document, and double-click it. (You can also just start a program by double-clicking its icon in these windows.)

These methods of getting down to work require several steps, but with Windows, you can speed things up by making the programs and documents you use most frequently immediately accessible. In this section, we'll examine a few simple techniques for instant access.

Using Shortcuts

For ultimate convenience, you can create a shortcut to any program, folder, document, or Web site and place it on the Quick Launch toolbar as a button or on the desktop as an icon. Clicking the button or double-clicking the icon starts the program, takes you directly to the folder's window, and opens the document in the appropriate application, or opens the Web site in your default Internet browser, depending on the nature of the shortcut.

Creating Quick Launch Toolbar Buttons

> **Ready-made shortcuts**
>
> If you install a new program on your computer, the program's setup utility might create desktop and Programs menu shortcuts for you. If your desktop and Programs submenu become cluttered with shortcuts you rarely use, you can delete the shortcuts without affecting their programs in any way.

Earlier in this course, you learned that you can use the buttons on the Quick Launch toolbar to start programs or display your desktop with only one click. In this section, you'll see how to add other shortcut buttons to the toolbar so that you have immediate access to the programs and tools you use most often.

CHAPTER 5 INCREASING YOUR EFFICIENCY 127

Before we play with buttons, let's see how to change the relative sizes of the Quick Launch toolbar and the taskbar:

1. Point to the vertical bar at the left end of the button display area of the taskbar.

   The pointer changes to a double-headed arrow.

2. Drag the bar to the right until the Quick Launch toolbar and the button area are about equal in size.

Now let's add a shortcut button for WordPad to the Quick Launch toolbar:

1. Right-click a blank area of the Quick Launch toolbar, and then click **Open** (or **Open Folder**) on the shortcut menu.

   A Quick Launch folder window like the one shown in this graphic appears:

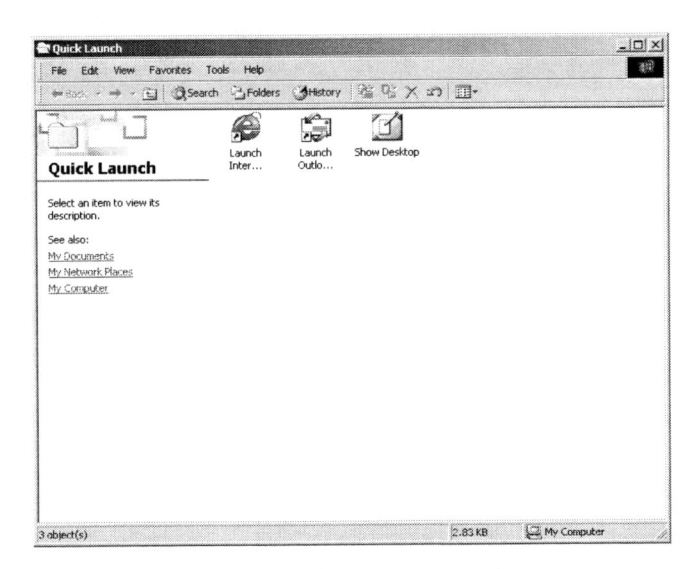

2. On the window's **File** menu, click **New** and then **Shortcut** to start the Create Shortcut Wizard.

3. On the wizard's first page, click the **Browse** button.

   The wizard displays the dialog box shown in the graphic on the next page.

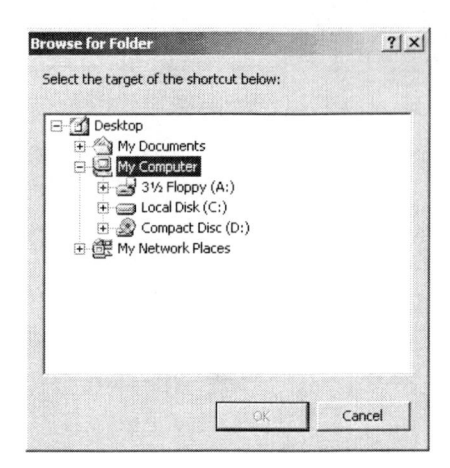

4. Double-click **Local Disk** (C:), **Program Files**, **Windows NT**, and **Accessories**. Then click **wordpad**, and click **OK**.

   The path *"C:\Program Files\Windows NT\Accessories\wordpad.exe"* appears in the "Type the location of the item" box, telling Windows where to look for the WordPad program when you click its shortcut.

5. Click **Next** to move to the next page of the wizard.

   The wizard suggests the name *wordpad* for the new shortcut.

6. Change the capitalization of the name to *WordPad*, and click the **Finish** button.

   Windows adds a WordPad shortcut icon to the Quick Launch folder window and a WordPad button to the Quick Launch toolbar, as shown in this graphic:

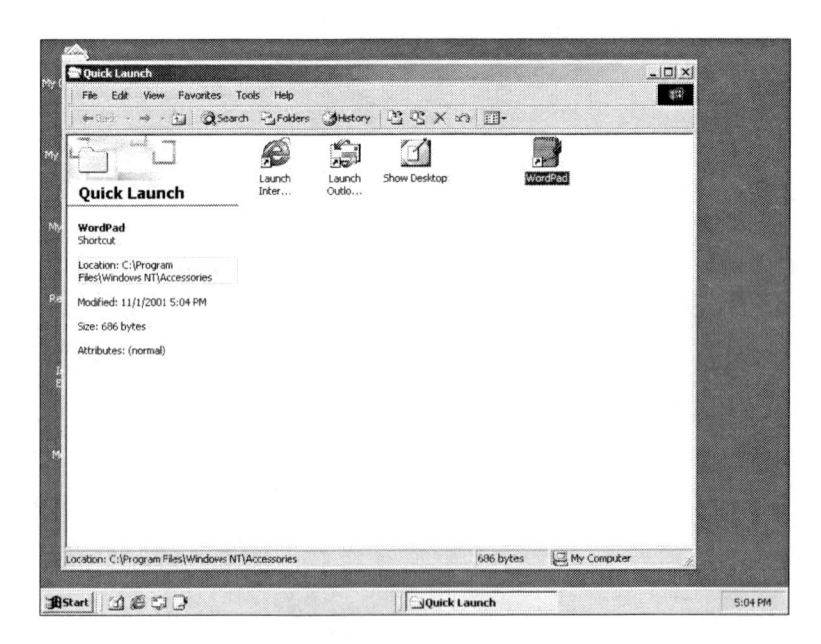

CHAPTER 5 INCREASING YOUR EFFICIENCY   129

7. Click the **WordPad** button on the Quick Launch toolbar to test the new shortcut.

   WordPad starts and displays a blank document window.

8. Close all open windows.

Having shown you the most reliable way of adding new buttons to the Quick Launch toolbar, we'll now show you a faster way that requires some care and precision on your part. Let's add a button for the Paint program that comes with Windows 2000 to the Quick Launch toolbar:

1. Display the **Start**, **Programs**, and **Accessories** menus.

2. Point to **Paint**, hold down the right mouse button, and drag the command over the Quick Launch toolbar without releasing the mouse button.

   This action is called *right-click-and-drag*.

3. Drag the link to the left end of the Quick Launch toolbar.

   Notice as you drag that a vertical bar indicates where the program's button will appear.

4. Release the mouse button when the vertical black bar is to the left of the Show Desktop button.

5. Click **Create Shortcut(s) Here** on the shortcut menu.

   The Quick Launch toolbar now looks like this:

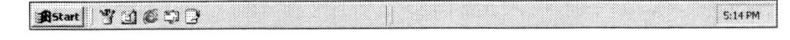

6. Click the **Paint** button to make sure the Paint program starts properly, and then close the Paint window.

CREATING DESKTOP ICONS

Now we'll create a desktop icon for the Calculator program. Here are the steps:

1. Open **My Computer**, and then size and position the window so that you can see a blank area of the desktop.

2. Double-click **Local Disk (C:)**, double-click **WINNT**, and if the contents of the folder are hidden, click **Show Files**.

3. Double-click **system32**, and if necessary, click **Show Files**.

4. Scroll the display of folders and files until you can see the **calc** (for Calculator) program.

5. Point to **calc**, and using the right mouse button, drag an image of the file onto the desktop, releasing the mouse button when the image is in a blank area.

6. Click **Create Shortcut(s) Here** on the shortcut menu.

   Windows creates a shortcut icon for the program on the desktop, as shown in this graphic:

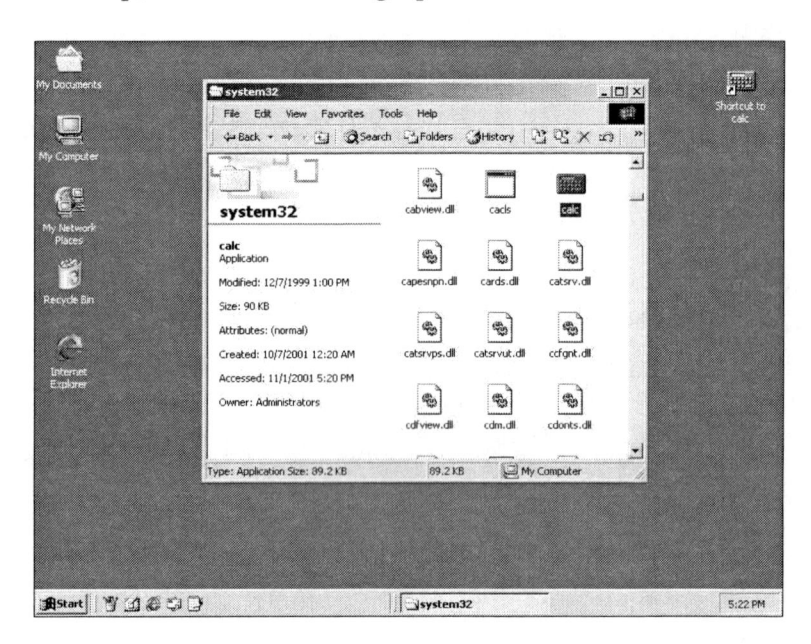

SHORTCUT ICONS VS. PROGRAM ICONS

Shortcut icons are distinguished from program icons by the small upward-pointing arrow in the bottom left corner. Whereas program icons visually represent their programs, shortcut icons are instructions to Windows. For example, Calculator's program icon is located in the WINNT\system32 folder on drive C, and if you move the program to another folder, its icon moves to the new location, too. However, if you create a shortcut icon to Calculator on the desktop, the icon doesn't indicate that the program itself is stored on the desktop. Instead, the shortcut icon stores the address of the program, and double-clicking the icon tells Windows to go to that address and start the program. Each program has only one program icon, but you can create many shortcut icons to that program and move them wherever you want. When you no longer need a particular shortcut, you can simply delete it without affecting the program or its other shortcuts in any way.

The arrow in the bottom left corner of the icon tells you that this icon is a shortcut to the program called *calc*, so you don't need the words *Shortcut to* in the name. Here's how to change the name:

1. With the icon selected, click the icon name.

2. Type *Calculator*, and press **Enter**.

Now let's try the shortcut:

1. Double-click the **Calculator** shortcut to start the Calculator program.

2. Click the buttons for **29.95**, click **x**, click **4**, and then click **=**.

   The display bar shows the cost (without sales tax) of four copies of the Training Edition of *Quick Course in Microsoft Office XP*: 119.8, or $119.80.

3. Close Calculator, and then close the system32 window.

Creating a shortcut for a folder or file is just as easy as creating a shortcut to a program. As an example, let's put the Directions folder and the North Directions document within easy reach:

1. Open **My Documents**, and then double-click **Staff Party** to display its contents in the open window.

2. Using the right mouse button, drag the Directions folder to the desktop, click **Create Shortcut(s) Here** on the shortcut menu, and change the name of the shortcut to *Directions*.

3. Close the Staff Party window.

4. Double-click the **Directions** shortcut on the desktop.

   Windows displays the contents of the **Directions** folder in the window without you having to go through My Computer and the higher-level folders.

5. If necessary, size the window so that you can see the desktop.

6. Using the right mouse button, drag **North Directions** to the desktop, click **Create Shortcut(s) Here** on the shortcut menu, and change the name of the shortcut to *North Directions*.

   The results are shown in this graphic:

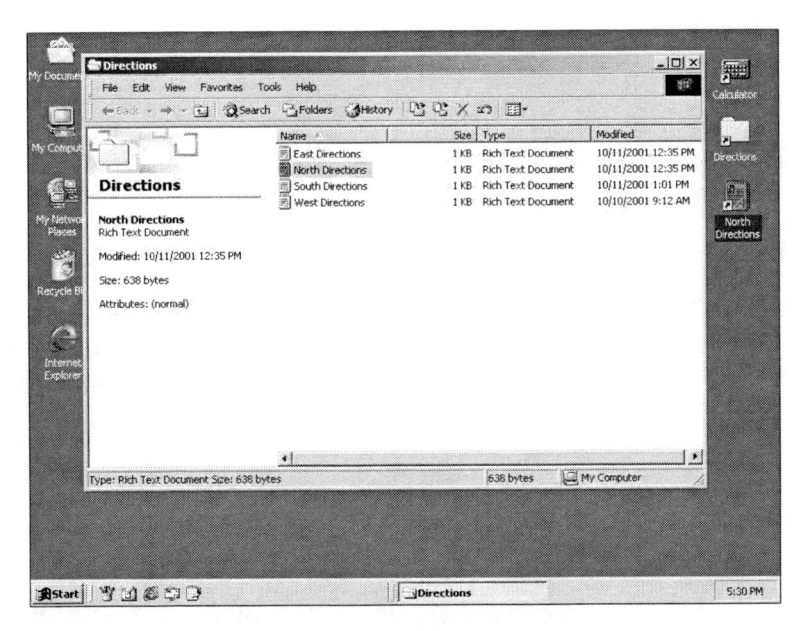

7. Double-click the **North Directions** shortcut.

   Windows starts your default word processor and opens the document.

8. Close the document.

USING THE CREATE SHORTCUT WIZARD

In our example, we select an object and then specify the location for its shortcut icon. But you can also select a location and then specify the object. Simply right-click the desktop or a blank area inside the folder where you want to create the shortcut, click New, and then click Shortcut on the shortcut menu. Windows starts the Create Shortcut Wizard, and you can follow the wizard's instructions.

You can create shortcuts within folder windows as well as on the desktop. For example, to create a shortcut for the North Directions document in the window for drive C, display both drive C and Directions windows, drag the North Directions document with the right mouse button from the Directions window into the drive C window, and then click Create Shortcut(s) Here on the shortcut menu.

Deleting Shortcut Icons and Buttons

When you no longer need immediate access to a program, folder, or document, you can delete its shortcut icon or button to free up space on the desktop or Quick Launch toolbar. Let's start by deleting a shortcut icon from the desktop:

1. Click the **North Directions** shortcut icon, and press **Delete**.
2. When Windows prompts you to confirm that you want to send the North Directions shortcut to the Recycle Bin, click **Yes**.
3. Close the Directions folder window.

Now let's free up some space on the Quick Launch toolbar:

1. Right-click a blank area of the Quick Launch toolbar, and click **Open** on the shortcut menu.

   The Quick Launch folder window appears, displaying the links for the buttons on the Quick Launch toolbar.

2. Click the **Paint** shortcut, press **Delete**, and confirm the deletion by clicking **Yes**.

   You can also select the icon and click the Delete button, or drag the icon to the Recycle Bin icon.

The Paint program is still safely stored in its original folder. When you delete a Quick Launch toolbar button, you are deleting a pointer to the address of the button's target, not the target itself.

Using Start Menu Shortcuts

When you work in a maximized window, you cannot see the desktop, so you cannot double-click any icons you might have placed there. You can either click the Show Desktop button on the Quick Launch toolbar to display the desktop, or you can use the Start menu to access a program or document.

The Start menu and its Programs submenus are collections of shortcuts that provide quick access to programs, folders, and

Shortcuts across the network

If you work on a networked computer and often open a file located on another computer, you can create a shortcut to the file on your desktop by dragging it from My Network Places. Then to open the file, simply double-click the shortcut. If you save changes to the file, Windows knows to save the file on the network computer from which you opened it.

CHAPTER 5 INCREASING YOUR EFFICIENCY

documents. You can add shortcuts to the Start menu itself or to its Programs submenu, as we show you here:

1. In the open folder window, click the **Up** button until you get to Local Disk (C:), and then double-click **WINNT** and **system32** to display the contents of the system32 folder.

2. Scroll the display until you can see the charmap (for Character Map) program.

3. Drag **charmap** over the **Start** button.

4. When the Start menu opens, release the mouse button.

    Windows adds a shortcut to the Character Map program to the menu, as shown in this graphic:

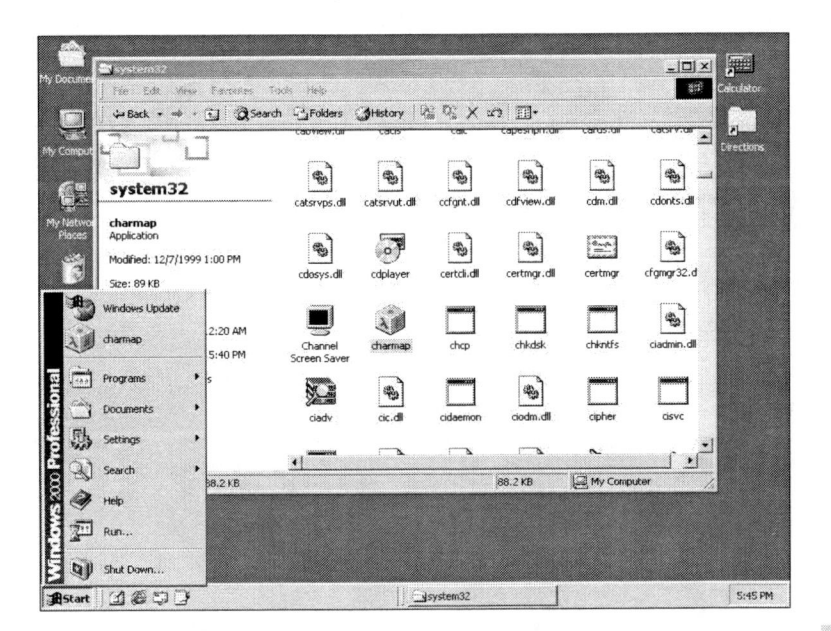

5. Close the window, which also closes the Start menu.

ADDING SHORTCUTS TO THE PROGRAMS MENU

Suppose you want to create a submenu from which you can easily access all the important documents you are working on, including the Directions documents. Here are the steps:

1. Right-click a blank area of the taskbar, click **Properties** on the shortcut menu to display the Taskbar and Start Menu Properties dialog box, and click the **Advanced** tab.

    You see the options shown in the graphic on the next page.

CHANGING THE START MENU ORDER

You can manually change the order of the shortcuts at the top of the Start menu and on the Programs menu and its submenus. Simply point to a shortcut, and drag it to its new location. As you drag, Windows displays a thick black line showing where the shortcut will move to when you release the mouse button. You can also drag a shortcut from the top of the Start menu to the Programs menu and vice versa.

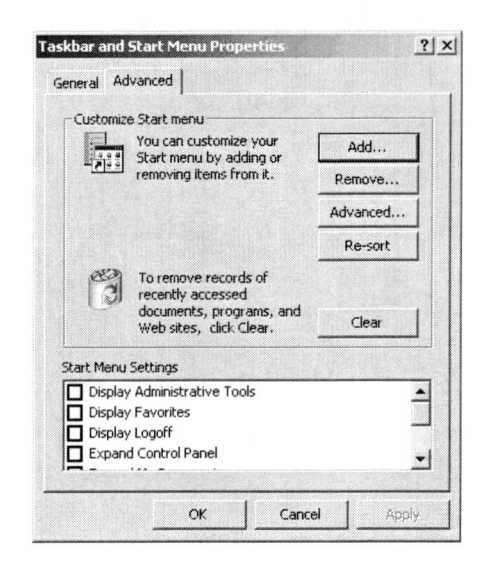

2. Click the **Add** button to start the Create Shortcut Wizard.

3. Click the **Browse** button.

4. In the Browse for Folder dialog box, double-click **My Documents**, then **Staff Party**, and then **Directions**.

5. Click **East Directions**, and click **OK** to close the Browse for Folder dialog box and enter the path of the selected document in the **Type the location of the item** text box.

6. Click **Next** to display the wizard page shown in this graphic:

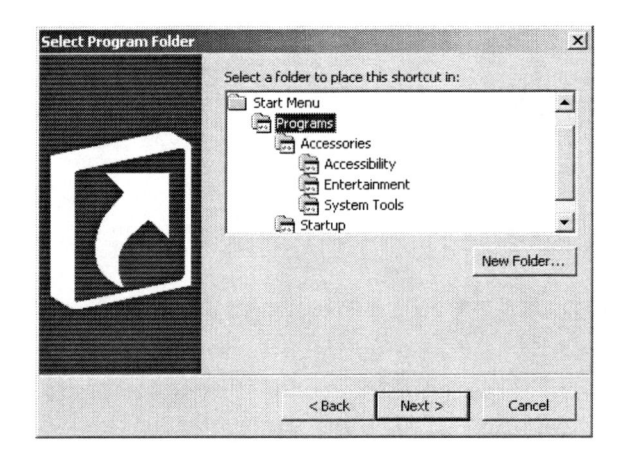

This wizard page displays all the possible locations you can select as a home for the shortcut to the selected document. Note that Programs is the only submenu on the Start menu to which you can add shortcuts.

7. With Programs selected, click the **New Folder** button.

CHAPTER 5 INCREASING YOUR EFFICIENCY 135

The wizard adds a new subfolder called *Program Group (1)* within the Programs folder and places it in alphabetical order in the folder tree.

8. Type *A Priority* as the new folder's name, and click **Next**.

   The wizard displays its last page, which is shown here:

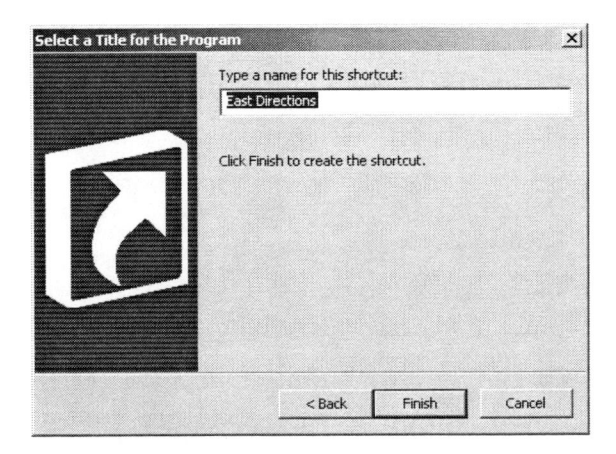

9. Click **Finish** to accept the suggested shortcut name, and then click **OK**.

   The Taskbar and Start Menu Properties dialog box closes. Now for the acid test.

10. Display the **Start**, **Programs**, and **A Priority** menus.

    The shortcut to the document is just waiting to be clicked, as shown in this graphic:

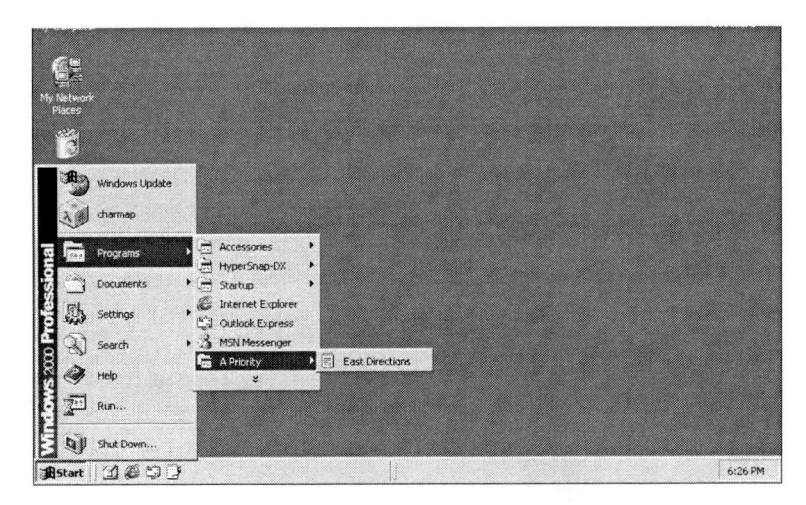

11. Click away from the menus to close them.

HIDDEN PROGRAMS SHORTCUTS

If you don't use a shortcut on the Programs submenu, after a while Windows hides the shortcut. You can redisplay the shortcut by clicking the double chevrons at the bottom of the Programs submenu.

ADDING SHORTCUTS TO THE STARTUP MENU

In Chapter 1, we mentioned that when you turn on your computer, Windows checks the Startup folder and starts any programs it contains without your lifting a finger. The shortcuts in this folder appear on the Startup submenu of the Programs menu. If you want a particular program to be available whenever you are working at your computer, it makes sense to add a shortcut for the program to the Startup folder. To demonstrate, here's how to put a shortcut for Calculator in this folder:

1. On the **Start** menu, click **Programs**.
2. Right-click **Startup**, and click **Open** on the shortcut menu.
3. Maximize the window.
4. On the **Start** menu, click **Programs**, and then click **Accessories** to display the Accessories submenu.
5. Using the right mouse button, drag the **Calculator** shortcut from the submenu into the Startup folder window.
6. Click **Copy Here** on the shortcut menu.

   Windows creates a copy of the Calculator shortcut in the Startup folder.
7. Close the Startup folder window.

To test this shortcut, restart your computer, like this:

1. On the **Start** menu, click **Shut Down** to display the Shut Down Windows dialog box.
2. Click **Restart** in the drop-down list, and then click OK.

   Windows shuts itself down, and restarts. After you log on, Calculator opens on the desktop.
3. Display the **Start**, **Programs**, and **Startup** menus.

   The Calculator shortcut is on the Startup submenu.
4. Click away from the menus to close them.

REMOVING STARTUP MENU SHORTCUTS

You now have instant access to Calculator through two shortcuts: one on the desktop and one on the Startup submenu. Let's eliminate the redundancy by removing the shortcut from the Startup submenu:

1. Display the **Start**, **Programs**, and **Startup** menus.

REORGANIZING START MENU SHORTCUTS

If you add a shortcut to the Start menu or Programs submenu and later decide you want to move it, right-click a blank area of the taskbar, and click Properties on the shortcut menu to open the Taskbar and Start Menu Properties dialog box. Click the Advanced tab, and then click the Advanced button. The contents of the Start Menu folder are displayed in a window. (This folder is buried deep inside the Documents and Settings folder.) You can then use normal techniques to display the contents of subfolders and move, copy, rename, and delete shortcuts.

CHAPTER 5 INCREASING YOUR EFFICIENCY 137

2. Right-click the **Calculator** shortcut, and click **Delete** on the shortcut menu.

3. Click **Yes** to confirm that you want to delete the shortcut.

   Removing the shortcut from the Startup menu does not close the Calculator window, nor does it in any way affect the Calculator program stored on your hard drive.

4. Click away from the Start menu to close it.

5. Close the Calculator window.

USING FAVORITES

If you want to be able to quickly access the documents in a folder but you don't want to clutter up the Start menu with shortcuts, you can add a shortcut to the folder to your list of favorite places. Follow these steps to add a Favorites menu to the Start menu and then add favorites to the new menu:

1. Right-click the taskbar, click **Properties**, and click the **Advanced** tab. Then select the **Display Favorites** check box in the **Start Menu Settings** list, and click OK.

2. Click the **Start** button, check that Favorites now appears on the Start menu, and then click a blank area of the desktop to close the menu.

3. Double-click the **Directions** shortcut icon on the desktop to display its contents in a window.

4. On the **Favorites** menu, click **Add to Favorites** to display the dialog box shown in this graphic:

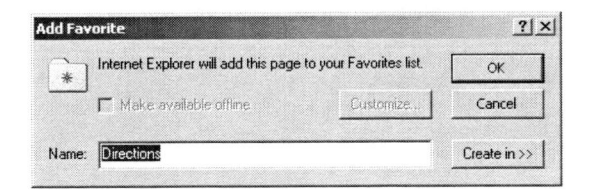

   ![Add Favorite dialog box with Name field showing "Directions", and buttons OK, Cancel, Create in >>]

5. Click **OK** to add a shortcut to the Directions folder to your favorites list.

6. Click the **Up** button to open the Staff Party folder window.

7. On the **Favorites** menu, click **Add to Favorites**, and click **OK** to make that folder a favorite as well.

8. Close the Staff Party window.

Now check the results:

1. Display the **Start** and **Favorites** menus, and then click **Directions** to return quickly to the Directions folder.

2. On the **Favorites** menu, click **Staff Party** to switch quickly to that folder.

3. Close the Staff Party folder.

DELETING FAVORITES

We already have a shortcut to the Directions folder on the desktop, so let's delete it from the favorites list:

1. On the **Start** menu, click **Favorites**, and then right-click **Directions** on the Favorites menu.

2. Click **Delete** on the shortcut menu, and then click **Yes** to confirm the deletion.

   The Directions folder is no longer on the Favorites menu.

3. Click away from the Start menu to close it.

MORE ABOUT...
Recycle Bin, page 62 and 88

If you decide later that you want to restore this favorite, you can open the Recycle Bin and retrieve it. Otherwise, it will be deleted completely when the Recycle Bin is emptied.

CREATING CUSTOM TOOLBARS

You've seen that the taskbar at the bottom of the screen provides an at-a-glance log of your open windows, and you've clicked its buttons to switch from one window to another. You've used the Start button as an easy way of accessing programs and documents, and you've tried out a couple of the buttons on the Quick Launch toolbar. In this section, we'll show you how to display other toolbars on the taskbar to provide quick access to the programs or documents you use most often. This type of toolbar has buttons based on the contents of a folder that you create on your hard disk, so first you need to set up the folder:

1. Display the contents of the My Documents folder.

2. Right-click a blank area of the window, and click **New** and then **Folder** on the shortcut menu. Name the new folder *My Programs*.

3. Double-click the **My Programs** icon to display that folder's contents in the window. (The folder is currently empty.)

4. Right-click a blank area of the My Programs window, and click **New** and then **Shortcut** on the shortcut menu to start the Create Shortcut Wizard.

5. Type the path *"C:\ProgramFiles\WindowsNT\Accessories \wordpad.exe"* in the **Type the location of the item** text box (don't forget the quotation marks), click **Next**, and then click **Finish** to store a shortcut to WordPad in the folder.

6. Repeat steps 4 and 5 to store a shortcut to Paint in the folder, typing *C:\WINNT\system32\mspaint.exe* in the **Type the location of the item** text box.

7. Close the window.

Displaying Custom Toolbars

Having set up the My Programs folder, you can make its contents available at any time by telling Windows to display the folder as a toolbar. Here are the steps:

1. Right-click a blank area of the taskbar, and click **Toolbars** and then **New Toolbar** on the shortcut menu.

   Windows displays the dialog box shown in this graphic:

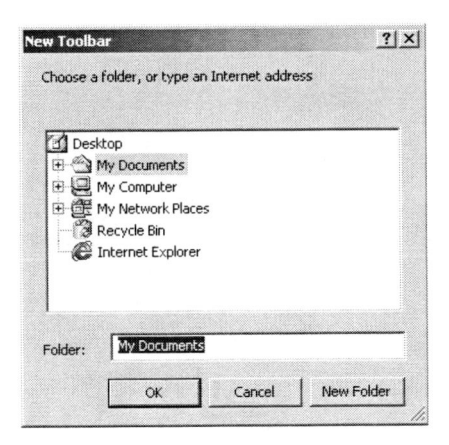

2. Double-click **My Documents**, **Staff Party**, and **Directions** to enter *Directions* in the **Folder** text box. Then click **OK**.

   Shortcuts to the documents contained in the Directions folder appear on your taskbar.

3. Repeat steps 1 and 2, this time double-clicking **My Documents** and **My Programs** in the New Toolbar dialog box.

   Your taskbar now looks something like the one shown in this graphic:

4. Click the **East Directions** button on the Directions toolbar to start your word processor and open that document. Then close the word processor's window.

Customizing the Taskbar

As you can see, the taskbar is now pretty crowded. To the right of the Start button is the familiar Quick Launch toolbar, and to the right of that is a blank area where buttons for open windows can be displayed. Next come the Directions and My Programs toolbars and the status area. Here are a couple of ways to set up the toolbars for maximum efficiency:

1. To see more of the Directions toolbar, point to the vertical bar at the left end of the My Programs toolbar, and drag it all the way to the right.

   The Directions toolbar expands as the My Programs toolbar contracts, so that they now look like the ones shown in this graphic:

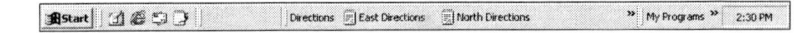

2. Click the chevrons (>>) at the right end of the My Programs toolbar.

   A list of the program shortcuts stored in the My Programs folder pops up.

3. Click away from the taskbar to hide the list.

4. Right-click the **My Programs** toolbar, and click **Show Title** on the shortcut menu to toggle it off. Repeat this step for the **Directions** toolbar.

5. Point to the taskbar's top border, and when the pointer changes to a two-headed arrow, drag upward until the bar doubles in height.

   When you release the mouse button, the toolbars take the form of two rows on the taller taskbar, making them easier to read.

> **THE ADDRESS, LINKS, AND DESKTOP TOOLBARS**
>
> You can display the Address, Links, and Desktop toolbars on the taskbar by right-clicking a blank area of the taskbar, pointing to Toolbars, and then clicking Address, Links, or Desktop to display the toolbar you want. (You can display the Address bar and Links toolbar in many windows, such as the My Computer and Recycle Bin windows.) In the Address bar, you can type the name of a folder or file and press Enter to open the folder or file, or you can type a Web address to open a Web site. The Links toolbar provides links to several important Web sites, and you can add your own links. The Desktop toolbar contains buttons for all the shortcuts on your desktop, giving you yet another way to access them.

6. Point to the vertical bar at the left end of any toolbar, hold down the left mouse button, and drag the toolbar wherever you want it. Then do the same with the other toolbars.

   Rearranging the toolbars can be tricky. Practice until you have a feel for this technique. For example, we arranged our toolbars as shown in this graphic:

Let's return the taskbar to its default state:

1. Right-click a blank area of the taskbar, and click **Toolbars** and then **Directions** on the shortcut menu to turn off the Directions toolbar.

2. Next, right-click the **My Programs** toolbar, and click **Close** on the shortcut menu.

3. If Windows prompts you to confirm that you want to close the toolbar, select the check box that tells Windows not to show the message again, and then click **OK**.

4. Resize the taskbar to its original one-row height.

Because the taskbar can easily become overcrowded, you have to plan ahead to ensure that any toolbars you add to it increase your efficiency enough to warrant setting them up. For example, you might create a Projects folder containing shortcuts to the documents you are currently working on, or a Log folder containing shortcuts to mileage or expense reports that you update several times a day. By analyzing your daily tasks, you'll probably find many creative ways to use taskbar toolbars to streamline your work.

WORKING FASTER

Hungry for more ways to speed up your daily work? This section looks at a few techniques that take advantage of some built-in Windows capabilities. We will use the WordPad and Paint programs for our examples, but you can use the same techniques with many commercial programs designed to work with Windows 2000.

FLOATING TOOLBARS
You can add toolbars to the desktop as well as to the taskbar. First create or open the taskbar toolbar as usual, and then drag the vertical bar at the left end of the toolbar onto the desktop, dropping it either in the middle or along the edge of the screen. Then right-click the toolbar, and click Auto-Hide or Always On Top on the shortcut menu to specify whether you can see the toolbar when windows are maximized.

CREATING INSTANT DOCUMENTS

You can start a new, blank document with a couple of clicks of the mouse button, without even opening the document's program. Here's how:

1. Right-click a blank area of the desktop, and click **New** on the shortcut menu.

   The submenu that Windows displays varies depending on what programs you have installed.

2. Click **Rich Text Document**.

   You now see a new icon on the desktop, similar to the one shown in this graphic:

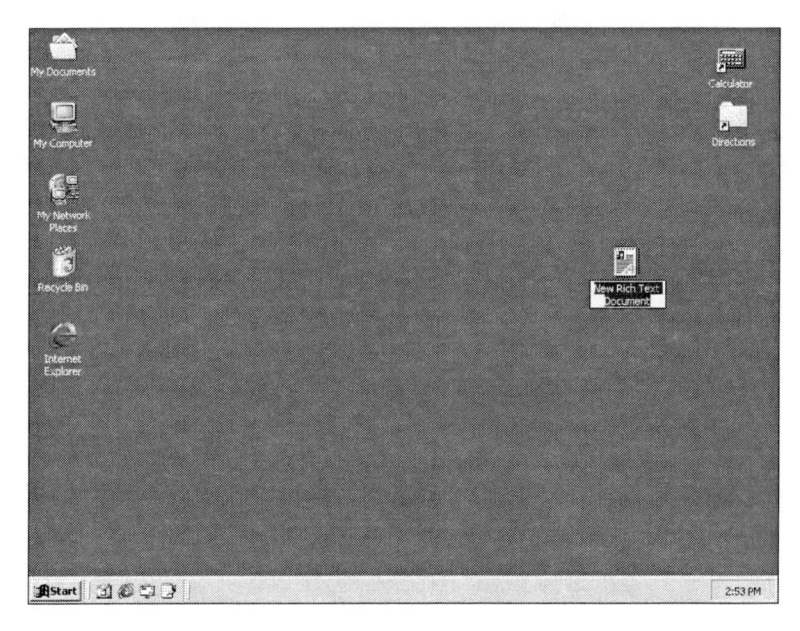

3. Type *Map* as the icon's new name, and press **Enter**.
4. Double-click the icon.

   Windows starts your word processor and opens the blank Map document.

5. Type *Here is a map to Adventure Works*.
6. Click the **Save** button.
7. Close the document's window.

For good measure, follow these steps to create another instant document, this time in a folder:

TWO DOCUMENTS WITH THE SAME NAME?

You can't store two files with the exact same name in the same folder. However, the files we create here don't have the exact same name because the names have different extensions. These extensions tell Windows what type of program created the file.

CHAPTER 5 INCREASING YOUR EFFICIENCY 143

1. Double-click the **Directions** shortcut icon on the desktop to display the contents of the Directions folder.

2. Right-click a blank area of the folder window, click **New** and then **Bitmap Image** on the shortcut menu, and rename the file as *Map*.

3. Right-click the new file, and click **Open With** on the shortcut menu. Select **Microsoft Paint** in the Open With dialog box, and then click **OK**.

4. Use the **Line**, **Pencil**, **Ellipse**, and **Text** tools to create a "map" that is similar to this one:

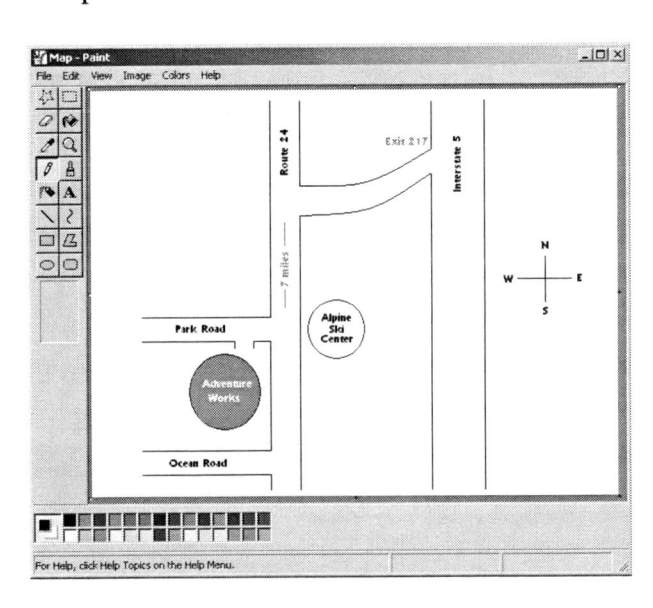

USING THE PAINT TOOLS

Paint offers lots of tools to help you create your own works of art. Before selecting any tool, first select a color from the color palette at the bottom of the Paint window. Next, click the drawing tool you want in the toolbox along the left side of the window. Included are a text tool; tools for drawing freehand, straight, and curved lines; tools for painting and airbrushing lines; and tools for drawing various geometric shapes. To zoom in for a closer look at a section of your drawing, click the Magnifier tool, and then click the area you want to examine. You can change the zoom percentage by selecting a magnification from the list below the toolbox. (This list has different options depending on the tool selected.) To zoom back out, click the Magnifier tool again, and then click your drawing. To change an object's color, click the Fill With Color tool, select a color from the color palette, and then click the object. To cut or copy part of a drawing, you can use either the Free-Form Select or Select tools to drag a border around the object, and then click Cut or Copy on the Edit menu. To erase part of a drawing, use the Eraser tool. If you want to stretch or rotate the drawing, experiment with the commands on the Image menu. If you make a mistake, you can undo the last action by clicking Undo on the Edit menu. To save, open, or print a Paint file, the procedure is the same as in any other Windows program.

You can hold down the Shift key while dragging the Pencil tool to draw straight lines. Don't worry about including all the details shown in our graphic. The goal is not to teach you how to use Paint, but to create a simple graphic for future examples.

5. Save the graphic, and close the Paint window.

In the next section, we'll use the two documents you just created to demonstrate a few other ways to save time.

Associating Documents with Programs

Double-clicking a document's icon simultaneously starts the program with which the document was created and opens the document. Windows keeps a list of which file types are associated with which programs, but sometimes is unable to open a document if it has no record of a particular file type. Instead, it displays an Open With dialog box and asks you to select the program you want to use to open the document. And sometimes Windows opens the document with a program that is different from the one you want, because that's the program associated with the document's file type in the list. In either case, you'll need to set the record straight. As an example, let's make sure that Rich Text Format documents, which are identified by the *.rtf* extension after their file names, are opened with WordPad, and that Bitmap Image documents, which are identified by the *.bmp* extension, are opened with Paint.

Unassociated files

Anytime you try to open a file that is not associated with a particular program, Windows displays the Open With dialog box. Here, you can select a program from the list, or you can click the Other button and navigate to the program you want. After choosing the program you want to use, click OK to open the file. To make sure that Windows always opens that particular file type with the program you designated, select the "Always use this program to open these files" check box before clicking OK.

Extensions

An extension is a three-character suffix that is added to the end of a file name and separated from the name by a period. Extensions are not case-sensitive—files with an extension of *.rtf* or an extension of *.RTF* are the same. Back in the old days, extensions were sometimes used to categorize and identify files; for example, *.ltr* might have been used to signify a letter. Because you can use long file names in recent versions of Windows, extensions now have a different purpose. A program adds its extension to the file name when the file is first saved, and Windows uses this extension to identify which program to open when you double-click the file's icon. (If you manually add a different extension, you will quite often end up with both yours and the program's, separated by periods—and that's not a good idea!) Depending on the settings in the Folder Options dialog box, you might not be able to see file extensions. To hide or display extensions, open My Computer, click Folder Options on the Tools menu, and then deselect the "Hide file extensions for known file types" option in the Advanced settings list on the View tab.

Chapter 5 Increasing Your Efficiency

1. In the open window's **Tools** menu, click **Folder Options** to display the Folder Options dialog box.

2. Click the **File Types** tab to display the options shown here:

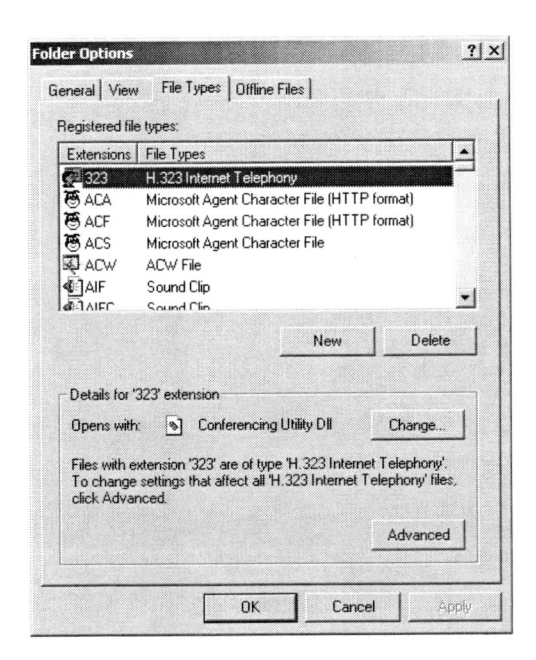

3. Scroll the **Registered file types** list, and select **Rich Text Document**.

   The Details area tells you which program will be used to open this file type.

Sending Documents

In your Documents and Settings folder is a SendTo folder containing shortcuts to programs and storage locations where you can send documents. You can add shortcuts to this folder and then use the SendTo command as an alternative to associating file types. For example, if you want to open a particular RTF document in WordPad instead of your word processor, you can add a WordPad shortcut to your SendTo folder and then use the SendTo command to open the document. (If your SendTo folder contains a shortcut to your printer, you can use the SendTo command to send files to the printer without opening them.) To set up a SendTo shortcut, first click Folder Options on the Tools menu of the My Computer window, click the View tab, click "Show hidden files and folders," and click OK. Then double-click Local Drive (C:), Documents and Settings, your personal folder, and SendTo. Right-click the window, and click New and Shortcut. Then click Browse, locate and select the program you want to add, click Next, and click Finish. To open a document, right-click the document, and click SendTo and the shortcut.

Other File Type Options

In addition to editing existing file types, you can add and remove file types. To add a new file type, click the New button. Windows displays the Create New Extension dialog box, where you can enter the specifications of the new file type. To remove a file type from the Registered file types list, select the file type and click the Delete button. Windows then displays a warning asking if you are sure you want to delete the type. If you know you will never need to open files of this type, click Yes.

4. If the associated program is not WordPad, click the **Change** button to display the dialog box shown in this graphic:

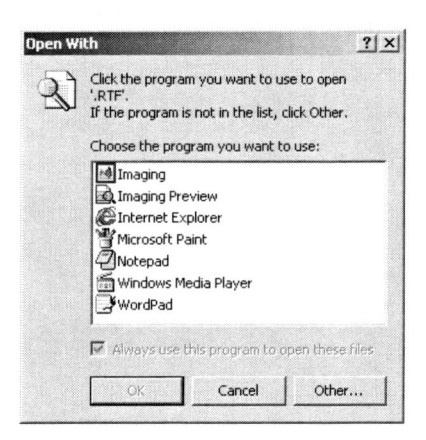

5. Click **WordPad** in the **Choose the program you want to use** list, and click **OK**.

6. Repeat steps 3 through 5 to make sure the **Bitmap Image** file type is associated with **Microsoft Paint**.

7. Click **Close** to close the Folder Options dialog box.

8. Test your association by double-clicking the **Map** graphic and one of the **Directions** documents. Then close all open windows.

If necessary, return these associations to their former programs when you have worked your way through the course.

REUSING INFORMATION

If you followed along with the examples in Chapter 2, you know that it's easy to reuse the same information in different documents. You simply select the information in the desired source document and click Copy on the Edit menu. Then you open the document in which you want to paste the information, click an insertion point, and click Paste on the Edit menu.

However, the power of Windows 2000 far exceeds this simple kind of copying and pasting. With Windows, you can build documents that are patchworks of pieces created in different programs, while maintaining the association of the pieces with

CHAPTER 5 INCREASING YOUR EFFICIENCY 147

the programs that created them. Here is a quick overview of this concept so that you can decide when and how to use it.

Windows treats files or parts of files as objects—for example, a block of text, a graphic, a table, and a chart are all objects. The program that creates the object is called the *server*, and the original file is called the *source document*. The object can be used by another program called the *client*, and the file in which the object is used is called the *client document* or the *container document*.

To create a document by piecing together bits of various source documents, you can *link* an object to the document you are creating or you can *embed* the object. When you link an object, you need both the source document and the container document to be able to display the object. When you embed an object, it becomes part of the container document and you no longer need the source document.

So how do you know when to link and when to embed? If the object is used in more than one document and is likely to change, it is best to create the object in its own source document and then link the object where it's needed. If the object is used in only one document or is not going to change, embedding might be the best way to go, because embedded information can be edited in the container document without the source document having to be present. You should bear in mind, however, that documents that contain embedded objects can get very large.

So that's the scoop on objects. Now let's see how you might go about using them. First, we'll take the graphic you created in Paint and embed it in a Directions document:

1. Open the **Directions** folder, and double-click the **North Directions** document to open it in WordPad.

2. Maximize the WordPad window if necessary, press **Ctrl+End** to move to the end of the document, and press **Enter**. Type *Here is a map:* and press **Enter** twice.

3. On the **Insert** menu, click **Object** to display the dialog box shown in the graphic on the next page.

OTHER PROGRAMS
Although the instructions given here are specific to WordPad, the procedure is similar for other Windows applications that support linking and embedding. To link or embed an object in another program, look for an Object or Insert Object command, and follow the directions given in the dialog box, using Help if necessary. (Some programs also create links by using a Paste Special command on the Edit menu.)

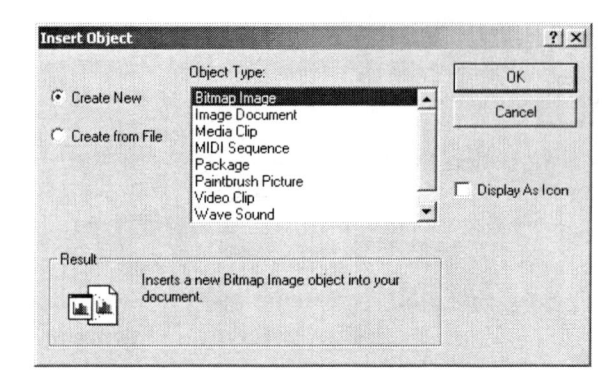

4. Select the **Create from File** option, and when the dialog box changes to let you enter the name of the document you want to insert as an object, click the **Browse** button.

5. In the Browse dialog box, navigate to the **Directions** folder, and double-click the **Map** graphic.

   You return to the Insert Object dialog box with the document's path in the File text box.

6. Click **OK**.

   The dialog box closes, and you return to the North Directions document, where the map has been embedded in a large frame, as shown here:

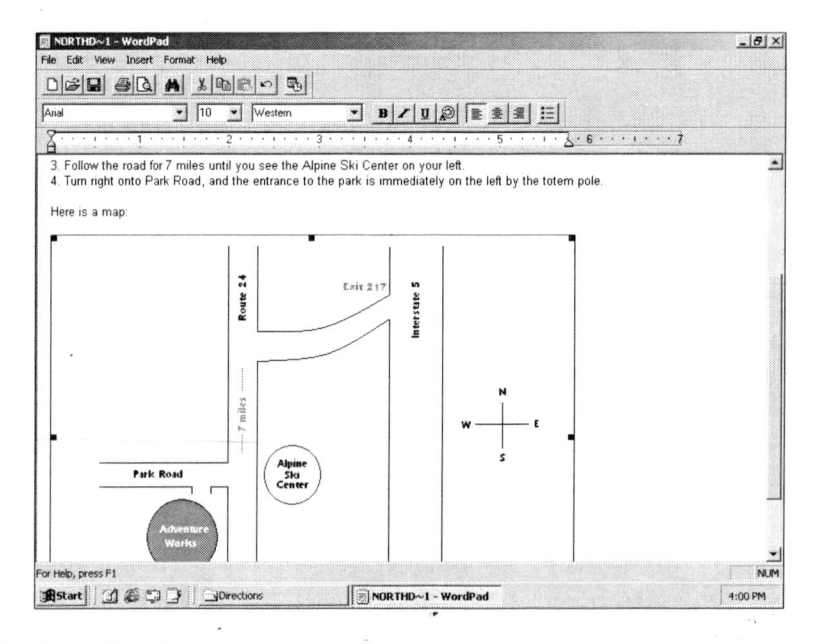

7. Save the document.

Now suppose you need to change Ocean Road in the map to Ocean Avenue. Instead of making the change in Paint and then re-embedding the object in North Directions, you can change the street name using Paint's tools without leaving WordPad, like this:

1. Double-click the map object.

   The screen looks like this:

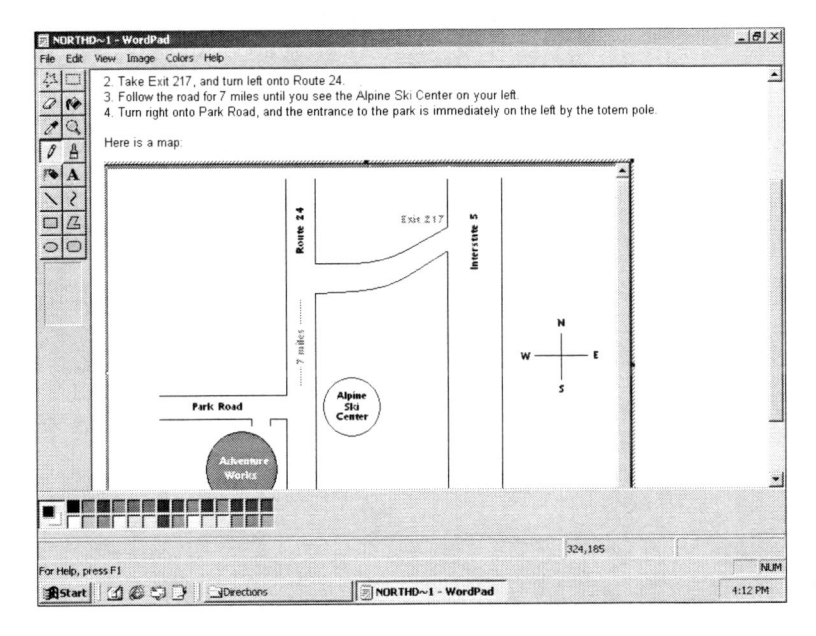

   As you can see, the menu bar has changed, and the window has many of the characteristics of a Paint window, even though the title bar shows that you are still in WordPad.

2. If you know how to use the **Eraser** and **Text** tools, change **Ocean Road** to *Ocean Avenue*.

   If you don't, use the Pencil tool to make a squiggle anywhere on the map. You just need to demonstrate that when you embed an object, you can change it using the program that created it, even though the object is now stored in another document.

3. Click outside the graphic's frame to see the result. Save the document, and then close WordPad.

CREATING NEW OBJECTS

When you click Object on the Insert menu, you have the option of creating a new object of the type specified in the Insert Object dialog box. For example, with the Create New option selected on the left and Bitmap Image selected in the Object Type list, clicking OK displays an empty frame in the open North Directions document, and Paint's menus and tools appear. You can then draw the map object directly in the frame. Clicking outside the frame removes Paint's menus and tools but leaves the map object in place as part of the document. You can edit the map later by double-clicking it to redisplay Paint's menus and tools.

Instead of embedding the map as a graphic object, you can embed it in your document as an icon. Follow these steps to see the difference:

1. Open the **South Directions** document, press **Ctrl+End** to move to the end of the document, and press **Enter**.

2. Type *Double-click this icon to see a map:* and press **Enter** twice.

3. On the **Insert** menu, click **Object**, select the **Create from File** option, browse to **Directions**, and double-click the map.

4. Select the **Display As Icon** check box, and click **OK**.

   The result is shown in this graphic:

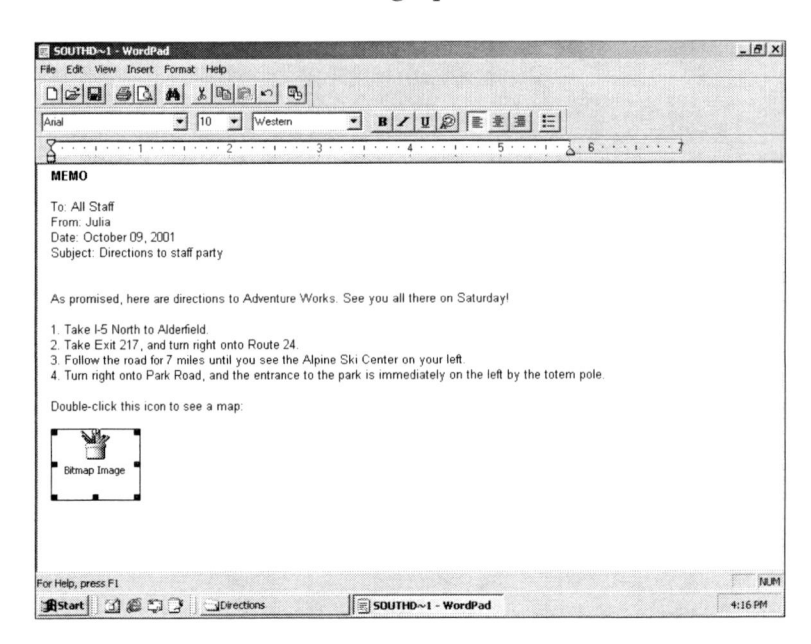

5. Save the document, and then double-click the icon.

   A Paint window opens displaying nothing but the map. Notice that the original Map graphic was not affected by the changes you made to the map object in the North Directions document.

6. On the Paint window's **File** menu, click **Exit & Return to South Directions** to return to the document.

7. Close the WordPad window.

WHAT EXACTLY ARE YOU EDITING?

Whenever you make changes to an embedded object (one that is not linked to its source document), you are changing the version of the object that is stored in the open container document. Your changes do not affect the original source document at all.

CHAPTER 5 INCREASING YOUR EFFICIENCY   151

Now let's link the map to two different documents, first as a graphic object and then as an icon:

1. Open the **East Directions** document, press **Ctrl+End**, press **Enter**, type *Here is a map:*, and press **Enter** twice.

2. On the **Insert** menu, click **Object**. Then in the Insert Object dialog box, click the **Create from File** option, browse to **Directions**, and double-click the map.

3. Select the **Link** check box, and click **OK**.

4. Save the document.

5. Click the **Open** button on the toolbar.

6. If necessary, display the contents of the **Directions** folder in the Open dialog box, and select **Rich Text Format** from the **Files of type** drop-down list. Then double-click **West Directions** to open that document.

7. Press **Ctrl+End**, press **Enter**, type *Double-click this icon to see a map:*, and press **Enter** twice.

8. On the **Insert** menu, click **Object**. Then click **Create from File**, browse to **Directions**, and double-click the map.

9. Select both the **Link** and **Display As Icon** check boxes, and click **OK**.

   A shortcut icon to the Map graphic now appears at the bottom of the document.

10. Save the document, and close the WordPad window.

Now suppose that Exit 217 on the map should be Exit 216. Because the inserted maps in the East Directions and West Directions documents are linked to the source Paint document, you can edit the Map graphic in Paint, and the change will be reflected in each of the two linked documents. Follow these steps to see this in action:

1. Double-click **Map** in the Directions folder to open the map in Paint. Then use the **Eraser** and **Text** tools to make the necessary changes (or make a squiggle or two with the **Pencil** tool), save the map, and close Paint.

2. Open the **East Directions** document.

   Windows displays a message box stating that it is updating ActiveX objects.

3. When the message box disappears, scroll down the window.

4. If the linked object doesn't reflect the changes you made to the Paint document, on the **Edit** menu, click **Links** to display this dialog box:

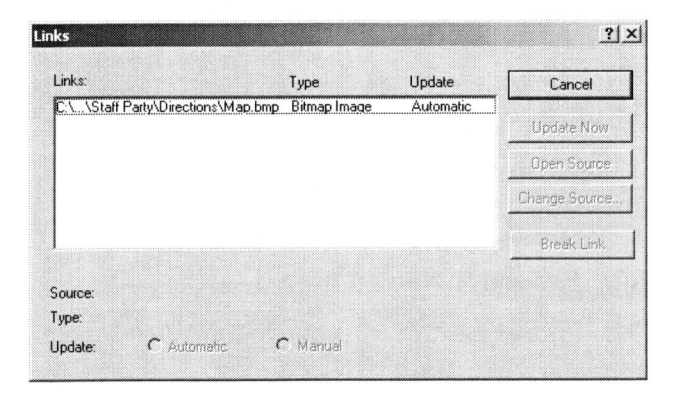

   ![Links dialog box showing C:\...\Staff Party\Directions\Map.bmp as a Bitmap Image with Automatic update, and buttons for Cancel, Update Now, Open Source, Change Source, and Break Link]

5. Select the link to **Map**, click **Update Now**, click **Close**, and then save the East Directions document.

6. Now open the **File** menu, and click **West Directions**.

   Most Windows programs store the names of documents you worked with most recently at the bottom of the File menu, so that you can quickly access a document again by clicking the document's name.

7. Double-click the **Map** icon.

   A Paint window opens with the new version of the map displayed.

8. Tidy up the desktop by closing all open windows, saving any changes if prompted.

Depending on the programs you are using, you might find that inserting objects in documents sometimes doesn't work quite as well as you would like. Or you might find that it works well under certain circumstances, such as when the source document is open, and not so well under others, such as when the

WHAT ARE ACTIVEX OBJECTS?

ActiveX objects are used primarily by Internet Explorer but also by Windows 2000 to add dynamic, interactive elements to documents. You can think of ActiveX objects as mini-programs, or *applets*, which perform discrete functions. In this case, the object's function is related to the updating of the linked graphic.

source document is closed. However, if you need to create dynamic documents that contain objects from different programs, it is worth taking the time to experiment a bit so that you understand how the process works in the particular programs you use most often.

That's it for this chapter on efficiency. We hope being aware of some of the possibilities will help you make your time at the computer more productive.

Customizing the Way You Work

We discuss how to add hardware and install programs, how to set up the screen the way you want it, and how to customize the taskbar. Then we cover other common adjustments that you can make to tailor your computer to your own way of working.

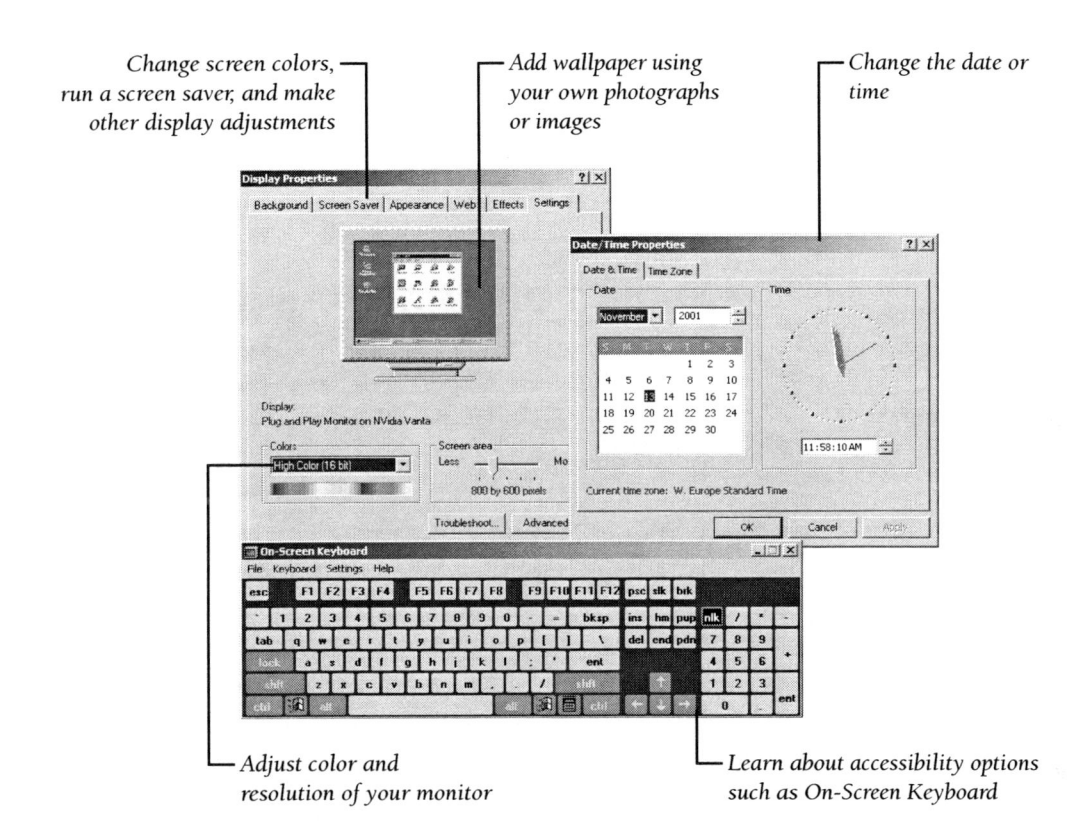

Change screen colors, run a screen saver, and make other display adjustments

Add wallpaper using your own photographs or images

Change the date or time

Adjust color and resolution of your monitor

Learn about accessibility options such as On-Screen Keyboard

In this chapter, we give you a brief overview of the tools in Windows 2000 that you can use to change your computer's setup. We've left this discussion until now because we feel you are unlikely to need these tools when you first start using Windows. Moreover, if you are working on a network, your network administrator might not allow you to make some changes. No matter what your particular situation, you can look through this chapter to learn about the available settings. Then, if you are allowed to experiment, you'll know where to start.

First, we'll briefly discuss how to add or remove hardware and programs.

Adding or Removing Hardware

If you add new hardware to your computer, such as a sound card, modem, or CD-ROM drive, you will want Windows to recognize this new device. *Plug and Play* technology makes adding new hardware a snap. With Plug and Play technology, as the name implies, you still have to physically attach new hardware to your computer, but then you're ready to go; you no longer have to fuss around with drivers and setup programs. When you turn on your computer, Windows 2000 recognizes the new device, takes care of setting it up, and installs any programs necessary to make the new hardware work, prompting you for files if necessary.

Sounds great, right? Unfortunately, there are a couple of potential snags. To take full advantage of this technology, you must have Plug and Play support in these areas:

- Your computer's BIOS. The BIOS (basic input-output system) is a program built into your computer, and you usually don't have to worry about it. If you purchase a computer with Windows 2000 already installed, or if you upgrade a relatively new computer from Windows 98, the BIOS has Plug and Play support.

- The hardware device. Any new hardware device supports Plug and Play if it has a Windows logo on the box. Microsoft allows hardware manufacturers to display this logo only if the hardware has Plug and Play capability.

Although Plug and Play devices are the easiest to install because they practically install themselves, installing devices that are not Plug and Play compatible is not very difficult. Windows 2000

USB and FireWire support

Windows 2000 supports both universal serial bus (USB) and FireWire technologies. USB is a type of hardware that makes adding multiple devices to your computer much easier. FireWire is similar to USB but works at a higher speed. Both allow you to chain devices together, and each uses a standard connector type; however, USB and FireWire connections cannot be interchanged. With USB or FireWire installed in your computer, you can attach a USB or FireWire device simply by plugging its cable into a compatible port. (You can attach and detach devices while your computer is running.) Windows will then recognize the device and install the appropriate driver for it.

CHAPTER 6 CUSTOMIZING THE WAY YOU WORK 157

includes an Add/Remove Hardware Wizard that makes installing and uninstalling devices relatively easy. To start this wizard, click Settings and then Control Panel on the Start menu, and then double-click the Add/Remove Hardware icon. The wizard guides you through the process of adding, troubleshooting, unplugging (temporarily) or uninstalling (permanently) a hardware device.

When you use the Add/Remove Hardware Wizard to add a hardware device, Windows searches your computer for new devices and then displays a list of any it finds. To have Windows install the correct driver, select the device you want to add from the list, and click Next. Then follow the wizard's instructions to complete the process.

If Windows can't locate the new device, you can select from an extensive list of hardware types, manufacturers, and models. Windows can then usually install the new hardware correctly.

If the hardware you are adding is not listed in the wizard's database and a driver did not come with the device, contact the device's manufacturer and ask for a Windows 2000 driver and the instructions for installing it. (The easiest way to do this is to visit the manufacturer's Web site and download the driver directly onto your computer. Most hardware manufacturers have easy-to-find driver download areas on their Web sites.)

The Add/Remove Hardware Wizard also makes it much easier to troubleshoot or temporarily unplug an existing device. The wizard displays a list of all the devices installed on your computer from which you can choose the specific device you want to reconfigure.

Here's how to install a hardware device that is not Plug and Play compatible:

1. Open **Control Panel**, and double-click the **Add/Remove Hardware** icon.

   The Add/Remove Hardware Wizard starts.

2. Click **Next**.

3. Select the **Add/Troubleshoot a device** option, and then click **Next**.

   When the wizard doesn't find any Plug and Play devices to install, it displays a list of the devices that are already installed on your computer.

4. In the **Devices** list, click **Add a new device**, and click **Next**.

5. Select the **No, I want to select the hardware from a list** option, and click **Next**.

   The wizard displays a list of all the types of hardware devices you can install on your computer system, like this:

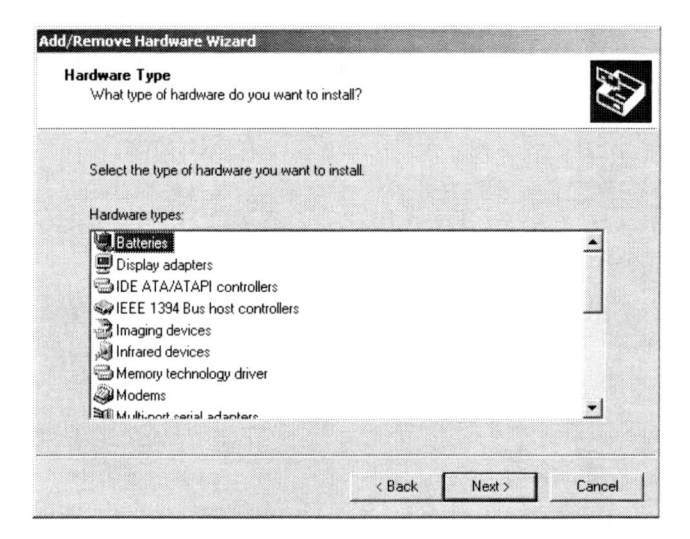

   ![Add/Remove Hardware Wizard - Hardware Type dialog showing a list of hardware types including Batteries, Display adapters, IDE ATA/ATAPI controllers, IEEE 1394 Bus host controllers, Imaging devices, Infrared devices, Memory technology driver, Modems, and Multi-port serial adapters]

6. Click the type of hardware you want to install, and click **Next**.

   The wizard displays a list of manufacturers and models of that type of hardware.

7. Click the manufacturer, click the model, and then click **Next**.

   The wizard displays information about the selected hardware device.

8. Click **Next** to install the device, and then click **Finish** to close the wizard.

If you are going to completely remove a device from your computer, here's how to tell Windows that the device is no longer available:

1. Open **Control Panel**, and double-click the **Add/Remove Hardware** icon.

   The Add/Remove Hardware Wizard starts.

2. Click **Next**.

3. Select the **Uninstall/Unplug a device** option, and click **Next**.

4. Select the **Uninstall a device** option, and click **Next**.

The wizard displays a list of all the devices installed on your computer system, like this:

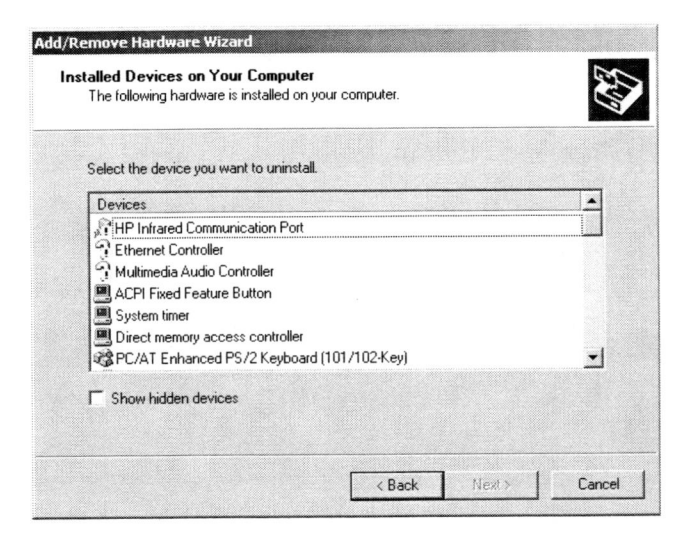

[Screenshot of Add/Remove Hardware Wizard showing Installed Devices on Your Computer]

Before you go any further, here's a word of warning: Don't play around where Windows and devices are concerned. Using this wizard to tell Windows that you have removed a hardware device is relatively straightforward, but don't do it unless you really don't need the device anymore.

5. Click the device you want to uninstall, and then click **Next**.

6. Select the **Yes, I want to uninstall this device** option, and click **Next**.

   The wizard uninstalls the device and its supporting files.

7. Click **Finish** to close the wizard.

ADDING OR REMOVING PROGRAMS

Gone are the days when adding a program to your computer was a just a simple matter of copying the program to your hard drive. Nowadays, almost every application includes a setup program that copies all the necessary pieces to the correct locations and alerts Windows to their existence. If you remove an application, not only must its files be deleted from your hard drive, but ideally, Windows should remove all references to the application from its system files. Similarly, if you add or remove any programs that come with Windows 2000, Windows needs to be notified so that it can do the necessary housekeeping.

ADDING OR REMOVING APPLICATION PROGRAMS

To install a new application program from a floppy disk or CD-ROM, follow these steps:

1. Open **Control Panel**, and then double-click **Add/Remove Programs**.

   This Add/Remove Programs window appears:

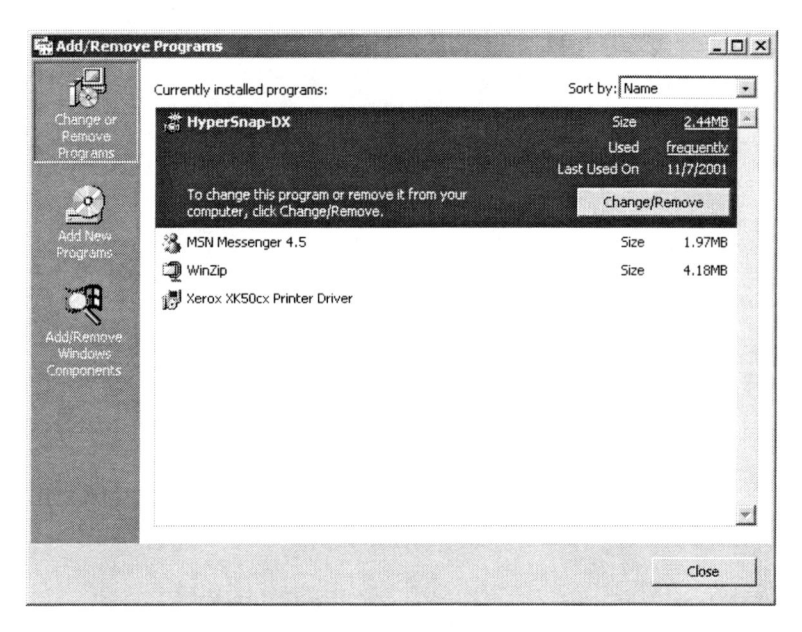

   [screenshot of Add/Remove Programs window]

2. Click **Add New Programs**, and then click **CD or Floppy** to start the installation wizard.

   The wizard searches the CD-ROM and floppy drives for a setup program, and then prompts you to confirm that it should run the program.

3. Click **Finish**.

   The program's setup program takes over from the installation wizard, prompting you for any information it needs.

If the application program comes with an uninstall utility, the installation wizard adds the utility to a list of programs that can be removed. To remove (*uninstall*) a program, follow these steps:

1. Open **Control Panel**, and double-click **Add/Remove Programs**.

   Windows displays a list of programs that can be changed or uninstalled, as shown earlier.

2. Click the program you want to remove in the list box, and click the program's **Remove** or **Change/Remove** button. (The

button's name changes depending on the program's installation options.)

Windows uninstalls the program. You might be prompted to confirm the uninstallation process.

3. Close the Add/Remove Programs window.

If the program you want to remove is not listed in the Add/Remove Programs window, look for an uninstall application in the folder where the program is stored. (It will most likely be called *Remove* or *Uninstall*.) If you don't find anything there, check the program's documentation, or call technical support for that particular program.

ADDING OR REMOVING WINDOWS COMPONENTS

To simplify the process of installing Windows 2000, the setup program offers a *typical installation* that includes all the vital Windows components plus a selection of useful mini-programs, called *applets*. As you work with Windows, you might find that you need an applet that was not initially installed, or maybe that you never use an applet that was installed. With Windows, you can add or remove this type of program at any time, provided you have permission to change your setup in this way.

Here are the steps for adding or removing a component:

1. Double-click **Add/Remove Programs** in the Control Panel window, and click **Add/Remove Windows Components**.

   After checking your computer for installed components, Windows displays a dialog box like the one shown in this graphic:

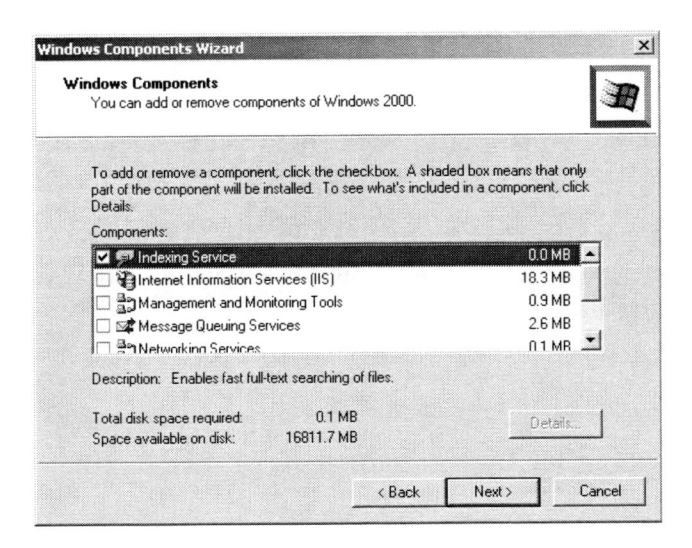

In the Components list, Windows displays its optional components by category. Categories with all components installed display a check mark in a white check box, whereas categories with only some components installed display a check mark in a gray check box. On the right side of the Components list, Windows displays how much hard disk space the components in each category will use.

To add or remove an entire category, you select the check box to the left of the category's name. To add or remove individual items, you click the category name, and then select the check boxes of the individual components.

2. Click the **Internet Information Services (IIS)** category name to select that category.

   Don't click the check box, or you will select the entire category. (If you click a check box that contains a check mark, you will deselect the entire category.)

3. Click the **Details** button. Windows displays the Internet Information Services (IIS) dialog box shown in this graphic:

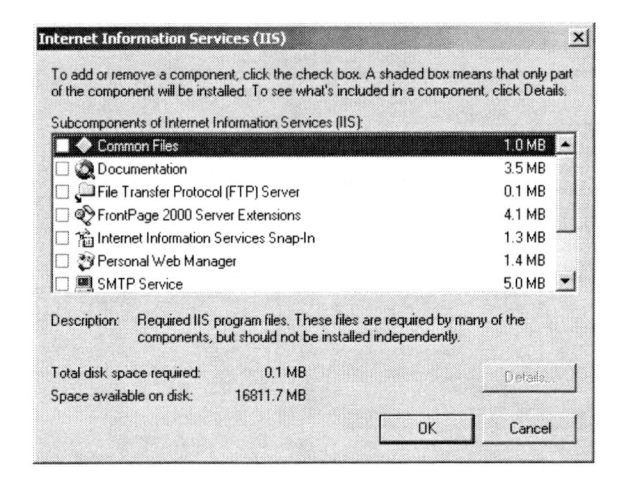

   Each of the components you see here can be installed individually.

4. Click the name of each subcomponent (not its check box), and notice the descriptions that are displayed below the Subcomponents list.

5. Click **Cancel** to close the dialog box, and then click **Cancel** again to close the Windows Components Wizard.

6. Close both the Add/Remove Programs window and the Control Panel window.

TAILORING THE DISPLAY

You can tailor the look of your computer display by changing its resolution, color scheme, screen saver, and other visual settings. To access the dialog box where you make these adjustments, you could double-click the Display icon in the Control Panel window, but here's a faster way:

1. Right-click a blank area of the desktop, and click **Properties** on the shortcut menu.

2. Click the **Settings** tab to display these options:

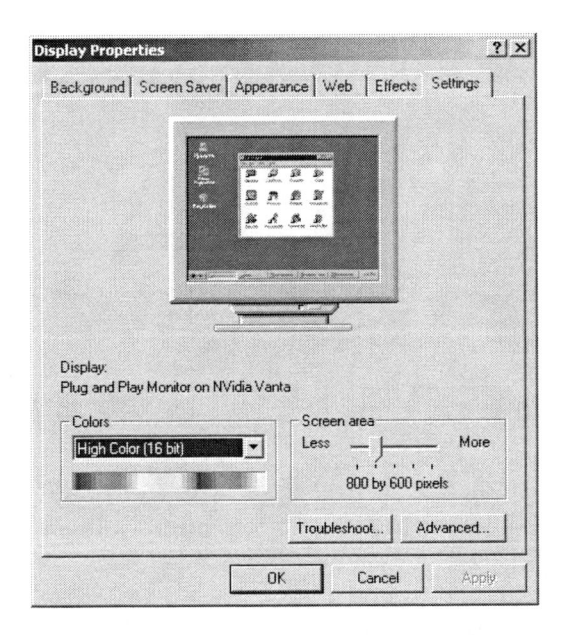

CHANGING THE NUMBER OF COLORS AND THE RESOLUTION

The options available on the Settings tab of the Display Properties dialog box reflect the capabilities of your monitor and video card, which are specified below the image of the screen.

ADVANCED DISPLAY SETTINGS

On the Settings tab of the Display Properties dialog box, you can click the Advanced button to open a dialog box with more detailed settings. On the General tab, you can alter the appearance of fonts and specify whether to restart the computer after you change settings. On the remaining tabs, you can change your adapter, monitor, and performance (how your graphics hardware components are used), as well as the default color profile for your monitor.

Here's how to check the possibilities and change the settings if necessary:

1. In the **Colors** area, click the down arrow to the right of the box to see the available choices, and then click whichever setting is already highlighted.

   For now, you should retain the existing configuration and experiment with different color settings later. Changing the settings changes the number of colors Windows displays. The range might be from 256 to over 16 million.

2. In the **Screen area** section, make a note of the current setting. Then drag the slider to the left or right to reduce or increase the screen resolution, and click **Apply**.

   As you drag, Windows displays the selected number of pixels wide by number of pixels high. When you release the mouse button, you might see the dialog box shown in this graphic:

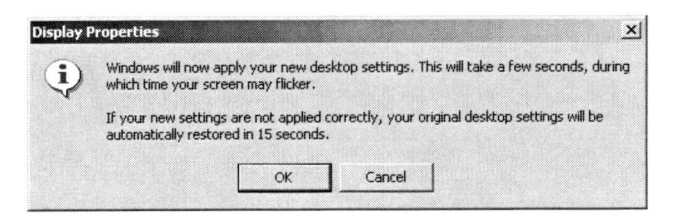

> **SEE ALSO...**
> Changing the color scheme, page 170

> **MORE ABOUT...**
> Pixels, page 8

3. If you see this dialog box, click **OK**.

4. Experiment with different display settings. When you are finished, click **OK** to apply the settings you want.

The graphics in this book are shown at 800 by 600 pixels. If you choose a different resolution, your graphics might look different from ours.

CHANGING THE BACKGROUND

You can easily change the pattern of your desktop or add a picture or an HTML document as background wallpaper. (Beware: large, colorful wallpaper files can really eat up memory, so you

Chapter 6 Customizing the Way You Work

might want to skip the wallpaper.) First, let's change the pattern of the desktop:

1. With the **Display Properties** dialog box open, click the **Background** tab to display these settings:

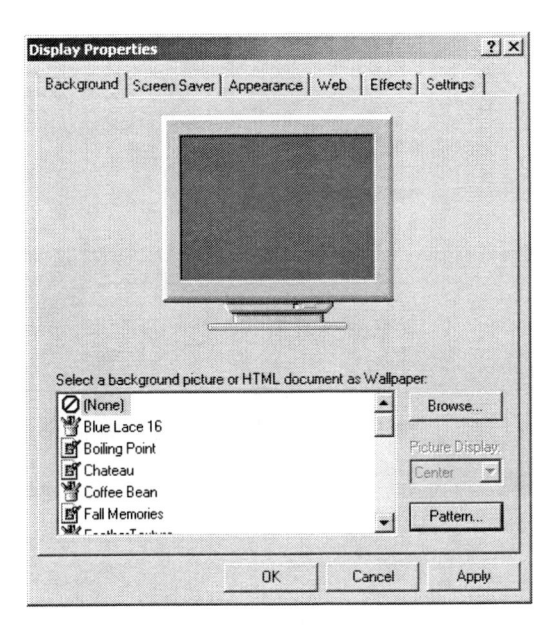

2. Click the **Pattern** button to display this dialog box:

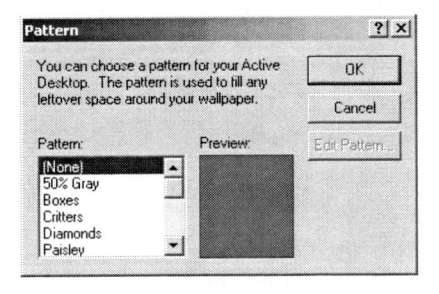

3. Click the various pattern names in the list and notice their effect on the sample screen shown to the right of the list.

4. When you have finished exploring, select **Thatches**, and click **OK**.

5. Back in the Display Properties dialog box, click **Apply**.

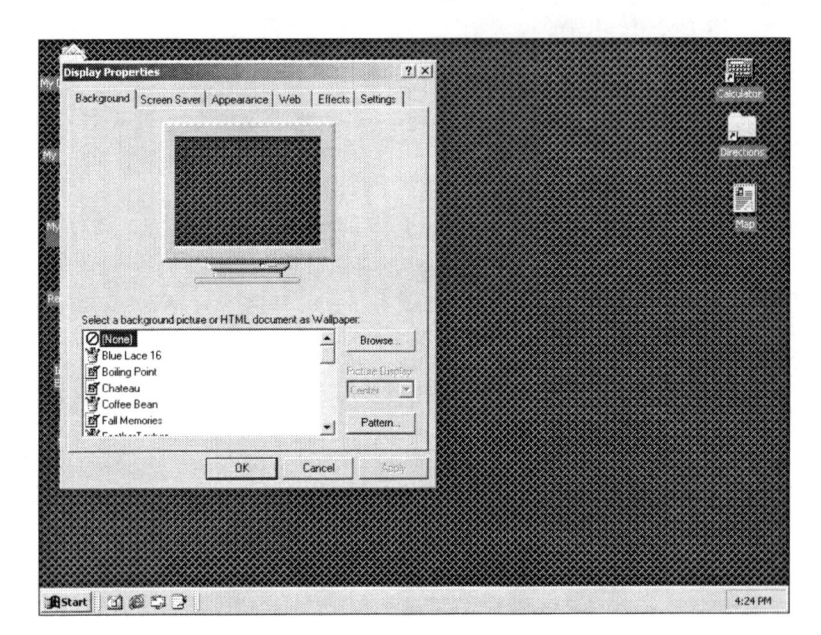

Your screen will look something like this:

Now let's try wallpapering the background with a graphic:

1. On the Background tab of the Display Properties dialog box, click some of the wallpaper names, noticing their effect on the sample screen.

   Some of the wallpaper pictures are photographs and others are computer-generated graphics. The picture type is indicated by the small icon preceding the name.

   The photographs are displayed at the full size of the monitor's screen, but you can choose different ways of displaying the graphics. By default, they are centered on the screen, and your selected background pattern is visible around the edges. If you prefer, you can stretch the graphic to cover the entire screen, or you can tile the screen with multiple copies of the graphic—both these settings hide the background pattern completely.

2. Click **Soap Bubbles**, and look at the effect on the preview screen in the dialog box.

3. Click the down arrow to the right of the **Picture Display** box, and click **Stretch** in the drop-down list.

> **USING YOUR OWN PHOTOGRAPHS OR GRAPHICS**
>
> If you want to use a digital image of a loved one or a favorite pet or place as your desktop wallpaper, click the Browse button on the Background tab of the Display Properties dialog box, locate the image file you want to use, and click Open. The image is added to the list in the Display Properties dialog box, and you can then use it as wallpaper in the normal way.

CHAPTER 6 CUSTOMIZING THE WAY YOU WORK   **167**

The centered graphic is stretched to cover the entire screen, completely obscuring the Thatches pattern you selected earlier. You can see a few dozen bubbles in the graphic.

4. Click **Tile** in the **Picture Display** drop-down list.

    The preview screen changes to display multiple copies of the original graphic, producing hundreds of bubbles.

5. In the list of backgrounds, click **Paradise**, and click **OK**.

    You might see a dialog box like this one:

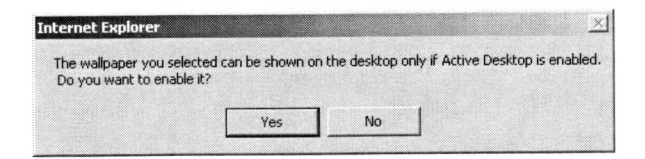

6. If you see the dialog box, click **Yes**.

    Your screen now depicts an idyllic paradise, like this:

7. If you don't like your screen's new look, reopen the Display Properties dialog box and try a different background, or return the pattern and wallpaper settings to (**None**), as we did.

Displaying a Screen Saver

Using the Display Properties dialog box, you can specify whether Windows should display a moving picture or pattern during periods of screen inactivity. In the old days, a moving display, or *screen saver*, saved power and helped prevent static screen objects (such as window title bars and menu bars) from "burning" their image into the monitor. Today's monitors, however, automatically turn off the image after a period of inactivity, and screen savers are used mostly for fun and for personalizing your display. They also hide your work in progress from passersby. Here's how to activate a screen saver:

1. In the **Display Properties** dialog box, click the **Screen Saver** tab, which looks like this:

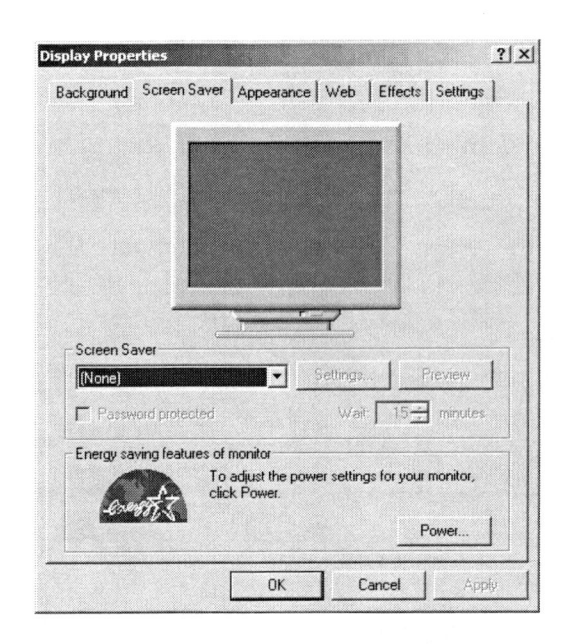

Power management

To optimize your computer's power consumption, you can choose a *power scheme*—a collection of settings for power usage. Open Control Panel, and double-click Power Options to open the Power Options Properties dialog box. On the Power Schemes tab, select one of six typical usage settings, or you can modify one of the predefined settings and save a personalized power scheme. On the Advanced tab, you can elect to display a power meter in the taskbar status area, and you can specify that Windows prompt you for a password when your computer is activated from standby or hibernation mode. You can also specify what you want to happen when you press your computer's power button, and if your computer has a "sleep" mode, what happens when you press the sleep button. On the Hibernate tab, you can enable the Hibernation feature, which powers down your computer after periods of inactivity but ensures that data isn't lost. This is one of the special power-saving features of Windows. If your computer is connected to an uninterruptible power supply (UPS), you can monitor the status of the UPS device on the UPS tab.

Chapter 6 Customizing the Way You Work

2. Click the down arrow to the right of the **Screen Saver** box, and then click **3D FlowerBox (OpenGL)** in the drop-down list.

   The sample screen shows what the screen saver looks like, but you can also click the Preview button to see its effect on the full screen. (After you click the Preview button, moving the mouse returns you to the Display Properties dialog box.)

3. Watching a flying object might give you motion sickness, so click the **Settings** button in the **Screen Saver** area to display the dialog box shown in this graphic:

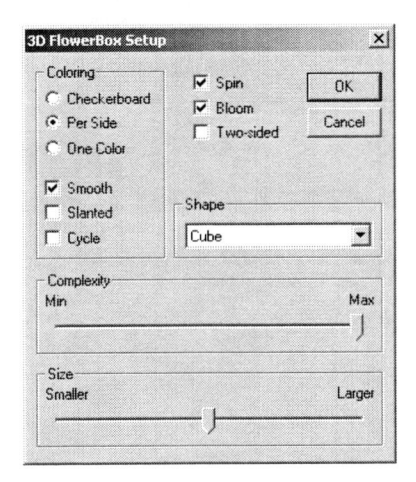

4. Experiment with the options in this dialog box, clicking **OK** to view their effects in the sample screen.

5. When the screen saver is the way you want it, change the **Wait** setting to **5**.

TEXT SCREEN SAVERS

Windows provides two text-based screen savers called 3D Text and Marquee Display that, when activated, display words on your screen. You can use these screen savers to remind yourself of an important event or task, or a favorite motivational phrase. To create a text screen saver, open the Display Properties dialog box, click the Screen Saver tab, select 3D Text from the Screen Saver drop-down list, and then click the Settings button. Type up to 16 characters in the Text box (for example, *Go Seahawks!*). For longer messages (up to 254 characters), use the Marquee Display screen saver. You can adjust the size, speed, resolution, and spin of the text, and change its font and style. Click OK to return to the Display Properties dialog box, where you can preview the text screen saver before putting it into effect.

USING OTHER SCREEN SAVERS

Many screen saver programs are available on the Web for free, or you can buy them in computer stores. If you download or purchase a screen saver, you can install it using Add/Remove Programs in the usual way. Then activate the screen saver by double-clicking the Display icon in Control Panel, and on the Screen Saver tab, selecting the new screen saver in the drop-down list.

This setting controls the number of minutes of inactivity after which Windows should turn on the screen saver. You can type the number directly in the box, or click the up arrow to raise the counter number and the down arrow to lower it.

6. Click **OK** to apply your changes and close the dialog box.

Changing the Color Scheme

Some colors are easier on the eyes than others. You might find the default screen colors tiring, especially if you use Windows a lot, or you might simply want a change. To create a different effect, you can change the entire color scheme or change the colors of specific Windows elements, such as the desktop and the active title bar. (If you have a visual impairment, you can create a high-contrast screen.) Let's experiment a bit with the screen colors:

1. Right-click the desktop, click **Properties**, and then click the **Appearance** tab to display these settings:

> **More About...**
> Accessibility options, page 184

> **Using multiple monitors**
> Windows 2000 supports the use of more than one monitor at a time (up to ten). You can either view different windows on different monitors, or stretch a single window (such as a particularly wide Excel spreadsheet) across multiple monitors. You could use a second monitor to display your e-mail if you receive e-mail constantly throughout the day and don't want to interrupt the work you are doing to read it. Multiple monitors are also useful for desktop publishing and presentation graphics. After you have set up the monitors, you can customize their displays by opening the Display Properties dialog box and making adjustments on the Settings tab. You can set different screen resolutions and color depths for each monitor, optimizing its display for its primary usage. See Windows Help for more information.

2. Click the down arrow to the right of the **Scheme** box, and click **Desert** in the list of preset color schemes.

   In the area above the list, Windows shows how the screen will look with that color scheme.

3. Click the down arrow to the right of the **Item** box, and select **Menu** from the list. Then click the **Color** box, and select the pale gray in the top row of the palette.

4. Next, click the **Active Window** title bar in the preview pane.

   The setting in the Item box changes to Active Title Bar.

5. Change the **Color** setting to purple (the last color in the fourth row of the color palette) and the **Color 2** setting to magenta (to the left of purple).

   Notice that in the preview pane, the title bar's colors are gradually shaded from purple on the left to magenta on the right.

6. Change the font of the active title bar by selecting **Times New Roman** from the **Font** drop-down list. Then change the size to **11** and the color to **yellow**.

7. To save your custom color scheme, click the **Save As** button, type **!Mine** in the **Save Scheme** dialog box, and click **OK**.

   Preceding the name with an exclamation mark ensures that the new scheme will appear at the top of the Scheme drop-down list.

8. To implement the new color scheme, click **OK**. If you would rather ignore the new scheme and leave the current one in place, click **Cancel**.

Playing with colors can be fun, and we encourage you to experiment with this feature. You can return to the default color scheme any time you want by selecting Windows Standard from the Scheme drop-down list.

Accessing the Web from Anywhere

The Web desktop is designed to put the resources of the Web or your organization's intranet at your fingertips. Follow these steps to see what's available:

1. Open **My Computer**.

2. If the Address bar is not visible, on the **View** menu, click **Toolbars** and then **Address bar**.

3. Repeat step 2 to turn on the **Links** toolbar.

4. Point to the **Links** toolbar, and drag it down to display it underneath the Address bar at the top of the window, as shown in the graphic shown on the next page.

INTRANETS

Using Internet technology, many companies have set up Internet servers and created intranets that are accessible only to authorized employees (no matter where they are physically located). The intranet enables people to easily access company information, exchange ideas, and collaborate on projects. A system of security firewalls ensures that the intranet information is available only to the people in the company who are authorized to access it, not to general Internet users.

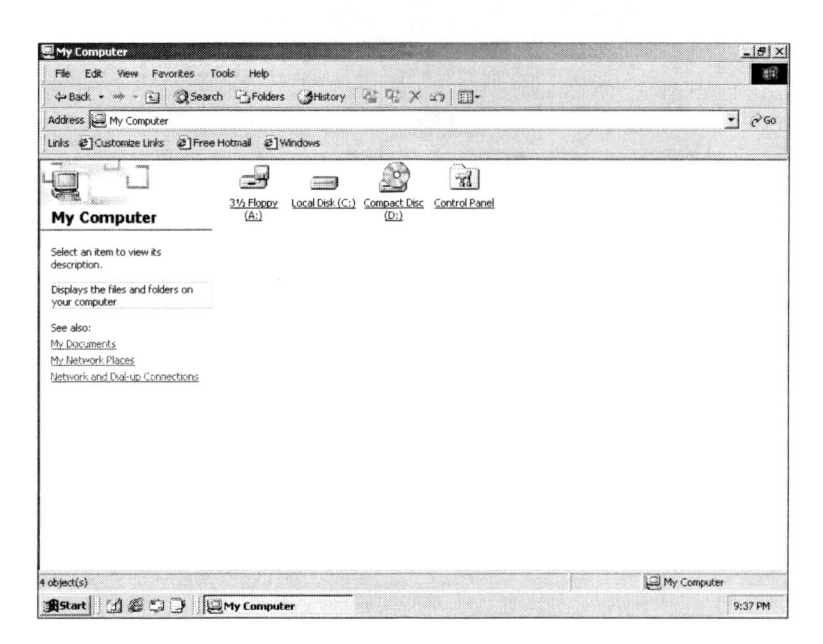

5. Without clicking anything, run the pointer slowly over the buttons on the Links toolbar to display pop-up boxes containing the Web addresses (*uniform resource locators*, or URLs) of the links.

More About...
Connecting to the Internet, page 98

6. If you are connected to the Internet, take a moment to explore the buttons on the Links toolbar, which provide one-click access to the Web.

   If you click a button without being connected to the Internet, one or more dialog boxes might appear. Close the dialog boxes without making any changes, or select the option to stay offline. Close any open Web browser windows when you're done looking at them.

Adding buttons to the Links toolbar
If you want to add a new shortcut to the Links toolbar, open the Web page you want to link to, and then drag its icon from the Address bar onto the Links toolbar. Alternatively, you can drag a shortcut from your desktop, from a Web page, or from your list of favorites onto the Links toolbar.

Internet Explorer
Once you are connected to the Internet, you can use Internet Explorer, Microsoft's Web browser, to access and view information available on the Web. This browser is included with Windows 2000 and can be accessed by double-clicking its icon on the desktop or clicking its button on the Quick Launch toolbar. Windows also opens Internet Explorer when you click buttons on the Links toolbar, click Web sites on the Favorites menu, or type a Web address in the Address bar. You are free to install and use other browsers if you prefer—doing so will not affect the performance of Windows. (For more information on how to use Internet Explorer, check out *Quick Course in Microsoft Internet Explorer*, another book in this series.)

CHAPTER 6 CUSTOMIZING THE WAY YOU WORK 173

7. On the **View** menu, click **Explorer Bar** and then **Favorites**.

   Again, if a message box prompts you to connect to the Internet, continue working offline.

   The Explorer bar opens on the left side of the window, displaying the same Favorites list you see when you display the Favorites menu.

8. On the Explorer bar, click the **Links** folder to display the links shown in this graphic:

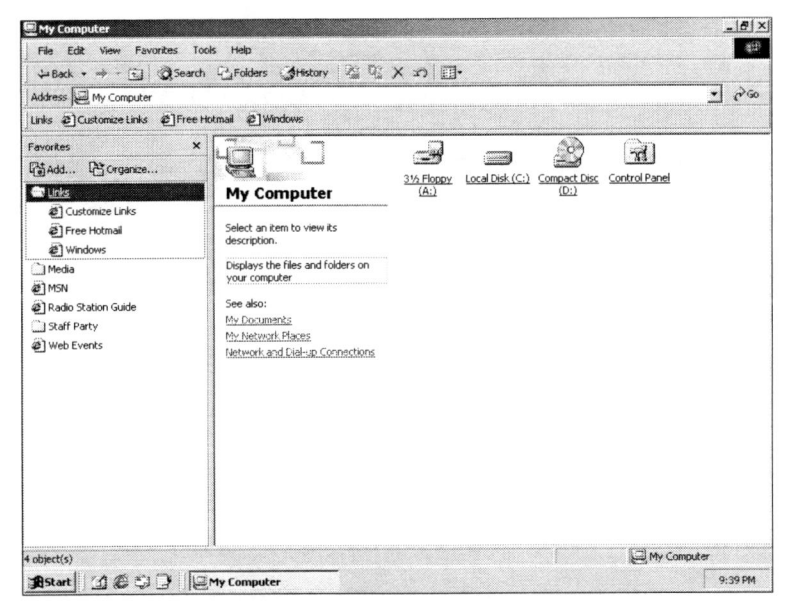

   If you are working offline, the links are a light gray color to indicate that they are currently unavailable. The same links are available through the Explorer bar's Favorites view, the Links toolbar, and the Favorites menu.

9. Click the Explorer bar's **Close** button to turn off the bar.

Here's another way that Windows makes Web resources instantly available to you:

1. On the **Favorites** menu, click **Radio Station Guide**.

   If your computer is currently connected to the Internet, the WindowsMedia.com Web site opens and displays a list of radio stations. You can also search for stations based on format, band, language, location, call sign, frequency, or keyword.

   You can add stations to your Favorites list for easy access next time you feel like a little musical distraction.

WINDOWS MEDIA PLAYER

The widespread availability of audio and video clips (as well as the development of new, inexpensive technologies for creating your own multimedia projects) created a need for a method of organizing and easily accessing multimedia files. Windows 2000 comes with Windows Media Player 6.4, which provides tools to accomplish this type of task. To start the program, display the Start, Programs, Accessories, and Entertainment menus, and click Windows Media Player. You can download the latest version of Windows Media Player from within the program. To upgrade from within the program, start Windows Media Player, and then click Check for Player Upgrade on the Help menu. If the resulting dialog box tells you there is a new version, click Upgrade Now to go to the Windows Media Download Center on the Web. (You need Internet access to do this.) In the Download Center, locate the latest version designed for the Windows 2000 operating system, and click Download Now to install it on your computer. If you prefer to visit the Web site, go to *http://www.microsoft.com/windows/windowsmedia/* for downloads and other information about the Windows Media Player.

2. If your computer has speakers, listen to a radio station over the Internet by selecting it and clicking **Play**.

3. Close the open windows.

Customizing the Taskbar and Start Menu

As you have seen while working through this course, the taskbar is an important element of the Windows 2000 interface. Because you use it so frequently, you can customize it for maximum convenience. You learned how to add and remove Start menu items and how to add toolbars to the taskbar in Chapter 5. Here, we'll look at ways to manipulate the taskbar itself.

> **See Also...**
> Start menu shortcuts, page 132
> Taskbar toolbars, page 141

Moving the Taskbar

Although the taskbar appears at the bottom of your screen by default, it doesn't have to stay there. Try this:

1. Point to a blank area of the taskbar, and drag the pointer to the top of the screen.

    The taskbar jumps into place at the top of the screen, and the items on your desktop move to accommodate the change, as shown here:

2. Drag the taskbar to the left side of the screen to see how Windows adjusts the width of the bar, and rearranges your screen again, like this:

CHAPTER 6 CUSTOMIZING THE WAY YOU WORK 175

3. Drag the taskbar to the right side of the screen.

4. Drag the taskbar back to the bottom of the screen.

   When you release the mouse button, the taskbar returns to its original size and location.

CHANGING TASKBAR AND START MENU PROPERTIES

In addition to changing the location of the taskbar, you can change its look. Follow these steps:

1. Right-click the taskbar, and click **Properties** on the shortcut menu.

   Windows displays the dialog box shown in this graphic:

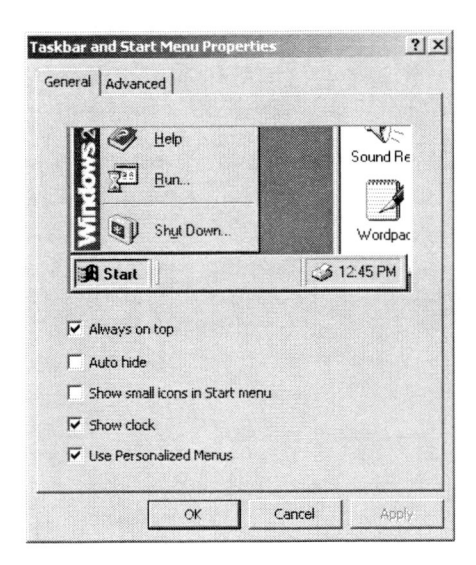

2. On the **General** tab, deselect the **Always on top** check box.

   The window in the sample screen now overlaps the taskbar.

3. Select the check box again to turn the option back on.

   The taskbar in the sample screen now overlaps the window. You will probably want to leave this check box selected so that the taskbar is always at hand.

4. Select the **Auto hide** check box.

   The taskbar has disappeared from the sample screen, leaving only a dotted outline. This setting is useful when you want to maximize windows to occupy as much of the screen as possible.

5. Click **OK** to close the dialog box.

6. Click the desktop to make the taskbar disappear from the screen.

7. Point to the bottom edge of the screen to pop the taskbar into view. Then move the pointer elsewhere to hide the taskbar.

Now let's experiment with more settings:

1. Point to the bottom edge of the screen to display the taskbar, click the **Start** button, click **Settings**, and then click **Taskbar & Start Menu** to redisplay the Taskbar and Start Menu Properties dialog box.

2. Deselect the **Auto hide** check box.

3. Select the **Show small icons in Start menu** check box.

   As you can see in the sample screen, small icons take up less room. In addition, the Windows 2000 banner is no longer displayed on the side of the Start menu, saving you further screen "real estate."

4. Toggle the **Show clock** check box off and on again, noticing the effect in the sample screen.

   You might want to turn off the clock if you have many windows open and you want to make room for their buttons on the taskbar.

5. Click the **Advanced** tab, and look through the check boxes that are available to you in the **Start Menu Settings** area.

   Changing the way the Start menu behaves is as simple as selecting or deselecting a check box in this list. Although you will not make any changes to these settings as part of this exercise, it is important to know what changes you can make, so that you can personalize your Windows 2000 computing experience whenever you want.

6. When you are finished looking at the settings, click **Cancel** to close the dialog box without making any changes.

Making Other Adjustments

With Windows 2000, you rarely need to live with a setting that annoys you or interferes with your work. Do you travel across time zones and need to adjust your computer's clock? Do you want to switch the left and right mouse buttons? Is your keyboard's repeat rate too fast or too slow? Then this section is for you. We'll explore two categories of customization: first, the settings that you are most likely to want to change and are most likely to be able to experiment with; and second, the settings that you are unlikely to want to change and that only experienced users should mess with (provided, of course, that they have the proper permissions).

Many of the adjustments we discuss in the following sections are made using the tools in Control Panel. As you'll see, we don't deal with the tools in the order in which they appear in Control Panel, and we don't deal with some of the more technical ones at all. But by the end of this chapter, you'll have a good idea of the range of customization possibilities available to you and know where to look when you want to change something.

Some of the settings we cover here are fairly easy to change, and experimenting with them can't harm your system. (As you work through the following examples, bear in mind that you can actually implement a change by clicking OK or pressing Enter in a dialog box, or you can leave the current setting as it is by clicking Cancel or pressing the Esc key.) Other settings are more obscure, and you need to change them only rarely or perhaps never. If you want, you can just skim through this section, coming back to specific parts if you need to later.

CHANGING THE DATE OR TIME

The time is displayed by the clock in the status area at the right end of the taskbar, and the date is displayed in a pop-up box when you point to the time. You can set your computer's date, time, and time zone through the Date/Time Properties dialog box. To open this dialog box, you can double-click Date/Time in the Control Panel window; double-click the clock in the status area; or right-click the clock and click Adjust Date/Time on the shortcut menu. Let's try the last method:

1. Right-click the clock in the status area at the right end of the taskbar.

2. Click **Adjust Date/Time** on the shortcut menu.

   Windows displays the dialog box shown in this graphic:

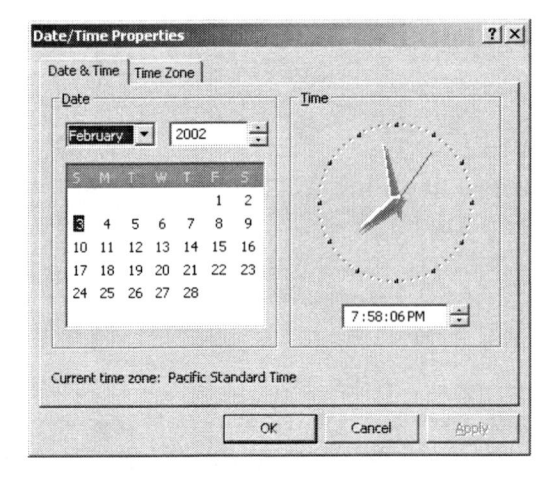

3. On the **Date & Time** tab, click the down arrow to the right of the box that displays months, and select **January** from the drop-down list.

4. In the box that displays years, click the up arrow to increase the year by one.

5. On the calendar, click the 1st day of the month.

6. If the time needs adjustment, select the hour, minutes, seconds, or AM/PM in the spin box that displays the time, and type a new entry.

   You can also select each component of the time and use the spin box's arrows to change it.

CHAPTER 6 CUSTOMIZING THE WAY YOU WORK

7. If you want to change the time zone, click the **Time Zone** tab, and select the zone you want from the drop-down list.

8. Assuming you don't really want to change the date, time, or time zone, click **Cancel**.

If you want, you can change the format in which dates, times, currencies, and other numeric values are displayed. Double-click Regional Options in Control Panel, and on the General tab, select a language and location in the "Your locale (location)" drop-down list, as shown here:

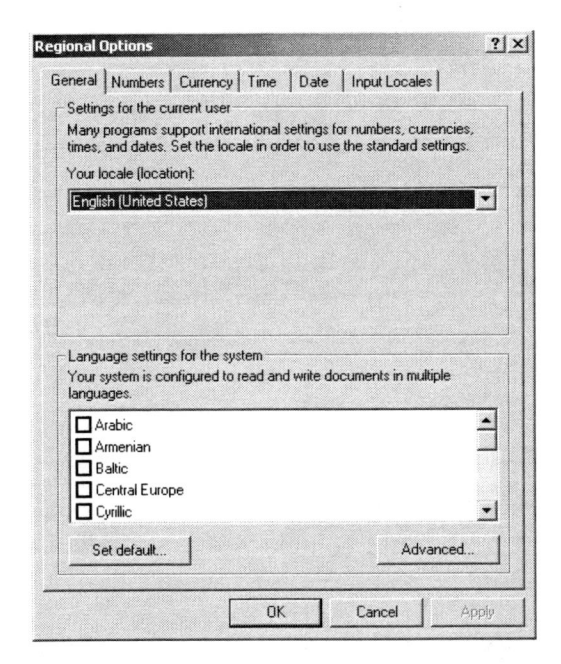

The selected language and location determines the way programs display and sort numbers, currency, dates, and times. (Changing the locale doesn't affect the language used in menus and dialog boxes, but if you have Windows 2000 Multilanguage Version installed, you can select a different language.)

You can also customize the display of numeric elements on the corresponding tabs of the Regional Options dialog box. Here's how to display dates with the day coming before the month:

1. Click the **Date** tab to display the settings shown in the graphic on the next page.

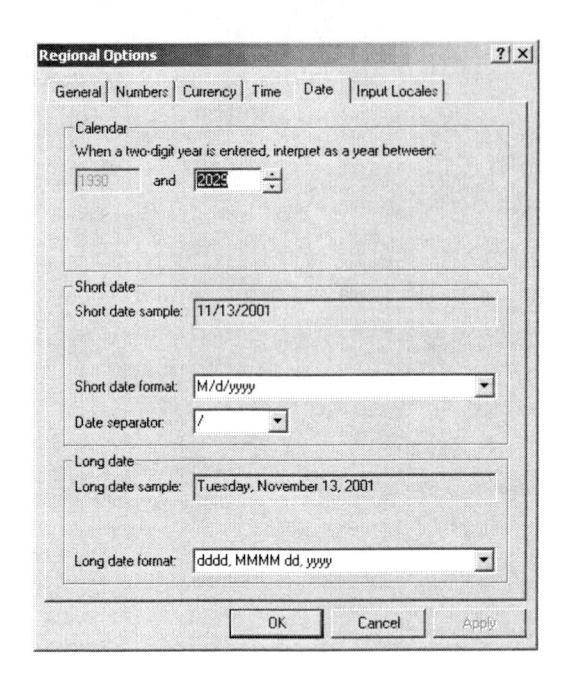

2. Click the arrow to the right of the **Long date format** box, select **dddd, dd MMMM, yyyy** from the drop-down list, and click **OK**.

ADJUSTING THE MOUSE BUTTONS

You can customize your mouse buttons for primary/secondary status, speed, and dragging technique. Here's how:

1. Open **Control Panel**, and double-click the **Mouse** icon to display this dialog box:

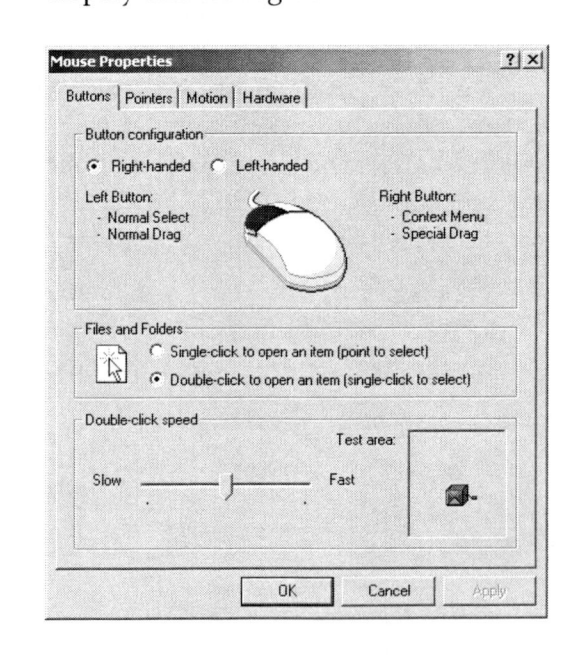

TWO-DIGIT YEARS

When you enter a year into the computer using only the last two digits, it is possible for misunderstandings to arise about which century the year belongs to. For example, if you enter a birth date as 02/28/01, was the person born on February 28, 1901 or February 28, 2001? You can set a 100-year span that allows your computer to interpret two-digit years correctly. Double-click Regional Settings in the Control Panel window, and click the Date tab. The default span is 1930 to 2029. Click the spin box's arrows to enter the desired ending year in the Calendar area, and click OK. For example, you would change the ending date to 2000 (or earlier) to have the computer interpret 02/28/01 as February 28, 1901.

2. On the **Buttons** tab, drag the slider in the **Double-click speed** area to the left.

   This will slow down double-clicking so that you can take more time between clicks and still have Windows recognize the action as a double-click.

3. Test your speed by double-clicking the toy in the **Test area**.

   The Jack-in-the-box jumps out of or into the box each time you double-click it at the correct speed.

4. Adjust the double-click speed to where you want it.

On the Buttons tab, you can also change the button configuration. If you find it easier to use the right mouse button as the primary button instead of the left, select the Left-handed option in the Button configuration area. The new primary button is indicated on the sample graphic but the setting isn't activated until you click Apply or OK. (Obviously, you then "right-click" with the left mouse button to display a shortcut menu.)

Adjusting the Mouse Pointer

In addition to changing the way the mouse works, you can also change the way it looks—or rather, the way it is represented on the screen. Here's how:

1. In the Mouse Properties dialog box, click the **Pointers** tab, which looks like this:

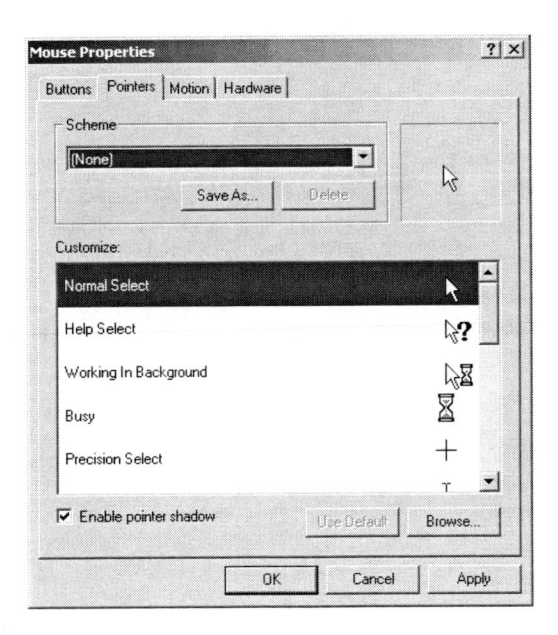

The variations of the pointer (the way it looks when different things are happening) are shown in the Customize box. You can scroll through them to see the different pointer states that are represented.

2. In the **Scheme** area, click the down arrow to the right of the text box to view the available pointer schemes.

3. Click **3-D Bronze**, and look at the more shapely representations of the pointer states in the **Customize** box.

4. Now click **Variations** in the **Scheme** drop-down list, and check out those representations.

   The Normal Select pointer displayed in the preview pane in the top-right corner of the tab is animated; it gradually changes from white to blue as you watch.

5. Click **Busy** in the Customize box.

   In the preview pane, you can see that the counter keeps track of the time that the pointer has been displayed.

6. Select **Dinosaur** in the **Scheme** drop-down list.

   The Busy pointer in the preview pane is now represented by a walking yellow dinosaur.

7. Click the banana that represents the **Unavailable** pointer to see its animation.

8. Double-click one of the pointers in the **Customize** box to see all the icons you could choose to represent that pointer state (there are nearly 200 choices), and then click **Cancel** so you don't make any changes.

9. Check out other schemes on your own. Then choose the pointer scheme you want to use, and click **Apply**.

In addition to changing the appearance of the pointer, you can change the pointer speed and acceleration, and specify that the pointer should move automatically to the default button in a dialog box. Try this:

1. In the Mouse Properties dialog box, click the **Motion** tab, which looks like this graphic:

CHAPTER 6 CUSTOMIZING THE WAY YOU WORK 183

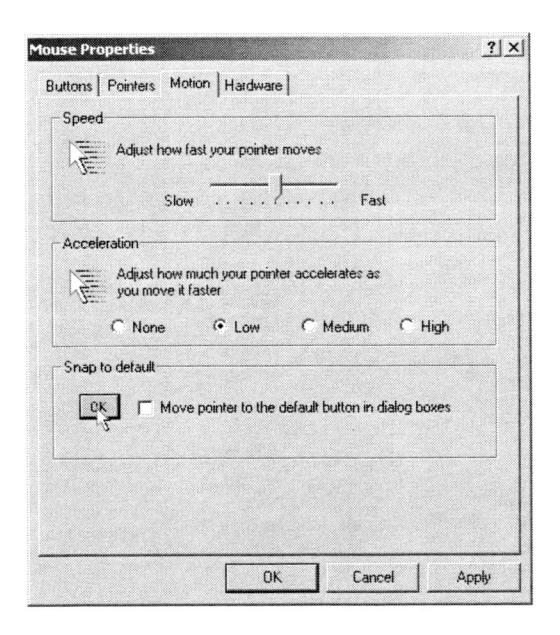

2. Move the **Speed** slider all the way to the left, and then move the mouse in a circle.

   The pointer moves extremely slowly.

3. Move the slider all the way to the right, and move the mouse in a circle.

   The pointer moves much faster.

4. Adjust the slider until the pointer is moving at the speed that is most comfortable for you.

5. Experiment with the other pointer movement options.

6. When you have the pointer options set the way you want them, click **OK** to close the dialog box and save whatever changes you made.

ADJUSTING THE KEYBOARD

If your keyboard repeats characters too fast or if the insertion point blinks too fast or too slowly, you can make adjustments in the Keyboard Properties dialog box. Let's experiment:

1. In Control Panel, double-click the **Keyboard** icon.

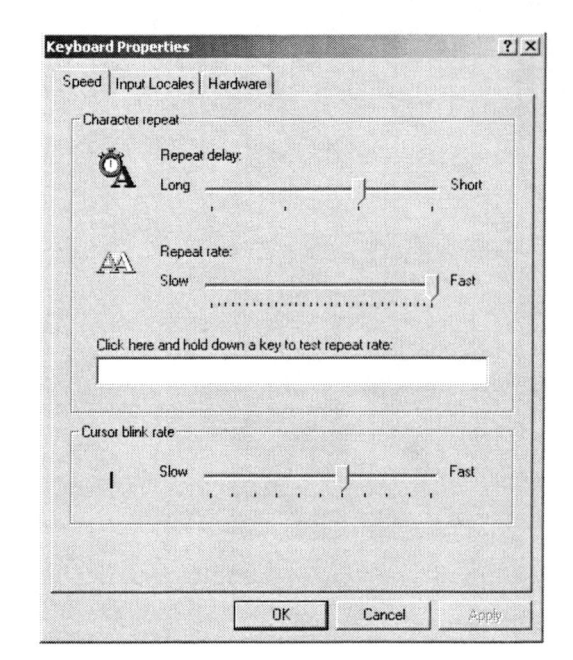

This Keyboard Properties dialog box opens:

2. Drag the **Repeat delay** slider all the way to the left to tell Windows to wait as long as possible before repeating a key you are holding down.

3. Drag the **Repeat rate** slider all the way to the left to tell Windows that after the initial delay, the rate at which it repeats the key should be as slow as possible.

4. Test the effect of your changes by clicking an insertion point in the text box below the **Repeat rate** slider and holding down any character key.

   Windows now responds very slowly to this keyboard action.

5. Adjust the **Repeat delay** and **Repeat rate** sliders until you find a speed to suit your typing style.

6. If you want, change the blink rate in the **Cursor blink rate** area.

7. Click **OK** to implement your changes, or click **Cancel** to discard them.

Accommodating Different Abilities

If you have a physical condition that makes using the computer difficult, you can configure the Windows 2000 accessibility options to work better for your vision, hearing, and mobility needs. To access the accessibility options:

1. Double-click **Accessibility Options** in the Control Panel window to display the dialog box shown in this graphic:

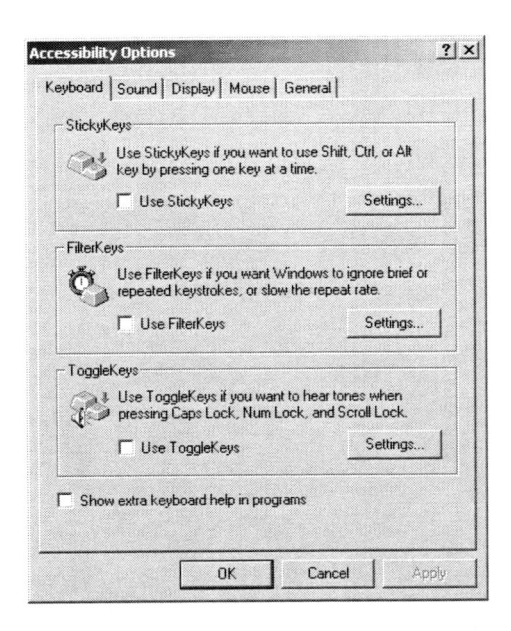

You can use this multi-tabbed dialog box to adjust several settings, including the following:

- **StickyKeys**. You can press the Ctrl, Alt, or Shift key and have the key remain active until you press a key other than Ctrl, Alt, or Shift. This feature is designed for people who have difficulty pressing more than one key at a time.

- **FilterKeys**. You can instruct the computer to ignore accidental or repeated keystrokes. (As you saw in the previous section, you can also adjust the keyboard repeat rate to avoid this problem.)

- **ToggleKeys**. The computer will emit one tone when you turn on the Caps Lock, Scroll Lock, or Num Lock key and another tone when you turn any of these keys off.

- **SoundSentry**. You can specify that a certain screen element (either the active caption bar, active window, or desktop) should flash whenever your computer makes a sound.

- **ShowSounds**. You can tell the programs you use to display text captions or informative icons for any sounds they make.

MORE ABOUT...
Changing screen colors and fonts, page 170

- **High Contrast**. You can tell Windows to use colors and fonts that make the screen easier to read. (You can also tailor the display yourself.)

- **MouseKeys**. You can commandeer the numeric keypad to control your mouse pointer.

- **SerialKey devices**. You can attach alternative devices to the computer's serial port if you have difficulty using a standard keyboard or mouse.

2. Explore the various sections of this dialog box to get a feel for the many accessibility options that are available.

3. When you are done, close the dialog box, and then close Control Panel.

USING MAGNIFIER

If your eyesight is poor or if you are working with projects that are difficult to see, you can use a Windows program called Magnifier to make parts of your screen more legible. To use Magnifier, follow these steps:

1. On the **Start** menu, click **Programs**, **Accessories**, **Accessibility**, and **Magnifier**.

2. If you see a message box about more powerful magnifier settings, click **OK**.

You now see the Magnifier window at the top of your screen, and the Magnifier Settings dialog box opens, like this:

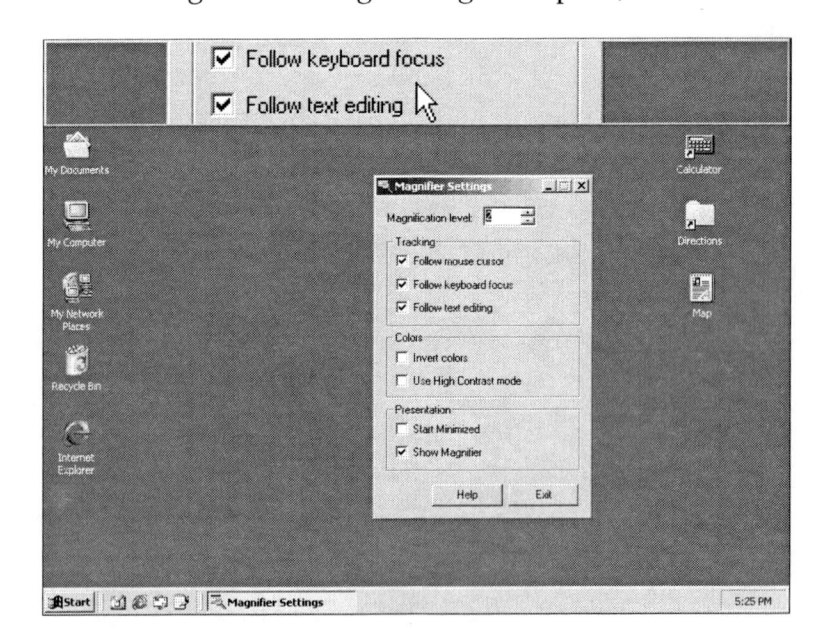

THE ACCESSIBILITY WIZARD
To adjust a number of vision, sound, or mobility settings, use the Accessibility Wizard, which helps you determine which settings to adjust. To start this wizard, just click Start, Programs, Accessories, Accessibility, and Accessibility Wizard. Select the smallest text size you can read, and then let the wizard walk you through the process of adjusting various settings. Clicking Finish in the wizard's last page implements your changes, but some basic accessibility features, such as large icons on the taskbar, are implemented as you go. Most of the changes made by the wizard can also be made individually in the Accessibility Options dialog box. However, you must use the wizard to adjust the text size.

In the Magnifier Settings dialog box, you can increase or decrease the magnification level, set tracking rules, and change the display colors. When you have the settings the way you want them, you then click the Minimize button to hide the Magnifier Settings dialog box under its button on the taskbar. As long as Magnifier is active, pointing to objects on the regular display makes them appear in a window at the top of the screen.

You can make the window bigger by dragging its bottom border. You can drag the Magnifier window away from the top of the screen so that it floats wherever you place it, or you can dock it against any of the four sides of your screen. When the Magnifier window is docked, any other open windows on your screen adjust themselves accordingly so that they aren't blocked by the Magnifier.

3. Experiment with Magnifier, and then right-click the **Magnifier Settings** button on the taskbar, and click **Close**.

USING THE ON-SCREEN KEYBOARD

You can use the On-Screen Keyboard, rather than using a traditional keyboard, to input text and commands, like this:

1. On the **Start** menu, click **Programs**, **Accessories**, **Accessibility**, and **On-Screen Keyboard**.

2. If you see a message box about other accessibility utilities, click **OK**.

The keyboard appears on your screen like this:

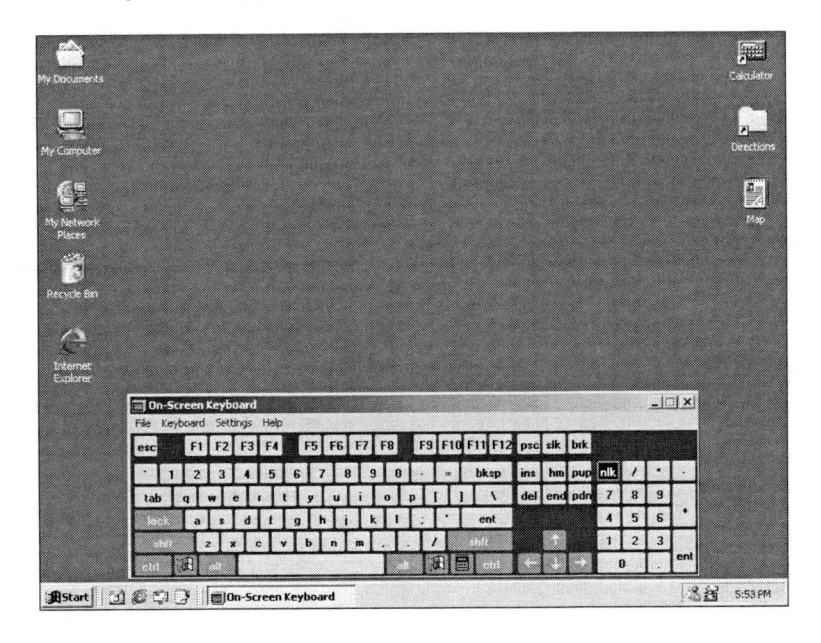

On the Keyboard menu, you can choose from a standard keyboard or an enhanced keyboard, which includes the numeric keypad and navigation keys. You can choose between the standard keyboard layout, in which the keys are offset from one another, and block layout, in which the keys are equally spaced in a grid. You also have three choices of keyboard—the U.S standard 101-key layout, the universal 102-key layout, and a 106-key layout that incorporates additional Japanese-language characters.

Characters on the on-screen keyboard can be selected in three ways:

- In clicking mode, you "click" the keys using the mouse or another pointing device.

- In scanning mode, On-Screen Keyboard highlights each row of the keyboard until you indicate the row that contains the key you want to type. It then highlights each key in that row until you indicate the specific key to type, and then starts over.

- In hovering mode, keys are selected after you point to them for a certain length of time.

You can switch between input methods by clicking Typing Mode on the Settings menu.

You can also change the font or size of the characters that are displayed on the keyboard, but keep in mind that the keys themselves don't change size, so you'll want to select a font size that fits on the keys.

3. Experiment with the On-Screen Keyboard, and then click the **Close** button to close the keyboard.

Adjusting Sounds and Audio Devices

If you have audio accessories on your computer, such as speakers or a microphone, you can fine-tune them by double-clicking Sounds and Multimedia in the Control Panel window to display this dialog box:

> **Multimedia programs**
> To access Windows's multimedia programs, display the Start, Programs, Accessories, and Entertainment menus. You can use the programs on the Entertainment menu to play DVDs, CDs, and audio and video clips; to record sounds; and to adjust your speaker volume. For more information, consult each program's Help menu.

Chapter 6 Customizing the Way You Work

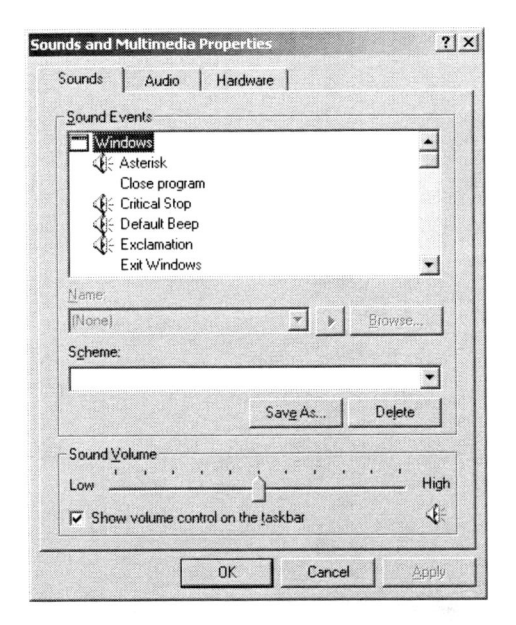

In the multi-tabbed Sounds and Multimedia Properties dialog box, you can change audio and voice settings, and you can inspect and adjust any multimedia devices attached to your computer.

If you have a sound card, you can assign sounds to system and application events. On the Sounds tab, you can select a sound scheme—a package of sounds that covers all the events that happen on your computer.

You can set the volume of sounds in the Sound Volume area of the Sounds and Multimedia Properties dialog box. If the "Show volume control on the taskbar" check box is selected, you can adjust the volume by clicking a speaker icon in the status area of the taskbar to display a slider, and then dragging the slider control up or down. To coax maximum audio performance from your computer, double-click the speaker icon in the status area to display a more complex Volume Control dialog box. This dialog box is also accessible by clicking the Advanced button on the Audio tab.

That concludes our quick tour of the Windows 2000 customization settings. You will probably want to experiment some more with the settings and dialog boxes we introduced to discover the configuration that best suits the way you work.

ASSIGNING INDIVIDUAL SOUNDS

To assign individual sounds to individual events, select an event from the Sound Events list, and then select a sound from the Name drop-down list, or use the Browse button to locate a sound file you have created.

Solving Common Problems

We discuss the steps you can take to reduce potential problems while working in Windows 2000. Included are discussions of backing up and restoring files; cleaning up, defragmenting and scanning hard disks for errors; and troubleshooting startup problems.

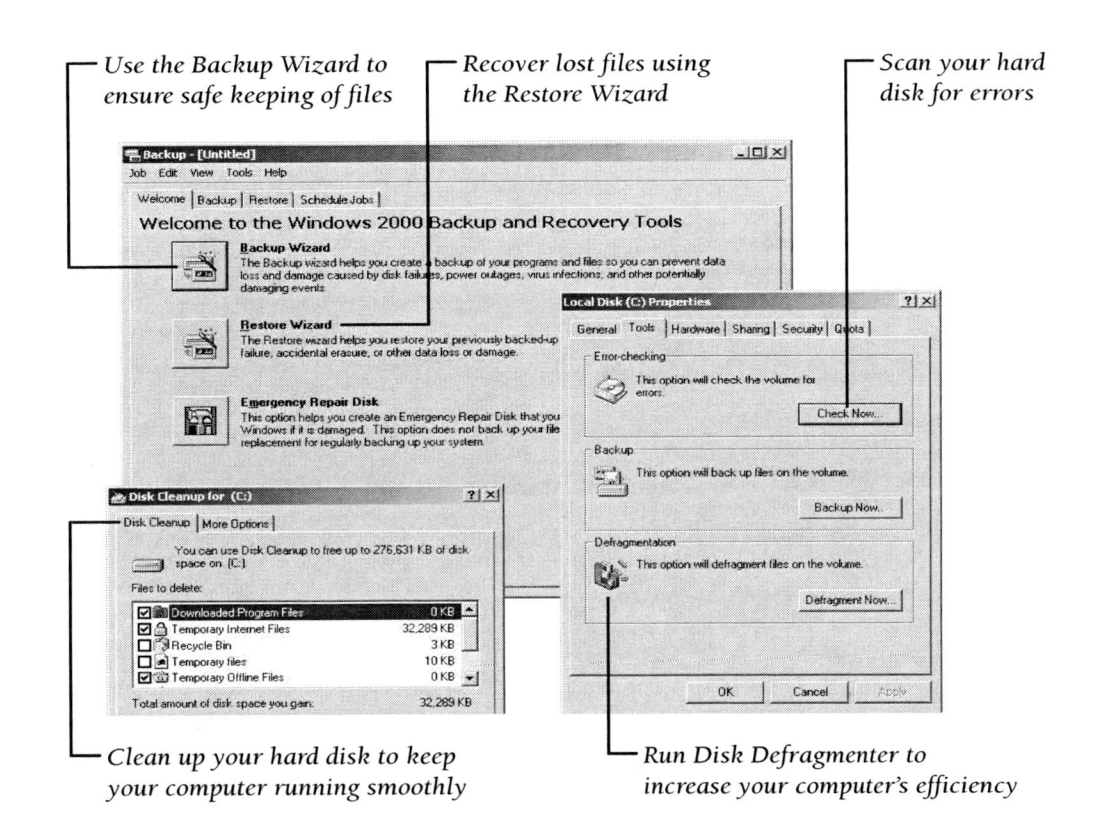

- *Use the Backup Wizard to ensure safe keeping of files*
- *Recover lost files using the Restore Wizard*
- *Scan your hard disk for errors*
- *Clean up your hard disk to keep your computer running smoothly*
- *Run Disk Defragmenter to increase your computer's efficiency*

In this chapter, we show you how to use some of the problem-solving tools that come with Windows 2000. As you work your way through our examples, your goal is twofold: You want to prevent problems from occurring (as much as possible), and you want to have a strategy in place for dealing with the problems that will inevitably occur. How well prepared you are for these problems could make the difference between a minor inconvenience and a major setback.

Many people have an aversion to thinking about problems before they happen. Others take Murphy's Law ("anything that can go wrong, will go wrong") quite literally and build contingency plans into every undertaking. Between the optimists and the pessimists, the rest of us hope for the best and try to learn from experience. Unfortunately, learning from experience can be painful (and expensive) where computers are concerned. Take our word for it: If you have important documents, data files, or projects that would be difficult or time-consuming to reconstruct, a little time spent planning ahead will pay big dividends in the event of software or hardware misbehavior, power outages, and unforeseeable disasters.

Backing Up Your Files

An effective plan for safeguarding your documents has two phases: First and most obvious, take steps to avoid losing them, and second, back them up regularly so that they are easy to recover if you do make a mistake.

Backing up is like flossing your teeth or taking out the garbage: necessary, but not exciting. It's easy to put it off. But we can't stress the point enough: If you don't do it, sooner or later something will go wrong, and you will lose valuable documents. Just as a bad dental checkup can induce people to start flossing, losing documents can overnight instill the habit of backing up.

The term *backing up* simply means making a copy of your data so that it is available if you have problems with your computer. Storing copies safely off your computer can reduce disasters to mere inconveniences and make recovering your work a matter of simply transferring the copies from disks, digital audio tapes, or CDs back onto your computer (or onto another computer in the event that yours is damaged). In addition to copying the data from your computer to another medium, consider storing the backup copy in another physical location, in case of a fire, flood, or other physical disaster. Taking some time to evaluate your needs and develop a simple and effective backup strategy can really pay off when the inevitable document loss occurs.

You can use regular or high-capacity disks, CDs, tapes, a removable hard drive, or another computer as the storage medium for backups. For our examples, we show you how to back up to your hard drive, but you'll easily be able to apply these techniques to other media.

Windows provides two methods for backing up documents:

- **Copying.** The simplest way to back up just a few documents is to copy them from their original location to the backup disk (or other medium).

- **Using the Backup utility.** If you get to the point where you are backing up large numbers of documents or single documents that use more than one disk, you will probably want to use the Backup program, which comes with Windows 2000. Backup employs a special coding system to compress files as it copies them, so the files take up less space. To restore the files back onto your hard drive in a usable format, use the Restore component of Backup. The Backup Wizard and Restore Wizard lead you through these processes with a minimum of difficulty.

Remember when we told you to store all your data files in subfolders of the My Documents folder to make backing up easier? Now you can see how this strategy pays off. If all your data is in one folder, you can quickly and easily back up just that folder.

In the following sections, you'll first create a full backup of the Staff Party subfolder of your My Documents folder and then you'll create an incremental backup, which safeguards any additions or changes made since the last full backup. Finally, you'll see how to restore files.

CREATING A FULL BACKUP

An important thing to keep in mind when selecting your backup medium is the size of the backup file. The copy of the data created by Backup takes up just about the same amount of space as the original data. If you run out of space on the backup medium, Backup will prompt you for additional disks or tapes until the backup is complete. However, this might mean that you need a lot of disks to complete a backup.

MORE ABOUT...
Copying files, page 83

MORE ABOUT...
Storage strategies, page 62

To experiment with Backup, you'll save a backup copy of your data on your hard drive, so you won't need a lot of disks and can see the correlation between the size of the original data and the backup data. When you are ready to create a backup file, follow these steps:

1. Click the **Start** button, and then click **Programs**, **Accessories**, **System Tools**, and **Backup**.

   The Backup window opens, displaying these options:

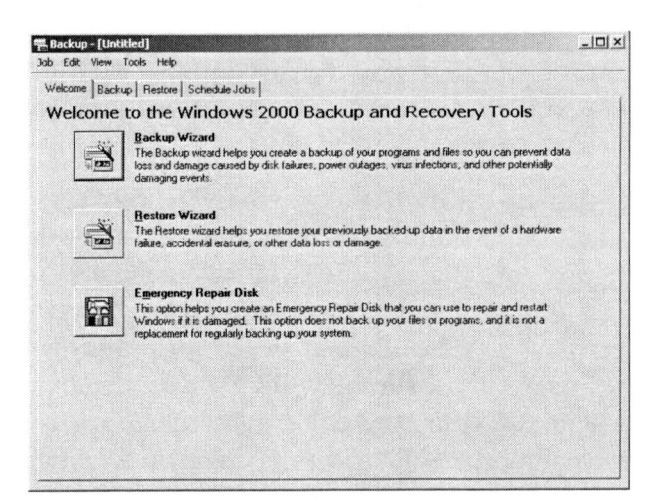

2. Click the **Backup Wizard** button, and when the wizard displays its welcome screen, click **Next**.

   You are given this choice of things to back up:

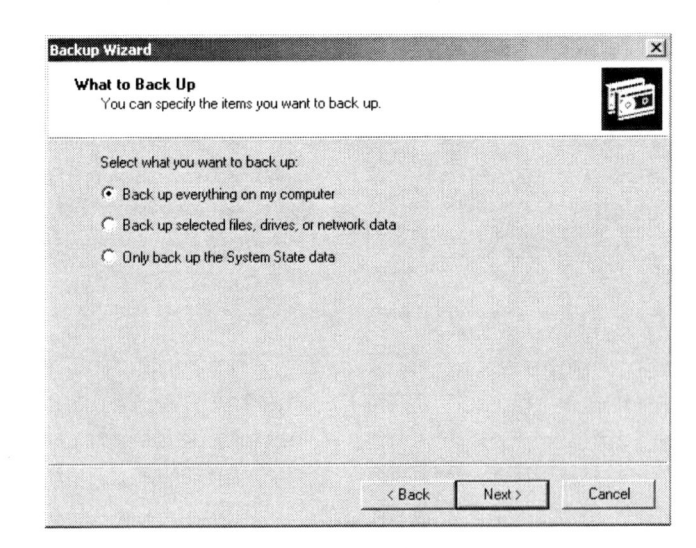

BACKING UP SYSTEM STATE DATA

If you select "Only back up the System State data," the Backup Wizard creates a file that contains all the System State data that is relevant for your computer. Most computer users will never use this file, but your network administrator might ask you to perform this type of backup.

Chapter 7 Solving Common Problems

3. You want to back up only the Staff Party folder, so select the **Back up selected files, drives, or network data** option, and then click **Next** to display this dialog box:

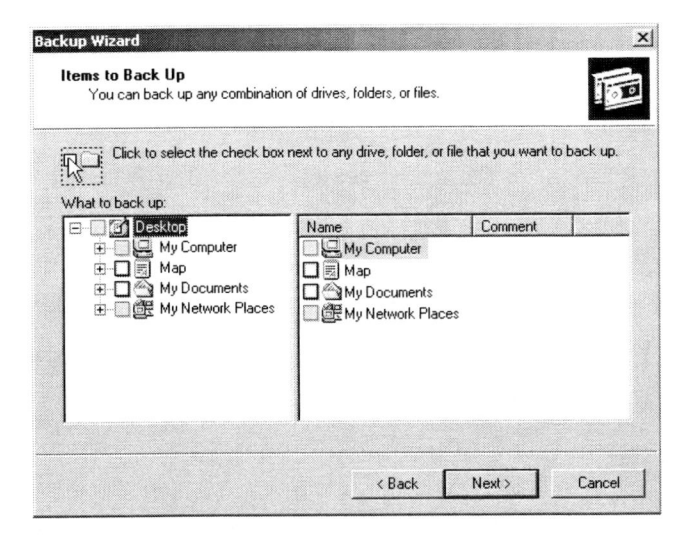

As you can see, this dialog box presents a tree diagram that is similar to the Folders list in My Computer. You can display folder contents in the left and right panes the same way you do in the My Computer window, except that when you point to a check box, the pointer changes to a check mark.

MORE ABOUT...
Browsing folders, page 65

4. Click the plus sign next to **My Documents** in the left pane to expand the folder, and then select the check box beside **Staff Party**, and click **Next**.

The wizard displays this backup location selection page:

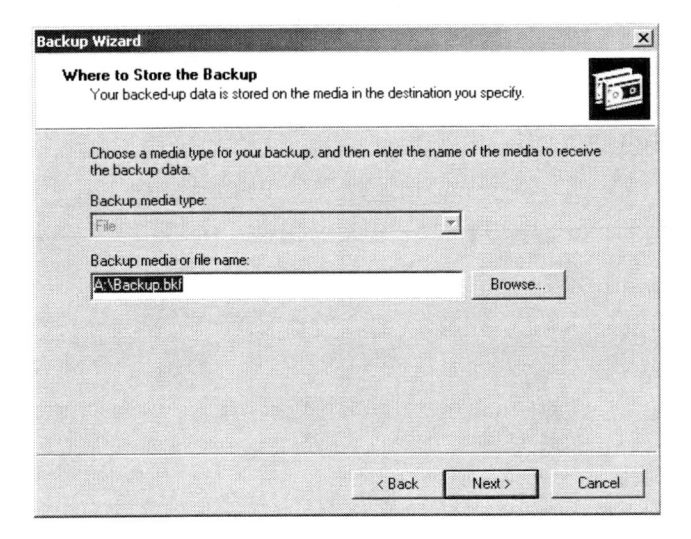

5. Click the **Browse** button, and in the Open dialog box, click the down arrow to the right of the **Look in** box, and then click **Local Disk (C:)** to display the contents of your hard drive.

6. Click the **Create New Folder** button at the top of the dialog box to make a new folder on drive C. Then with the folder name highlighted, type *Backups*, and press **Enter**.

   Your new Backups folder is created, without your ever leaving the Backup Wizard.

7. Double-click **Backups** to open the folder, type *Staff Party Full* in the **File name** text box, click **Open**, and click **Next**.

   The wizard checks that there are no problems with your settings and then displays a confirmation page.

8. Click **Finish** to begin the backup process.

   A **Backup Progress** dialog box is displayed while the backup is made. When the backup is complete, the dialog box looks something like this:

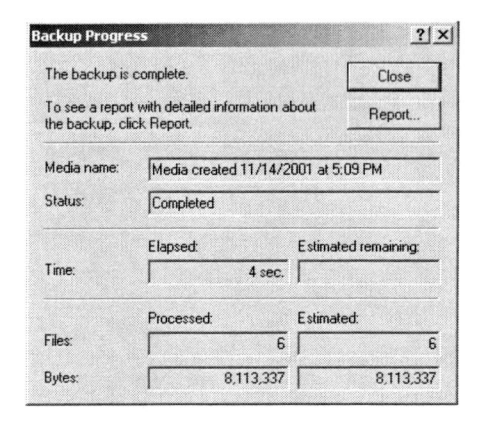

9. Click the **Report** button.

   A text file opens containing a report of how many files were processed and the space and time required.

RUNNING OUT OF SPACE

If you were doing a backup to a disk or tape and the medium ran out of space, a message box would prompt you each time a new disk or tape was needed. Each time this happens, eject your disk and label it (for example, *Backup Disk #1*), and then insert a new disk and click OK.

10. After reading the information, close the text file's window to return to the Backup Progress dialog box. Then close the dialog box, and close the Backup window.

Now let's look at the original data and the backup copy, and see how they compare:

1. On the desktop, double-click **My Documents** to open the My Documents window.

CHAPTER 7   SOLVING COMMON PROBLEMS   197

2. Right-click the **Staff Party** folder, and click **Properties** on the shortcut menu.

   The Staff Party Properties dialog box opens, displaying the total size of the folder and its subfolders.

3. Click **Cancel** to close the Staff Party Properties dialog box.

4. Click the **Up** button to display the Desktop folder.

5. Double-click **My Computer**, **Local Disk (C:)**, and then **Backups**.

   Your backup file looks like the one shown in this graphic:

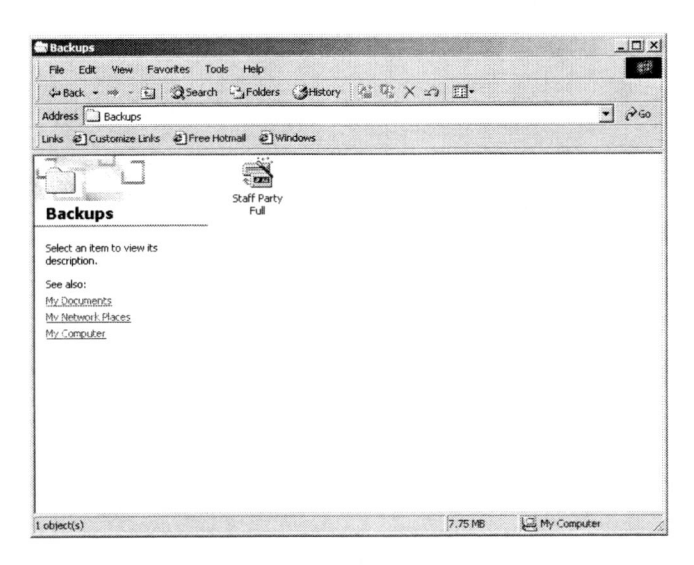

   [screenshot of Backups window showing Staff Party Full file]

6. Click **Staff Party Full** once to select it.

   The file's vital statistics are displayed on the left side of the window. In addition to your files and folders, the backup file contains extra information about where and when the data was backed up and how to restore it, so it is actually slightly larger than the original file. If you wanted to back up this particular folder to floppy disks, you would probably need several floppy disks to hold all the data.

CREATING AN INCREMENTAL BACKUP

Suppose you want to do a full backup of your My Documents folder every Friday, but on Monday, Tuesday, Wednesday, and Thursday, you want to back up only the files that have changed during the day. Here's how to create a backup job that will accomplish this task:

1. Double-click the **Staff Party Full** file to open the Backup window.
2. Click the **Backup Wizard** button, and when the wizard starts, click **Next**.
3. Select the **Back up selected files, drives, or network data** option, and then click **Next**.
4. On the Items to Back Up page, click the plus sign next to **My Documents**, select the **Staff Party** check box, click **Next**, and click the **Browse** button.

   The Open dialog box opens with your previous backup location displayed.
5. Change the name displayed in the **File name** box to **Staff Party Incremental**, and click **Open**.
6. Back on the Where to Store the Backup page, click **Next**.
7. On the confirmation page, click the **Advanced** button to open the Type of Backup page, which looks like this:

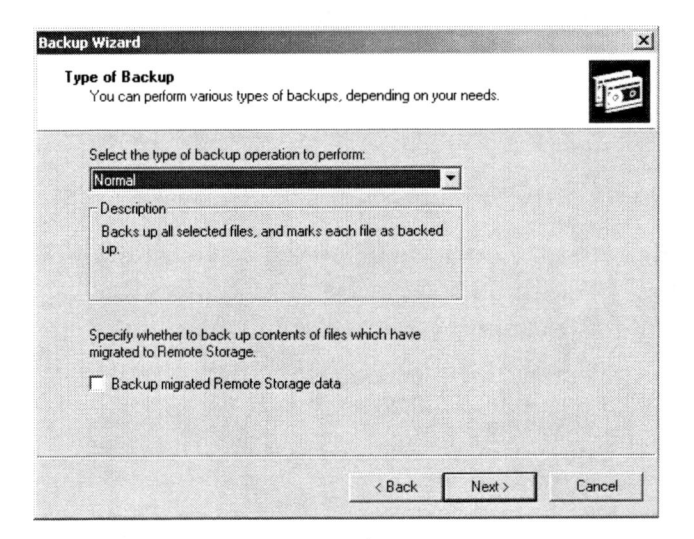

   ![Backup Wizard Type of Backup dialog]

The drop-down list setting is Normal, but you have four additional options: Copy, Incremental, Differential, and Daily. The *Copy* option creates a copy of your files and folders, without the additional backup information. *Incremental* backs up files that have changed since the previous incremental backup or since the last full backup if there have been no intervening incremental backups. *Differential* backs

CHAPTER 7   SOLVING COMMON PROBLEMS   199

up files that have changed since the last full backup; and *Daily* backs up files that were created or modified on the specific day that you are creating the backup file.

8. In the **Select the type of backup operation to perform** drop-down list, click **Incremental**, and then click **Next**.

   The How to Back Up page gives you these additional options:

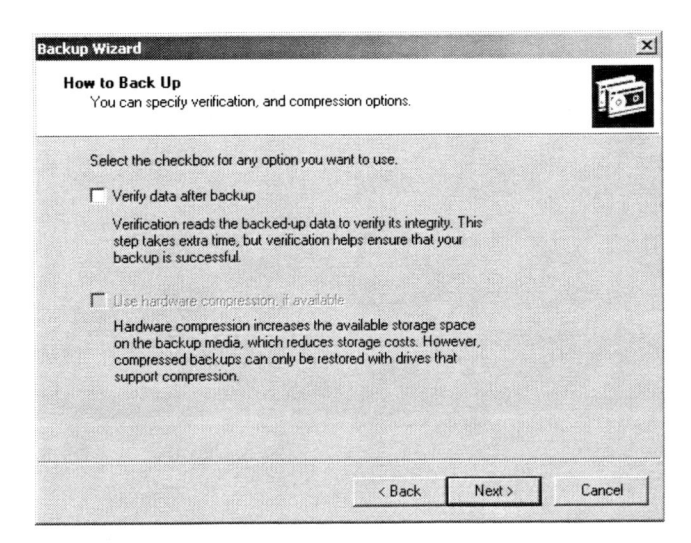

   ![Backup Wizard - How to Back Up dialog]

   The second check box is available only if your data backup drive supports compression.

9. Leave both options deselected, and click **Next**.

   You can specify whether you want to append the new backup to the original file, or to completely replace the original file on the Media Options page, shown here:

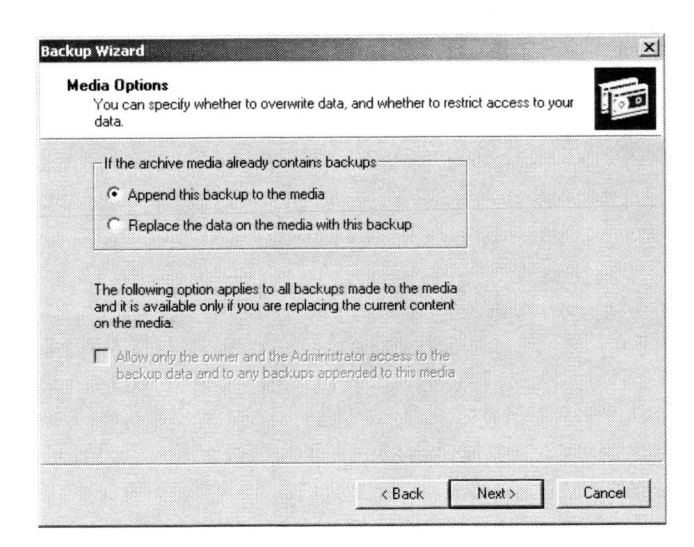

   ![Backup Wizard - Media Options dialog]

COMPRESSING BACKUPS

You can compress your backup file only if the hardware you are using for the backup supports compression. The most common type of compression-supporting hardware is a tape drive.

10. Leave the **Append this backup to the media** option selected, and click **Next**.

    The Backup Wizard prompts you to specify a label for the backup and the backup media:

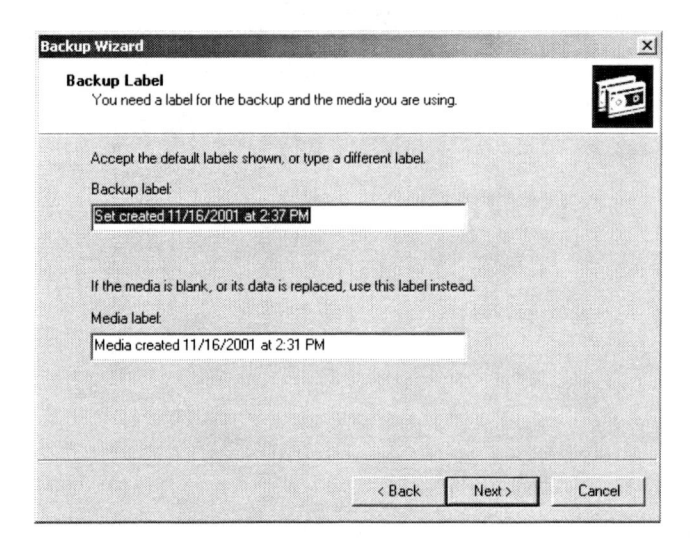

11. Accept the default setting, and click **Next**.

    The Backup Wizard gives you the option of scheduling your backup operations at a later time—or even scheduling a series of regularly occurring backups that happen without further instruction from you—on this page:

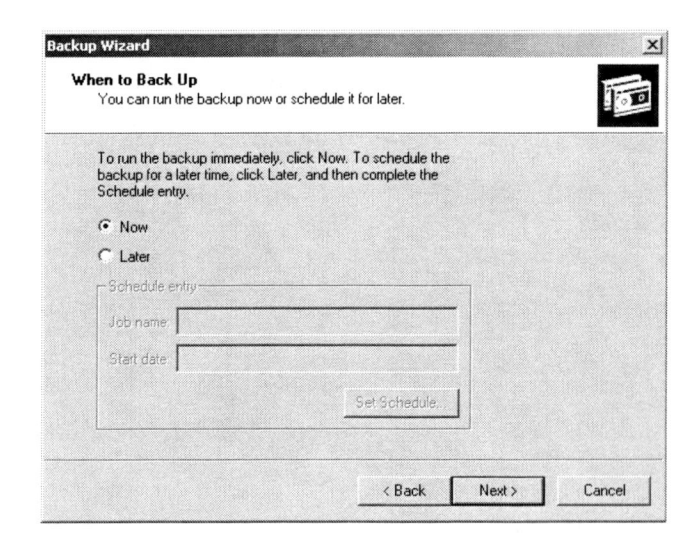

RUNNING THE BACKUP WIZARD LATER

If you click the Later option, you might be prompted to enter and confirm your password, and then you can enter a job name and set the backup schedule. You can schedule the backup to run once or regularly at specific times. If you schedule a regular backup, the backup is added to your scheduled tasks list. (See page 207 for more information.)

CHAPTER 7   SOLVING COMMON PROBLEMS

12. Leave the **Now** option selected, and click **Next**.
13. Click **Finish** to close the wizard and create the incremental backup file.
14. Close the Backup Progress dialog box.

RESTORING DOCUMENTS

If Murphy's Law proves correct, you will at some point need to restore your backup files. Let's give the restoration process a dry run. For the next example, you first need to simulate the accidental deletion of the documents from the Staff Party folder by changing the name of the folder. Then you will restore the backup file. Here's how:

1. In the Backups window, click the **My Documents** link at the left side of the window.
2. Rename the Staff Party folder as **Party**.

   Now that the Staff Party folder is "gone," you can restore it and its contents from the backup file you just created.

3. Click the **Back** button to move back to the Backups folder, and double-click **Staff Party Full**.
4. Click the **Restore Wizard** button, and then click **Next**.

   On the What to Restore page, the wizard displays descriptions of the available backup files, like this:

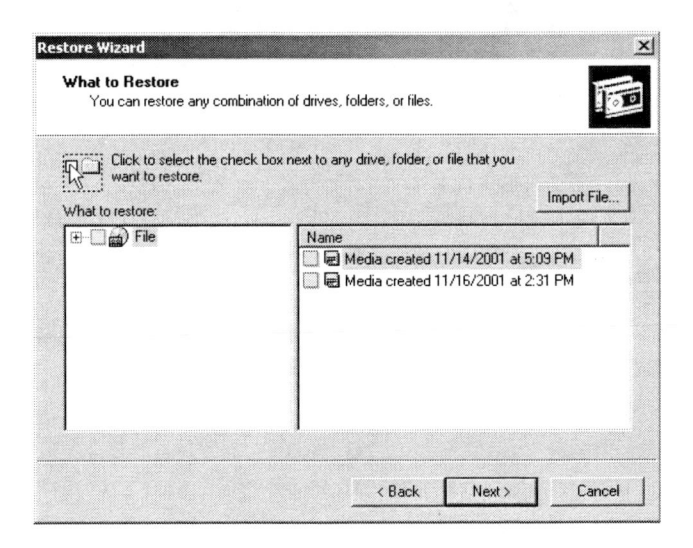

The check boxes next to the file descriptions are gray, meaning that you can't select them.

5. In the **What to restore** list, click the plus sign next to **File**, and then click the plus sign next to the first file description.

    The drive C backup has a white check box, which means you can select it.

6. Click the white check box to select it, click **Next**, and then click **Finish**.

7. In the Enter Backup File Name dialog box, change the file name that appears in the **Restore from backup file** text box to *Staff Party Full.bkf*, and then click **OK**.

    A Restore Progress dialog box just like the Backup Progress dialog box shown earlier is displayed.

8. When the restore process is complete, click **Close** to close the dialog box.

9. Open **My Documents**, which now contains the restored Staff Party folder as well as the renamed Party folder.

10. Close all the open windows.

From this simple demonstration, you can see how easily you can recover files in the event of a glitch, but only if you have taken the time to back up your documents.

OPTIMIZING YOUR HARD DISK

The risk of experiencing disk and file problems is greatly reduced if you regularly optimize your hard disk. In this context, optimization entails routinely deleting obsolete files, checking the integrity of your hard drive and file structure, and defragmenting the hard disk. We'll briefly cover these optimization procedures here, and then we'll show you how to use the Maintenance Wizard to automate these tasks.

SCANNING YOUR HARD DISK FOR ERRORS

AUTOMATIC SCANNING
If you turn off your computer without properly shutting it down, Windows might scan the hard disk for bad sectors the next time you turn on the computer, just to make sure an error on the disk did not cause the previous session's abrupt termination.

From time to time, you might experience difficulties with your computer that are caused by errors on the hard disk. These errors result from *bad sectors*—areas of the disk that have become corrupted because of physical damage. If your computer

CHAPTER 7 SOLVING COMMON PROBLEMS

seems to be acting weirdly, you can scan your hard disk to make sure that physical damage isn't causing the problem. Here's how:

1. On the desktop, double-click **My Computer**.

2. Right-click **Local Disk** (C:), and then click **Properties** on the shortcut menu.

3. In the Local Disk (C:) Properties dialog box, click the **Tools** tab to display these options:

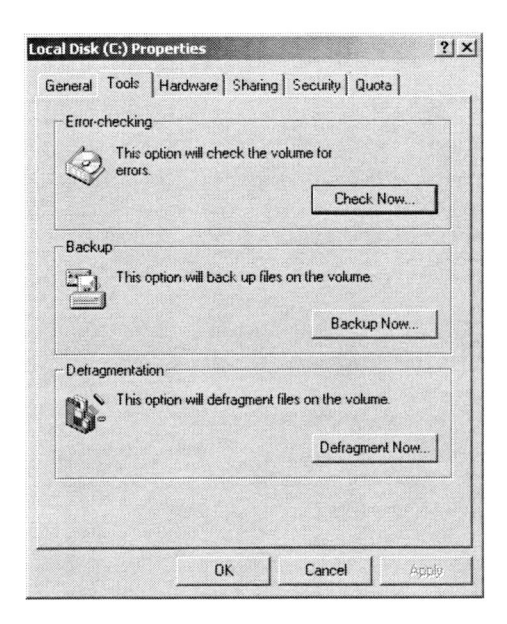

4. In the **Error-checking** area, click the **Check Now** button.

   You have these options:

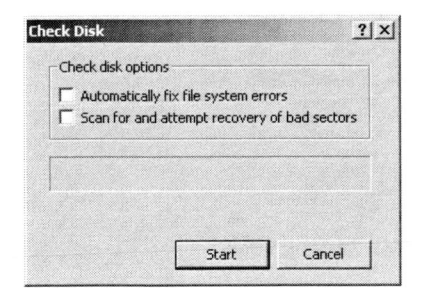

5. For the purposes of this exercise, leave both check boxes deselected, and click **Start**.

   A progress bar displays the status of the three-phase disk-checking operation, which might take a few minutes.

6. When the operation finishes, click **OK**, and then close the Local Disk (C:) Properties dialog box and the My Computer window.

USING DISK CLEANUP

Disk Cleanup identifies files that have been created behind the scenes but that neither you nor your computer is likely to need again. You can have Disk Cleanup delete the files to regain space on your hard drive. Here's how to run Disk Cleanup:

1. On the **Start** menu, click **Programs**, **Accessories**, **System Tools**, and then **Disk Cleanup**.

2. In the Select Drive dialog box, select the drive you want to clean up from the **Drives** drop-down list, and click **OK**.

   After Disk Cleanup checks your hard disk, a dialog box like this one appears:

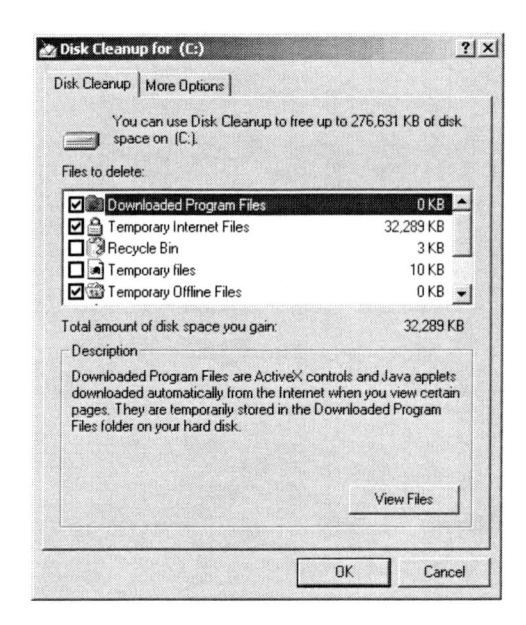

3. Deselect the **Downloaded Program File**s check box if it is selected, click **OK**, and then click **Yes** to confirm the deletions.

   Disk Cleanup now goes to work, freeing up space on your hard disk.

VIEWING BEFORE DELETING
You can click the View Files button to open a window where you can see all the files in the selected category before Disk Cleanup deletes them.

CHAPTER 7 SOLVING COMMON PROBLEMS 205

USING DISK DEFRAGMENTER

Though it might seem odd, the information in a specific document, file, or folder is not necessarily stored in one chunk, but might be scattered throughout your hard disk, which is divided into allocation units (sometimes called *clusters*), each with its own number. When you save a document, Windows starts storing it in the first available allocation unit and uses a sort of address book called the *file allocation table,* or *FAT,* to keep track of the unit in which the first part of the document is stored. When the unit is full, Windows looks for the next available unit and records its number, and so on, until the entire file is saved. After you've used your computer for a while, all the back and forth of saving, deleting, installing, and removing programs can make your hard disk look like a checkerboard of full and empty allocation units, making programs run less efficiently.

Windows comes with a Disk Defragmenter program that uses the FAT to find the scattered parts of each file and then stores the parts in a contiguous group of allocation units. Working with a program or document is then easier because its file is stored in one place, and Windows doesn't have to jump all over your hard disk to put the file together.

A complete discussion of the defragmentation program's options is beyond the scope of this book, but here are the basic steps involved:

1. With no other programs open, click the **Start** button and then click **Programs, Accessories, System Tools,** and **Disk Defragmenter.**

   The Disk Defragmenter window opens:

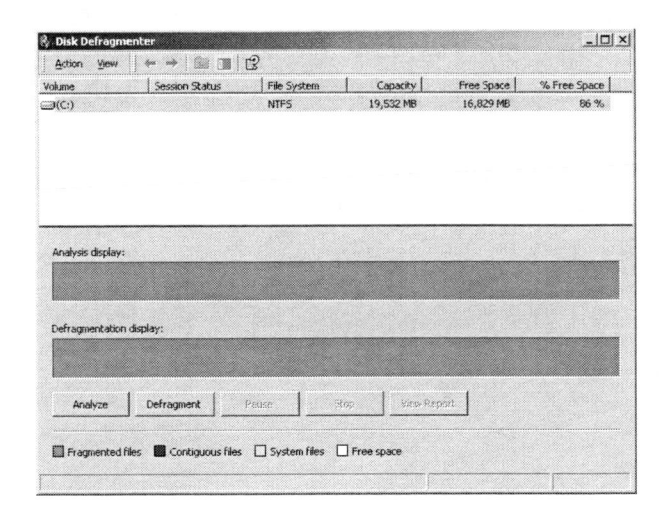

WHICH DISKS CAN BECOME FRAGMENTED?

The only disks that are analyzed and defragmented by Disk Defragmenter are your local hard disk drives. All computers have at least one of these, and some have more than one. Disk Defragmenter will not scan your floppy disk drive, CD-ROM drive, or DVD-ROM drive, because data is not stored on these drives in the same way it is stored on your hard drive, and thus is not at risk of fragmentation.

2. With drive C selected in the list, click the **Analyze** button.

   Disk Defragmenter analyzes drive C. When it is done, a message box indicates whether or not you need to defragment the drive, as shown in this graphic:

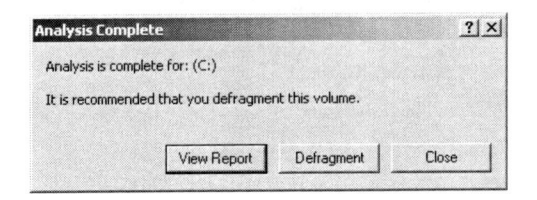

3. Click the **View Report** button.

   In the Analysis Report dialog box, you see a detailed report of what Disk Defragmenter found on your hard disk.

4. Close the report, and click **Defragment** to start the defragmentation process.

   The defragmentation process might take quite a while—up to an hour. You can watch the progress of the program in the Defragmentation display pane. The status bar at the bottom of the Disk Defragmenter window tells you exactly what is happening. When the process is complete, you can click the View Report button and scroll through a report about the defragmentation process.

5. Close the Disk Defragmenter window.

If your disk was severely fragmented, you'll notice that operations requiring hard disk access take less time than before.

SCHEDULING MAINTENANCE TASKS

You have seen how to check your hard disk for errors, and how to use Disk Cleanup and Disk Defragmenter to spruce up your hard disk and optimize its performance. You can schedule Disk Cleanup (and other programs) to be run on a regular basis, perhaps during non-working hours when these housekeeping chores won't interfere with your other tasks. Here's how to do it:

1. Click the **Start** button, and then click **Programs**, **Accessories**, **System Tools**, and then **Scheduled Tasks**.

CHAPTER 7 SOLVING COMMON PROBLEMS   207

The Scheduled Tasks window opens:

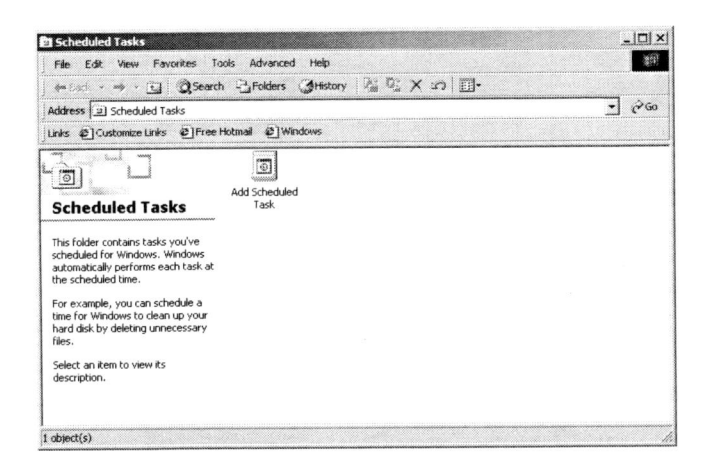

[Screenshot of Scheduled Tasks window]

If you already have any scheduled tasks, they are displayed here.

2. Double-click **Add Scheduled Task** to start the Scheduled Task Wizard, and then click **Next**.

The wizard generates a list of programs that can be scheduled, like this:

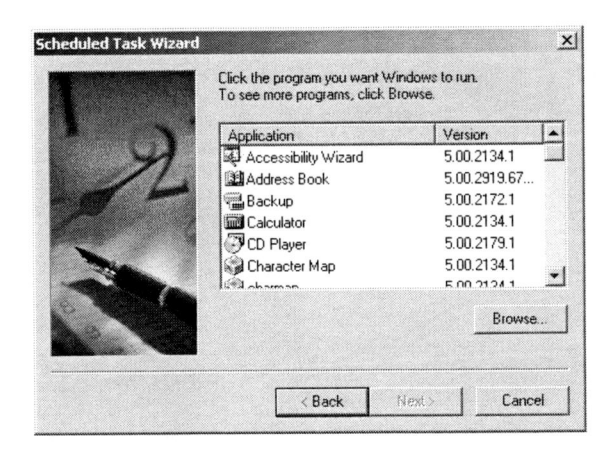

[Screenshot of Scheduled Task Wizard]

3. Scroll through the program list to see all the programs you can schedule. Then click **Disk Cleanup**, and click **Next**.

Your task scheduling options are displayed in the graphic shown on the next page.

SCHEDULING BACKUPS

You can schedule data backups to occur on a regular basis—whether daily, weekly, monthly, or every time you log on to your computer—using the Scheduled Tasks Wizard.

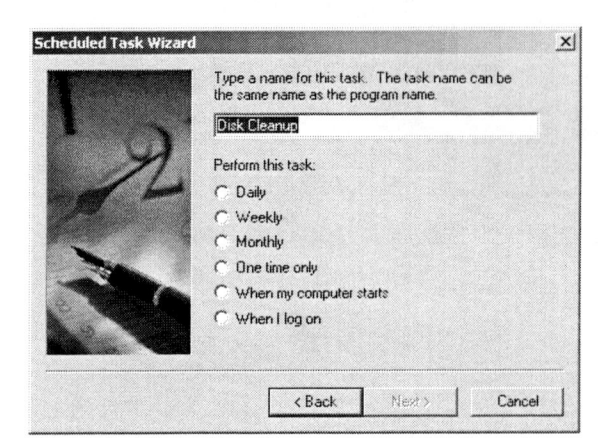

4. Select the **Weekly** option, and click **Next**.

5. Schedule the Disk Cleanup task to be performed every week at 7:00 P.M. on Tuesday, and then click **Next**.

6. Enter your user name and password where indicated, and then click **Next**.

7. Click **Finish** to add the Disk Cleanup task to your list of scheduled tasks.

   The wizard closes. Disk Cleanup is now shown in your list of scheduled tasks, like this:

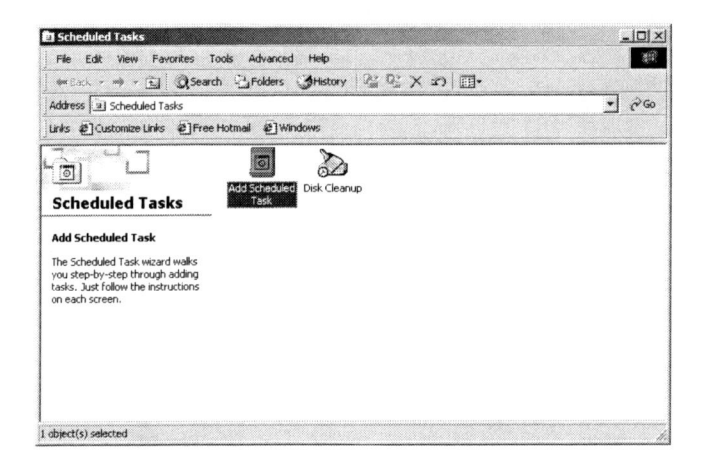

CHANGING SCHEDULED TASK SETTINGS

It's easy to change the settings of a scheduled task. Double-click the task to open it. Make your changes on the Task, Schedule, Settings, or Security tab of the dialog box, and then click OK to save your changes and close the dialog box.

8. Double-click the **Disk Cleanup** task, look at the settings on the **Schedule** and **Settings** tabs, and then close the Disk Cleanup dialog box and the Scheduled Tasks window.

Because you have scheduled the Disk Cleanup task to work its magic at night, you will obviously have to leave your computer on every Tuesday night, or the maintenance work won't get done. If you forget and turn off your computer for the night, you can run the task from the Scheduled Tasks window at any time by right-clicking the task and clicking Run on the shortcut menu.

TROUBLESHOOTING STARTUP PROBLEMS

If your computer doesn't start, or *boot*, properly when you turn it on, the glitch could be traceable to any number of problems that are way beyond the scope of this book. For the most part, you are probably better off calling in an expert than trying to sort things out on your own. However, one or two tricks of the trade might help you solve the problem yourself. At the very least, you might be able to retrieve any critical files that you haven't backed up, before someone starts dissecting your machine. And if you know about MS-DOS and its utilities, you might be able to go beyond the information we provide here and get everything working again.

CREATING AN EMERGENCY REPAIR DISK

An *Emergency Repair Disk* is a floppy disk that contains information about your computer. It can be used to repair your computer if it won't start, or if your system files are damaged or erased. You can also copy your registry settings to your Emergency Repair Disk in case they are lost. Although it is likely that you'll never need to use it yourself, an Emergency Repair Disk falls into the "nice to have when you need it" category. Here's how to create your own Emergency Repair Disk:

1. On the Start menu, click **Programs**, **Accessories**, **System Tools**, and then **Backup**.

2. Click the **Emergency Repair Disk** button.

3. Insert a floppy disk into your computer's floppy disk drive, and then click **OK**.

4. When the disk has been formatted, click **OK**, and then click the **Close** button to close the Backup utility.

5. Eject the floppy disk from your computer's floppy disk drive. Label the disk *Emergency Repair Disk*, and store it in a safe place.

USING SPECIAL START MODES

Windows 2000 has some useful programs that can help you solve startup problems, but to use them, you have to be able to get your computer up and running. As long as your computer will start, you can access a special menu that you use to log on to Windows in different modes. Not all the Windows functionality will be available, but in extreme cases, this might be the only way to get into a working version of Windows. It's best to know how to troubleshoot serious problems before you need to, so let's try it now:

1. Click the **Start** button, and then click **Shut Down**.

2. In the Shut Down Windows dialog box, click **Restart** in the drop-down list, and click **OK**.

   Windows shuts down, and then restarts.

3. Watch the screen carefully as Windows restarts. When you see the instruction to press a key to view advanced startup options, press the **F8** key.

   The Windows 2000 Advanced Options menu appears, listing several choices. (You might have to try this step a couple of times to press the key at the right time.)

   You see these startup options:

   - **Safe Mode.** Windows starts using the simplest hardware configuration (no fancy video drivers, no network, no CD-ROM drive, no printer, and so on).

   - **Safe Mode with Networking.** Windows starts using the simplest hardware configuration and network connections.

   - **Safe Mode with Command Prompt.** Windows starts with the simplest hardware configuration, and with the MS-DOS command prompt displayed instead of the Windows user interface.

   - **Enable Boot Logging.** While the system is starting, a list of all the drivers and services that are loaded (or not loaded) is created in a file called *ntbtlog.txt*. This log file might provide an indication of the cause of startup problems. Boot logging is automatically enabled in all three Safe Mode startup options.

Chapter 7   Solving Common Problems

- **Enable VGA Mode.** Disables any fancy video drivers and starts using only the basic VGA driver. VGA mode is automatically enabled in all three Safe Mode startup options.

- **Last Known Good Configuration.** Windows starts up using the registry information and drivers that were present the last time your computer was appropriately shut down.

- **Directory Services Restore Mode.** This option is available only on servers that are acting as domain controllers.

- **Debugging Mode.** Windows starts and sends debugging information to another computer that is connected to your computer with a serial cable (not over a network).

- **Boot Normally.** Windows starts as usual.

You can use the Up Arrow and Down Arrow keys to move between the startup options.

4. Select the **Boot Normally** option, and press **Enter**.

   Windows starts as usual.

5. Log on with your user name and password when prompted to do so.

Keeping Windows Up to Date

Because information technology is perpetually changing, it's essential to keep your system current. The easiest way to do this is through Microsoft Windows Update. Windows Update is a Web site run by Microsoft that serves as a centralized location for information services, support, and products pertaining to Windows application updates. At Windows Update you can find the latest Windows 2000 components and enhancements to keep your system running optimally.

Because Windows Update integrates with the Web, you can browse through their Product Updates catalog, select the components you need, and download and install them directly from the Web to your computer. The Support Information center provides Web-based help and support if you need additional assistance using Windows Update.

THE SYSTEM REGISTRY

The Windows system registry is a very important file stored on your computer that contains information about you, your computer, and every program that is installed on your computer. Some of the information is very simple, like your name, and some of it is very complex, like product IDs and default starting directories. The registry file is updated whenever you install a new program. An average computer user can go through his or her entire life without ever manually updating the registry file, and you should not make changes to it unless you know exactly what you're doing. If you'd like to look at your registry file, click Start, click Run, type *regedit* in the Open box, and then click OK. The registry is presented in a standard tree format, just like Windows Explorer Folders view.

What's especially handy about using the updates available for Windows 2000 is that most—if not all—the system checks and preparation legwork are automatically done for you. When you visit the Product Updates section of Windows Update, you see only updated features that you don't already have, so you can avoid unneeded duplication of files and components. Try this:

1. Make sure you have an active Internet connection, and then on the **Start** menu, click **Windows Update**.

   Your default Internet browser opens to display the Windows Update Web site, like this:

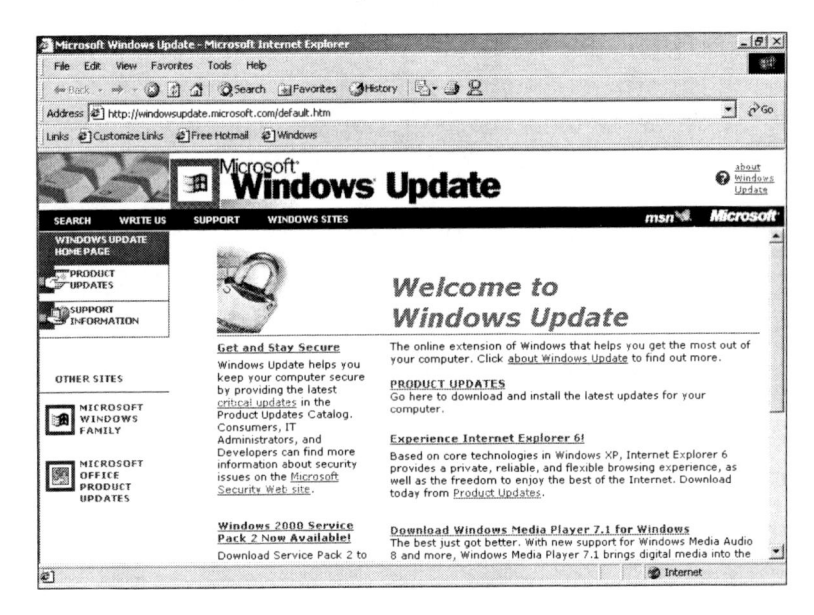

2. On the Windows Update home page, click **Product Updates**.

3. If you see a Security Warning dialog box, make sure the Windows Update Control Package is signed by Microsoft Corporation, and then click **Yes**. Windows Update scans your computer and creates a customized catalog of updates for your computer. These are divided into categories: critical updates such as bug fixes (corrections to the software), recommended updates, security updates, and so on, to help you choose which ones you want to install. Each available update is preceded by a check box. The check boxes of any critical updates are already selected.

4. Scroll through the available updates, and select the check boxes of the ones you want to download and install, and then click the **Download** button at the top of the page.

DIGITAL SIGNATURES

To let you know that the files you are downloading are authentic, Microsoft attaches a digital signature to the Windows Update Control Package. This signature is bound to the original files in such a way that it cannot be altered, replaced, or tampered with by anyone not authorized by Microsoft. Other software manufacturers also use this device to guarantee the origin of their files.

Chapter 7 Solving Common Problems

Windows Update displays a list of your selected updates.

5. Click the **Start Download** button to continue.

6. Click **Yes** if you are presented with a licensing agreement for the new Windows features.

   Windows Update downloads and installs your selected updates.

7. Restart your computer if you are prompted to do so.

That's all there is to it!

That's it for this chapter on problem solving. Hopefully, being aware of the potential problems we've discussed will help you avoid them altogether and make your time at the computer more productive. For more complex problems, you might have to use Web resources, call your computer's manufacturer or Microsoft for technical support, or visit your local repair shop.

Congratulations! You have now completed your *Quick Course in Windows 2000*. By now, you should feel comfortable with most of the components of Windows. With the basics you have learned here, together with the Help and Support features, you can now explore how to best make Windows 2000 work for you.

Index

A

access rights on networks 75
access to Web 171
accessibility options 184
Accessibility Wizard 186
activating windows 18
ActiveX objects 152
Add New Hardware Wizard 157
Add Printer Wizard 58
Address bar 91, 140
Address Book 103, 109, 111
addresses
   e-mail 96
   Web 172
Adjust Date/Time command 178
aliases 96
Align Right button 46
applications,
     adding/removing 160
application programs 4
Apply Stationery command 112
arranging
   icons 12, 13, 66
   windows 20
Attach File button 113
attaching
   files 113
   signatures 112
   stationery 112
   Web pages 113
autoarranging icons 13

B

background, changing 164
backing up files 192
backups
   full 193
   incremental 197
   scheduling 207
BIOS (basic input-output system) 156
blind carbon copies 109
Bold button 46
buttons 32
   command 39
   labels, turning on/off 69
   mouse, switching 181

option 39
Quick Launch toolbar 21, 126, 132
taskbar 15
toolbar 40, 45
ScreenTips 17

C

Calculator 48, 50, 51
carbon copies 109
CD-ROM drives 63
Character Map 52
characters, inserting 52
check boxes 39
clicking 5
clients/client documents 147
Clipboard 52
ClipBook Viewer 55
clock, hiding/displaying 176
closing
   menus, without choosing commands 33
   windows 11, 21
colors, screen
   changing 163
   changing scheme 170
combo boxes 39
command buttons 39
commands 33
   choosing
     with keyboard 35
     from shortcut menus 43
     with toolbar buttons 45
   groups of 35
   help with 34
   toggle 34, 35
   unavailable 35
Connect to the Internet icon 98
connecting
   to Internet 98
   to shared folders 76
connections, viewing 77
contacts 109
container documents 147
contracting
   tree diagrams 71
   windows 17

Control Panel 9, 10
copying 83, 85
correcting mistakes 36
Create New Folder button 42
Create Shortcut Wizard 127, 131, 134
Create Shortcut(s) Here command 129
custom toolbars 138
   displaying 139
customizing
   computer setup 156
   display 163
   My Computer 90
   Outlook Express 104
   taskbar 140, 174

D

data files 63
dates
   changing 178
   inserting 36
defragmenting hard disks 68
Deleted Items icon 121
deleting
   buttons from Quick Launch toolbar 132
   e-mail 120
   favorites 138
   files 15, 87
   folders 87
   icons 132
   Startup menu shortcuts 136
deletions, undoing 88
desktop 7, 62
   adding icons to 129
   changing 164
   displaying 21
   style, changing 8
   Windows Classic Desktop, displaying 11
desktop icons. *See* icons
Desktop toolbar 140
dialog boxes 10, 35
   components of 38
   tabs 36
digital signatures 212
disconnecting sharing 77

INDEX

disks
  defragmenting 205
  scanning 202
Disk Cleanup 204
display, customizing 163
displaying
  Address bar 91
  clock 176
  Control Panel 9
  desktop 21
  drive properties 68
  file details 69
  folders in Explorer bar 72
  information about drives 66
  network members 76
  rulers 34
  Start menu 9
  taskbar 176
  tip of the day 70
  Windows Classic Desktop 11
documents. *See also* files
  client 147
  container 147
  copying in same folder 85
  creating shortcuts for 131
  instant 142
  moving, with Folders pane 84
  naming 80
  opening 68, 126
    from Documents submenu 126
    from My Computer 126
    from My Network Places 126
    recently used 64
  organizing 81
  printing 56
    multiple copies 57
  restoring 201
  saving 40, 47
    in different folder 41
  searching for 65, 78
  selecting multiple 82
  sending 145
  source 147
  specifying program to open with 143
  storage location 81
Documents submenu, opening documents from 64, 126
domain names 97
double-clicking 5, 14
dragging
  icons 12
  to select 82
drivers 58
drives 63
  properties, displaying 66, 68

E

e-mail 94
  addresses 96, 98
  attaching
    files 113
    signatures 112
    stationery 112
    Web pages 113
  button labels, turning on/off 105
  deleting 120
  drafts 117
  Folder bar, turning on/off 104, 105
  formatting 109
  forwarding 118
  instant messaging 121
  internal 94, 95
  Internet 94, 95, 96
  marking messages 116
  message headers 116
  moving 119
  nicknames 112
  organizing 118
  Outlook bar, turning on/off 104
  preview pane, turning on/off 104
  reading 116
  receiving 115
  replying to 117
  scheduling delivery 115
  selecting messages 121
  sending 106
    from Address Book 111
    stored messages 114
  setting priority 108, 110
  setting up 98
  sorting 119
  status bar, turning on/off 104
  toolbar, turning on/off 104
  working offline 109
editing embedded objects 149
embedding
  icons 150
  objects 147
Emergency Repair Disk 209
Empty Deleted Items Folder command 120
executing. *See* starting
exiting. *See* quitting
expanding
  tree diagrams 71
  windows 17
Explorer bar 70
  displaying folder contents 72
  tip of the day, displaying 70
  tree diagrams, expanding/contracting 71
extensions 43, 65, 144

F

favorite Help topics 22
favorites 73, 137
  deleting 138
  displaying in Explorer bar 173
file names
  conventions 41
  length of 62
  portable 81
files 63. *See also* documents
  attaching 113
  backing up 192
  copying 83
  data 63
  deleting 15, 87
  details, displaying 69
  finding on networks 74
  moving 83
  names. *See* file names

files *(continued)*
　naming 80
　opening recently used 64
　organizing 62, 80
　program. *See* program files
　properties 67
　renaming 86
　restoring from Recycle
　　Bin 88
　searching for 65
　sharing 68
　storage location 81
　types 43, 65, 144, 145
　undeleting 88
FilterKeys 185
finding files on networks 74
FireWire 156
floppy disk drives 63
Folder Options command 145
folders 63
　copying 83
　　documents within 85
　creating 138
　　in Outlook Express 119
　　shortcuts for 131
　　shortcuts within 132, 139
　creating toolbars for 138
　deleting 87
　display, changing 69
　displaying toolbars for 139
　moving 83
　　up one level 68, 69
　My Documents. *See* My
　　Documents
　organizing 62, 80
　renaming 86
　selecting multiple 82
　sharing 74
　storage location 81
　structure, deciding on 80
　subfolders. *See* subfolders
　undeleting 88
　viewing details in 69
Folders pane 70
　moving documents with 84
　tree diagrams 70
font size, changing 54
fonts, sizing 54

formatting messages 109
Forward button 118
forwarding e-mail 118
frames, window 18

G
getting help. *See* Help
graphics as wallpaper 166
groups
　of e-mail addresses 110
　of commands 35

H
hard disk drives 63, 66
hard disks 66
　defragmenting 68
　scanning 202
hardware 4
　adding 156
　removing 158
Help 21
help
　with commands 34
　with programs 22
hiding
　Address bar 91
　clock 176
　taskbar 176
　windows 19
High Contrast 186
highlighting 37
History 73

I
icons 8, 14
　adding to desktop 129
　arranging 12, 13, 66
　deleting 132
　double-clicking 14
　embedding 150
　linking 151
　moving 12, 13
　My Computer 12
　My Network Places 14
　Recycle Bin 12
　shortcut 126
Inbox 103
　icon 106
insertion point 32

Install Wizard 160
instant messaging 121
internal e-mail 94, 95
Internet 16
　connecting to 98
　e-mail 94, 95
Internet Connection Wizard 99
Internet e-mail 96
Internet Explorer 172
intranets 171
inverting selection 83
ISPs 96

K
keyboard
　adjusting 183
　shortcuts 35
　starting programs with 47

L
labels, button, turning on/off 69
language, changing 179
Launch Outlook Express
　button 101
launching. *See* starting
Layout command 119
leaving. *See* quitting
Line Up Icons command 13
linking
　icons 151
　objects 147, 151
Links command 152
Links toolbar 140, 171
list boxes 38
loading. *See* starting
local printers 56
local storage 62

M
Magnifier 186
mapping network drives 74
maximizing windows 17
menu bar 32, 33
menu commands 9
menus 33
　closing without choosing
　　commands 33
　on menu bar 33
　opening 34

INDEX

message boxes 48
message headers 116
messages. *See* e-mail
Microsoft Backup 193
Microsoft Network (MSN) 103
Microsoft Outlook 101
Microsoft Word 64
Minimize All Windows
 command 20
minimizing windows 19
mistakes, correcting 36
monitors, multiple 170
mouse
 adjusting 181
 clicking. *See* clicking
 switching buttons 181
mouse pointer. *See* pointer
MouseKeys 186
Move To Folder command 119
MS-DOS programs, starting 30
MSN Messenger Service 121
multimedia devices,
 adjusting 188
multimedia programs 188
multitasking 47
music, playing 173
My Computer 66
 arranging icons in 66
 customizing 90
 icon 12
 opening documents from 126
My Documents 63
My Network Places 74
 icon 14
 opening documents from 126
My Pictures 63

N

names
 domain 97
 file. *See* file names
 user 97
naming files 80. *See also*
 renaming
network
 drives 74
 printers 58
 storage 62

networks
 access rights 75
 displaying members of 76
 finding files on 74
New Contact button 110
New Folder command 119
New Mail button 106
New/Folder command 138
New/Shortcut command
 127, 139
nicknames 112
NumLock 50

O

Object command 147
objects 43, 147
 creating new 149
 editing embedded 149
 embedding 147
 linking 147, 151
Open command 127
Open With command 143
opening. *See also* displaying
 documents 68, 126
 from Documents
 submenu 126
 from My Computer 126
 from My Network
 Places 126
 recently used 64
 menus 34
 Recycle Bin 14, 88
 windows, multiple 16
operating systems 4
option buttons 39
organizing
 documents 81
 e-mail 118
 files 62, 80
 folders 62, 80
Outbox 109
 icon 109, 115
Outlook bar 104
Outlook Express 94
 button labels, turning
 on/off 105
 creating folders 119
 customizing 104

Folder bar, turning
 on/off 104, 105
Inbox 103
moving around in 105
Outbox 109
preview pane, turning
 on/off 104
starting 101
status bar, turning on/off 104
toolbar, turning on/off 104

P

Paint 143
passwords 6, 100
Passport 121
pasting 54
paths 44, 63
people, searching for 78
photographs as wallpaper 166
Plug and Play 156
pointer
 clicking. *See* clicking
 vs. insertion point 32
power management 168
printers
 adding 58
 local 56
 network 58
printing 56
 documents 56
 multiple copies 57
 queues 59
priority of messages 108, 110
program files 63
program icons 32
programs
 adding 159
 application. *See* application
 programs
 help with 22
 MS-DOS 30
 quitting 59
 removing 159
 sharing information
 among 51
 specifying which to open
 document with 143

programs *(continued)*
  starting 126
    with keyboard 47
  switching between 48
  system. *See* system programs
Programs submenu 31
  adding shortcuts to 133
  starting programs from 126
Properties command 133

Q
queue 59
Quick Launch toolbar 8, 21
  buttons 21
    adding 126
  turning on/off 11
quitting
  programs 59
  Windows 2000 26

R
radio, playing 173
Radio toolbar 173
reading e-mail 116
receiving e-mail 115
Recycle Bin 15, 62
  opening 14, 88
  restoring files from 88
Recycle Bin icon 12
registry 211
removing
  hardware 158
  programs 159
  Windows components 161
renaming. *See also* naming files
  files 86
  folders 86
  shortcuts 130
Reply All button 117
Reply To Sender button 117
replying to e-mail 117
resizing windows 17
resolution, screen 8
  changing 163
restarting computers 136
restoring
  backups 201

files, from Recycle Bin 88
  windows 17
reusing information 146
Rich Text Format 43
right-aligning text 46
right-clicking 5
rulers 32, 34
running. *See* starting

S
Safe Mode 210
saving
  color schemes 171
  documents 40, 47
    in different folder 41
scanning disks 202
scheduling
  mail delivery 115
  tasks 206
screen
  changing
    background 164
    color scheme 170
    colors/resolution 163
  resolution 8
  savers 168
ScreenTips 17
scroll arrow 37
scroll bar 37
searching
  for documents 78
  for e-mail addresses 98
  for files 65
  for people 78
  Help 22
Select All command 121
selecting
  all 43
  by dragging 82
  inverting selection 83
  messages 121
  text 44
Send And Receive All
  button 115
Send And Receive
  command 109
Send button 109

sending
  documents 145
  e-mail 106
    from Address Book 111
  stored messages 114
Sent Items icon 121
SerialKeys 186
servers 147
Set Priority button 108
Set Priority/High command 108
setup, changing 156
shared folders, connecting to 76
sharing
  files 68
  folders 74
  information among
    programs 51
  stopping 77
shortcut icons 126
shortcut menus, choosing
  commands from 43
shortcuts
  adding to
    desktop 129
    Programs submenu 133
    Start menu 132
    StartUp menu 136
  attaching to e-mail 113
  creating
    for documents 131
    for folders 131
    within folders 132, 139
  deleting 132
  keyboard 35
  renaming 130
Show Desktop button 21
ShowSounds 185
shrinking windows 17, 19
Shut Down command 26, 136
shutting off Windows 2000 26
signatures, attaching 112
sizing
  fonts 54
  toolbars 127, 140
  windows 17
sliders 40
sorting files/folders 70

INDEX

sounds, adjusting 188
SoundSentry 185
source documents 147
special characters. *See* characters
spin boxes 40
Start button 8, 15
Start menu 15
   adding shortcuts to 132
   changing properties 175
   displaying 9
   reorganizing 136
start modes 210
starting
   Outlook Express 101
   programs 126
      from Programs submenu 126
      with keyboard 47
   Windows 2000 6
   WordPad 31
startup disk, creating 209
Startup menu
   adding/deleting shortcuts 7, 136
   starting from 210
stationery, attaching 112
status area 8
status bars 32
StickyKeys 185
stopping sharing 77
storage
   levels of 71
   local. *See* local storage
   locations 41
   network. *See* network storage
style, desktop, changing 8
subfolders 63
submenus 35
switching between programs 48
system programs 4
system registry 211

T

tabs 36
taskbar 8
   buttons 15, 18
   changing properties 175

customizing 140, 174
hiding/displaying 8, 176
moving 8, 174
Taskbar And Start Menu command 136
tasks, scheduling 206
text boxes 38
text, selecting 44
tiling windows 20
time
   changing 178
   inserting 36
tip of the day, displaying 70
title bars 32
toggle commands 34
ToggleKeys 185
toggles 35
toolbars 32
   buttons 40, 45
   changing size of 127
   creating 138
   displaying custom 139
   floating 141
   moving 141
   sizing 140
Toolbars/Links command 171
Toolbars/New Toolbar command 139
tree diagrams 71
troubleshooting startup problems 209

U

unavailable commands 35
Undo button 45, 88
Undo command 46
undoing
   deletions 88
   window arrangements 20
uniform resource locators (URLs) 172
USB 156
user names 97

V

viewing details in folders 69
Views button 69
viruses 116

W

wallpaper 166
Web addresses 172
Web pages, attaching 113
Windows
   adding components 161
   keeping up to date 211
   removing components 161
windows 16
   activating 18
   arranging 20
   closing 11, 21
   contracting/expanding 17
   frames 18
   hiding 19
   maximizing 17
   menu bars 32
   minimizing 19
   moving 17, 19
   moving between 68
   multiple 68
   My Computer. *See* My Computer
   opening multiple 16
   restoring 17
   shrinking 19
   sizing 17
   tiling 20
   title bars 32
Windows 2000
   starting 6
   turning off 26
Windows Classic Desktop, displaying 11
Windows Media Player 173
Windows Update 211
WordPad, starting 31
work area 32
Work Offline command 115
working offline 101, 109
   sending stored messages 114

About Online Training Solutions, Inc. (OTSI)

OTSI is a traditional and electronic publishing company specializing in the creation, production, and delivery of computer software and business training. OTSI produces the *Quick Course*® series of training products and the eclecticClassroom family of online learning environments. The principal authors of this book are:

Joyce Cox is the developer of the *Quick Course* series. She has 20 years' experience in writing about and editing technical subjects for non-technical audiences. For 12 of those years she was President of Online Press. She was also the first managing editor of Microsoft Press, an editor for Sybex, and an editor for the University of California.

Christina Dudley earned her publishing stripes at Online Press and has for the past several years been a lead writer for the *Quick Course* series. She writes from her home in Gig Harbor, Washington.

Joan Preppernau, a Vice President of OTSI, currently resides in Sweden. She is the primary author of *Windows XP Step by Step* and *FrontPage 2002 Step by Step* published by Microsoft Press. Prior to becoming involved as an author, Joan wore a variety of hats for OTSI, including data preparation manager, operations manager, web master, and technical editor.

Quick Course in Microsoft Windows 2000 was designed by **R.J. Cadranell**. The lead compositor was **Leslie Eliel**, the graphics were processed by **Liz Clark**, and the lead proofreader was **Gabrielle Nonast**. Other members of the OTSI team include:

Susie Bayers	**Aaron L'Heureux**
Nancy Depper	**Robin Ludwig**
Joseph Ford	**Lisa Van Every**
Jon Kenoyer	**Nealy White**
Marlene Lambert	**Michelle Ziegwied**

For more information about Online Training Solutions, Inc., visit *www.otsi.com*.